NEUROCOUNSELING
Brain-Based Clinical Approaches

edited by
Thomas A. Field · Laura K. Jones · Lori A. Russell-Chapin

AMERICAN COUNSELING
ASSOCIATION
2461 Eisenhower Avenue • Suite 300
Alexandria, VA 22314
www.counseling.org

NEUROCOUNSELING
Brain-Based Clinical Approaches

American Counseling Association

2461 Eisenhower Avenue, Suite 300 • Alexandria, VA 22314

Associate Publisher • Carolyn C. Baker

Digital and Print Development Editor • Nancy Driver

Senior Production Manager • Bonny E. Gaston

Production Coordinator • Karen Thompson

Copy Editor • Kathie Porta Baker

Cover and text design by Bonny E. Gaston

Library of Congress Cataloging-in-Publication Data

Names: Field, Thomas A., editor. | Jones, Laura K., editor. | Russell-Chapin
| Lori A., editor.
Title: Neurocounseling : Brain-based clinical approaches / edited by
Thomas A. Field, Laura K. Jones, Lori A. Russell-Chapin.
Description: Alexandria, VA : American Counseling Association, 2017. |
Includes bibliographical references and index.
Identifiers: LCCN 2016048751 | ISBN 9781556203640 (pbk. : alk. paper)
Subjects: LCSH: Counseling psychology. | Brain. | Neurophysiology.
Classification: LCC BF636.6 .N487 2017 | DDC 158.3--dc23 LC record
available at https://lccn.loc.gov/2016048751

We dedicate this book to everyone who has been working toward integrating neuroscience into the counseling field and to the next generation of counselors, eager to understand the bridge between brain and behavior.

TABLE OF CONTENTS

PREFACE

Many therapeutic fields are embracing principles of neuroscience in their practice, and such principles are rapidly influencing best practices. The counseling field is also beginning to consider how neuroscience and neurobiology can inform, explain, and enhance the theory and practice of counseling. Some leaders in the counseling field have already articulated that neuroscientific findings are becoming the "practice standards of the future" (Myers & Young, 2012, p. 21). In recognizing the growing influence of neuroscience on counseling practice, the American Counseling Association, Association for Counselor Education and Supervision, and American Mental Health Counselors Association have each established separate Neuroscience and Neurocounseling Interest Networks that work collaboratively to present a unified vision of how neuroscience can be used to explain and enhance counseling practice. The newly published 2016 Council for the Accreditation of Counseling and Related Educational Programs (CACREP) Standards (CACREP, 2015) contain nearly three times the number of references to neurobiology as the 2009 CACREP Standards (Jones, 2015). In addition, a growing number of counseling texts and national, regional, and state conference presentations have highlighted the integration of neuroscience into counselor practice. In this preface, we underscore how integrating neuroscientific principles related to the central nervous system and physiological processes underlying all human functioning into the practice of counseling can support and advance the profession (Beeson & Field, 2017).

2016 CACREP Standards

With that background in mind, this preface addresses the section of the 2016 CACREP Standards pertinent to the common core area of Professional Counseling Orientation and Ethical Practice (Standard II.F.1.):

- History and philosophy of the counseling profession and its specialty areas (Standard II.F.1.a.)

The preface also addresses the following 2016 CACREP Specialization Standard:

- Role of counselors and counselor educators advocating on behalf of the profession and professional identity (Counselor Education and Supervision, Standard VI.B.5.i.)

■ ■ ■

Definition of Counseling

Who are counselors? What do they do? What does it mean to be a counselor? How are we similar to and different from other mental health professions? How do advances in the field, such as neuroscience and neurobiology, pertain to counseling?

All of these questions are important to ponder throughout one's career, from new graduate student to experienced practitioner. As counselors consider who they are as professionals, neuroscience provides the information and tools to support their belief in certain core principles as foundational to counseling practice.

The field of counseling is unique among the mental health professions in its historical beliefs about the human condition and how to enhance optimal living. In 2010, a consensus definition of *counseling* was agreed on by multiple stakeholders in what was formally titled 20/20: A Vision for the Future of Counseling. The definition distilled into one sentence how the counseling profession could be defined: "Counseling is a professional relationship that empowers diverse individuals, families, and groups to accomplish mental health, wellness, education, and career goals" (para. 2). This definition identifies several important concepts as foundational to counseling practice: The professional relationship takes precedence; the goal of counseling is to empower people, especially those from diverse backgrounds, and address systemic barriers that prevent optimal health; and counseling assists people to achieve optimal mental health and wellness, not only to alleviate distress and mental disorders.

Neuroscience supports the importance of these concepts and provides models for how to implement them into counseling practice. As the chapters in this book elucidate, neuroscience can help counselors understand how relationships are forged, leading to deeper and more meaningful working relationships with clients; recognize the persisting impact of systemic barriers such as oppression, marginalization, and trauma on clients' ability to achieve their goals; and take a wellness and strengths-based perspective that serves to empower clients and increase optimal performance. In other words, neurocounseling is commensurate with the orientation and identity of the counseling profession.

Definition of Neurocounseling

The field of mental health services, including counseling, is rapidly evolving. One of the most important emerging trends in the field has been the integration of neuroscience into counseling practice (Beeson & Field, 2017). This new counseling approach has been termed *neurocounseling* (Montes, 2013). Neurocounseling has been defined as "the integration of neuroscience into the practice of counseling, by teaching and illustrating the physiological underpinnings of many of our mental health concerns" (Russell-Chapin, 2016, p. 93). Neurocounseling has a variety of uses. For example,

- Neurocounseling can be used by clinicians to understand how and why psychotherapy changes the brain (Russell-Chapin, 2016).
- Neurocounseling can help us better understand client concerns, conceptualize cases, and plan treatment by using a brain-based perspective.
- Neurocounseling can help clients understand their experience through brain-based psychoeducation.
- Neurocounseling provides counselors with a more holistic, wellness-based, and mind–body integrative approach to client work.
- Technical approaches such as biofeedback and neurofeedback can be used to determine the physiological and neurological underpinnings of a client's distress and dysfunction (assessment) and can help clients to modify physiology and brain waves to enhance their functioning and reduce distress and dysfunction (intervention).
- Neurocounseling approaches such as biofeedback and neurofeedback can also be used to improve optimal performance, not only to modify distress and dysfunction.

For some clinicians, neurocounseling can be used as part of what the clinician is already doing, as another tool in the toolbox (i.e., an adjunctive strategy to psychotherapy). However, neurocounseling can also entirely change the way clinicians conceptualize client cases, conduct assessments, and select interventions. For example, Lori A. Russell-Chapin wrote in 2016, "For decades, my goal was to assist clients in changing their unwanted thoughts, feelings and behaviors. Today . . . the overarching goal of all my counseling is to help clients to improve their emotional and physiological self-regulation" (p. 94).

Purpose of This Text

As counselors learn more about neuroscience, they are in need of guidance regarding how to integrate this new brain-based knowledge into counseling practice with clients. The ability to translate complex knowledge to clients is a separate skill set that requires the ability to distill rather than dilute information. Counselors whose case conceptualizations are becoming informed by neuroscientific knowledge also require guidelines regarding how to apply these concepts in clinical practice.

The purpose of this text is to provide a resource for how neuroscientific concepts can be translated and applied to the counseling field, with the objective of both explaining and enhancing the theory and practice of counseling. In doing so, we hope to provide guidance and facilitate learning about how counselors are integrating neuroscience into their work, with the hope of better understanding and identifying methods for effectively and responsibly incorporating key principles of neuroscience into the profession. To advance this effort, we use the new 2016 CACREP Standards as our markers of learning to ensure that CACREP-accredited programs (and all programs) have the information needed to apply neuroscientific concepts to all the major areas of counseling practice.

While writing and editing this text, we also understood that for some counselors, especially those for whom science and research are not strengths, neuroscience can be an overwhelming and frightening concept. The scientific terminology, complex anatomy, and technology-based brain measurements may seem irrelevant to daily counseling practice with clients who bring forth deep existential human struggles that cannot be easily quantified. The specialized knowledge required to be a neuroscience-savvy practitioner may also seem outside the scope of counseling practice.

With that in mind, the purpose of this text is to provide counselors with guidelines, ideas, and tips on how to become effective and skillful neuroscience-informed counselors. We have purposefully asked each author to convey these concepts in a way that is understandable yet retains important information (distill, not dilute). The chapters are organized so that you will understand foundational neuroscience concepts that inform client case conceptualization (e.g., human development, social and cultural background) before learning how to approach assessment and intervention from a neurocounseling perspective.

We hope that this text will be useful not only to current counseling practitioners but also to current master's-level students in counseling programs. In that regard, the book addresses the 2016 entry-level educational standards of the main accrediting body of the counseling profession, CACREP. Each of the eight common core areas of counseling knowledge and skills are covered (professional counseling orientation, social and cultural foundations, human growth and development, career development, helping relationships, group counseling and group work, testing and assessment, research and program evaluation). We also address several 2016 CACREP Standards that are integrated into the eight common core standards, such as the impact of crises, disaster, and traumatic events; the neurobiology of addictions; wellness and optimal performance; and psychopharmacology. Some chapters also address doctoral-level 2016 CACREP Standards for counselor education and supervision. We are proud that this text is the first publication to discuss the application of neurocounseling and neuroscience to the CACREP Standards specifically. In addition, the text represents the first publication to broadly address the application of neurocounseling and neuroscientific concepts across the core counseling curriculum, an approach that provides a practical, comprehensive model for the integration of neuroscience into counseling practice.

In addition to being an adjunctive text for all common core courses in the master's-level counseling curriculum, this text can also serve as a primary resource for counseling students (both master's and doctoral level) who are taking specialization courses in neuroscience, neurocounseling, brain and behavior, biological basis of behavior, and so forth. Finally, the text could also be a resource for counselor educators and supervisors who want to learn more about neuroscientific applications to counseling practice. As such, it is broadly designed for practicing counselors in the field, counselor education students in training, and counselor educators and supervisors.

Text Organization and Chapters

The text is divided into five sections. The first section reviews foundational information about neuroanatomy and neurophysiological development across the life span before exploring the impacts of social and cultural issues such as marginalization, oppression, and traumatic stress on neurophysiological functioning. The second section applies foundational knowledge from the first section to counseling relationships and assessments. Chapters emphasize the role of attentional processes in empathy and microskills, along with establishing safety within the counseling environment, neuroscience-informed counseling theory, completing a comprehensive neurocounseling assessment, and assessing for client wellness and enhancing optimal performance.

The third section addresses specialization areas related to neuroadaptation and addiction processes. Chapters examine the neuroscience of substance use and psychopharmacological intervention. The fourth section uses information from earlier chapters to explore a neuroscience-informed approach to specialized counseling modalities such as group counseling and career counseling. The fifth section describes a brain-based approach to conducting research and evaluating neurocounseling programs, and the final chapter provides guidance on integrating neuroscience into counseling practice. Ten tips are provided for counselors, with information from all prior chapters applied to the case study presented later in this preface.

Text Features

As editors, we sought to ensure that each chapter made direct connections between the content and clinical practice. As an anchor for the content knowledge, each chapter references a case study to ensure the material is relevant to client work. This preface starts that trend by presenting a case study that includes reflection questions that are further explored in the final chapter. Reflection questions are integrated throughout each chapter so that you can pause and consider how the content knowledge that has been covered could be relevant to the client case being discussed. We encouraged authors to share their own brain-based approach to the case study presented in their chapter so that you can consider how to use the information presented with clients in your own unique way. A few quiz questions are included at the conclusion of each chapter so that you can test your knowledge. The quiz answers are located at the back of the text. A glossary is also provided at the conclusion of the text so that you can evaluate whether you understand the concepts taught in the chapters. You are encouraged to return to sections of the chapter in which those terms are described if you are not confident in your knowledge.

 Clinical Case Study

> Muna is a 42-year-old Iraqi woman who is experiencing anxiety at her new job in an accounting firm. Muna lives and works in a metropolitan area of a large U.S. city. She is also struggling with feelings of inadequacy related to her long-standing dating relationship of nearly a decade. Her family lives in Iraq, and she emigrated to attend a U.S. college in her early 20s. She lives in constant dread of her family finding out that she is living with her boyfriend outside of marriage. She has been drinking alcohol to cope, mostly at night (four to five units). Muna also struggles with sleep at night, usually only getting 3 to 5 hours. She sometimes binge eats when she wakes up at night. Muna has a past diagnosis of attention-deficit/hyperactivity disorder and takes 20 mg of Adderall twice a day. In terms of her medical history, Muna was born prematurely at 28 weeks but otherwise has no history of medical issues. When asked about her family history, Muna mentions that she experienced psychological abuse from her father throughout her childhood. She is very warm and engaging during the initial interview, though her nonverbal fidgeting suggests she is somewhat anxious.

Concluding Thoughts

Over the course of the subsequent chapters, you will learn information that will help you conceptualize, assess, and intervene with this client on a deeper level. You will learn possible answers to important questions such as the following:

- How might the client's premature birth be playing into her current struggles?
- Which areas of her brain are being compromised?
- How does anxiety "happen" in the body?
- Why might the client struggle to think her way out of anxiety?
- What is the potential impact of emotional abuse on the client's functioning?
- How can stimulants interact with alcohol?
- How can the client tame anxiety without using alcohol?

In the final chapter of this text ("Ten Practical Guidelines for Neurocounseling"), we review each of these questions on the basis of knowledge you will acquire from each of the chapters that precede it.

As Lori likes to say, once you have learned about how the brain works in relationship to physical and emotional health, you cannot go back. We are confident that this knowledge will forever change how you approach case conceptualization, assessment, and intervention in clinical practice. We hope the subsequent chapters will be your starting point on this journey.

References

Beeson, E. T., & Field, T. A. (2017). Neurocounseling: A new section of the *Journal of Mental Health Counseling*. *Journal of Mental Health Counseling, 39*(1), 71–83. http://amhcajournal.org/doi:10.17744/mehc.39.1.06

Council for Accreditation of Counseling and Related Educational Programs. (2009). *2009 CACREP accreditation manual*. Alexandria, VA: Author.

Council for the Accreditation of Counseling and Related Educational Programs. (2015). *2016 CACREP standards*. Retrieved from http://www.cacrep.org/wp-content/uploads/2012/10/2016-CACREP-Standards.pdf

Jones, L. K. (2015). The evolving adolescent brain. *Counseling Today, 57*(7), 14–17.

Kaplan, D. M., Tarvydas, V. M., & Gladding, S. T. (2014). 20/20: A vision for the future of counseling: The new consensus definition of counseling. *Journal of Counseling & Development, 92*, 366–372. http://dx.doi.org/10.1002/j.1556-6676.2014.00164.x

Montes, S. (2013, December). The birth of the neurocounselor. *Counseling Today, 56*(6), 32–40.

Myers, J. E., & Young, S. J. (2012). Brain wave feedback: Benefits of integrating neurofeedback in counseling. *Journal of Counseling & Development, 90*, 20–28. http://dx.doi.org/10.1111/j.1556-6676.2012.00003.x

Russell-Chapin, L. A. (2016). Integrating neurocounseling into the counseling profession: An introduction. *Journal of Mental Health Counseling, 38*, 93–102. http://dx.doi.org/10.17744/mehc.38.2.01

About the EDITORS

The three editors of this text are the three chairs of the respective Neuroscience Interest Networks. Lori A. Russell-Chapin is the chair of the American Counseling Association (ACA) Neurocounseling Interest Network. Laura K. Jones is the chair of the Association for Counselor Education and Supervision (ACES) Neuroscience Interest Network. Thomas A. Field is the chair of the American Mental Health Counselors Association (AMHCA) Neuroscience Interest Network. We are excited about what neuroscience can bring to the counseling field and how it can be used in a manner that both honors its unique professional identity and keeps the field at the cutting edge of client care.

Thomas A. Field, PhD, LMHC (WA), LPC (VA), NCC, ACS,

is an associate professor in the Master of Arts in Counseling program at the City University of Seattle. Thom holds a PhD in counseling and supervision from James Madison University. He has 10 years of counseling experience with more than 1,000 clients in a variety of settings, including outpatient, inpatient, schools, and private practice. He maintains a small private practice to inform his work as a counselor educator. His research and clinical interests include the neuroscience of counseling practice, clinical mental health counseling and supervision, and social justice and advocacy issues in counseling. Thom has published on the neuroscience of counseling in peer-reviewed journals and has presented at national conferences on the integration of neuroscience into counselor preparation and practice. Thom is currently part of a research team (Eric Beeson, Thom Field, Laura Jones, Raissa Miller) that is studying the development of an emerging counseling theory called *neuroscience-informed cognitive behavior therapy*. Thom is the current chair of the AMHCA Neuroscience Interest Network and is also a member of the ACA and ACES Neuroscience/Neurocounseling Interest

Networks. He is also the associate editor of the Neurocounseling section of the *Journal of Mental Health Counseling* along with Eric Beeson. In 2013, Thom was the first-ever recipient of the 2013 AMHCA Dissertation Research Award.

Laura K. Jones, PhD, MS, NCC, ACS, is an assistant professor at the University of North Carolina at Asheville. She holds a PhD in counseling and counselor education from The University of North Carolina at Greensboro, as well as an MS in psychology-cognitive neuroscience from the University of Oregon. She uses her training in both disciplines to inform her research, clinical, and pedagogical practices. Laura's primary interest lies in the confluence of neuroscience and counseling, with specific interest in the intentional and informed integration of neuroscience into the counseling field and counselor training programs, as well as in the neuroscience of trauma and recovery as it relates to elucidating the impact of trauma on interpersonal relationships; perceptions of safety following trauma; and efficacious interventions for survivors. She has presented at numerous national and international conferences on the integration of neuroscience into clinical practice and has authored and coauthored publications and book chapters detailing the application of neurophysiology to clinical mental health counseling and trauma and crisis intervention. Laura serves as the chair of the ACES Neuroscience Interest Network, is a member of the ACA Neurocounseling Interest Network, and is coeditor of the monthly column in Counseling Today titled "Neurocounseling: Bridging Brain and Behavior."

Lori A. Russell-Chapin, PhD, NCC, CCMHC, LCPC, BCN, is a professor of counselor education at Bradley University in Peoria, Illinois. Lori earned a PhD in counselor education from the University of Wyoming and a master's in counselor education from Eastern Montana College. Currently, Lori teaches graduate counseling courses in Bradley University's campus-based and online brain-based master's programs. She codirects the Center for Collaborative Brain Research, a partnership among Bradley University, OSF Saint Francis Medical Center, and the Illinois Neurological Institute. Lori has authored or coauthored seven books ranging in topic from practicum–internship supervision to neurotherapy and neurofeedback. Lori is the chair of the ACA Neurocounseling Interest Network and coeditor of the monthly column in *Counseling Today* titled "Neurocounseling: Bridging Brain and Behavior." Lori edits the monthly magazine for AMHCA, *The Advocate*. She is an award-winning researcher and teacher at Bradley University and the recipient of the AMHCA Outstanding Counselor Educator of the Year.

About the CONTRIBUTORS

We are very fortunate to have been able to gather together some of the best minds (pun intended!) within the field of neurocounseling to share with you their expertise related to core counseling content areas. The authors who contributed to this book are listed in alphabetical order.

Eric T. Beeson, PhD, is a core faculty member at The Family Institute of Northwestern University and currently works part time at an integrative clinic that provides biofeedback, neurofeedback, and counseling services to clients.

Theodore J. Chapin, PhD, is the president and clinical director of Resource Management Services, a private business consulting and counseling firm in Peoria, Illinois. He is board certified in neurofeedback.

SeriaShia Chatters, PhD, is an assistant professor in the Department of Educational Psychology, Counseling, and Special Education at The Pennsylvania State University. She works in a neurofeedback lab and leads a neurofeedback research team with her colleague, Carlos P. Zalaquett, in the College of Education.

Thomas Daniels, PhD, is a retired professor of psychology at Memorial University of Newfoundland (Grenfell Campus). He is internationally known for his work in microcounseling and microskills.

Joel F. Diambra, PhD, is associate professor and director of graduate studies in the Educational Psychology and Counseling Department at the University of Tennessee at Knoxville. Before becoming an academic, Joel worked as an employment specialist for clients who had sustained a traumatic brain injury.

Kathryn Z. Douthit, PhD, is an associate professor and chair of counseling and human development at the University of Rochester. Before her counseling training, she earned an MA in microbiology and immunology.

Sean B. Hall, PhD, is an assistant professor of counselor education and clinic director for the University of Alabama at Birmingham. He earned his doctorate in counseling, specializing in clinical mental health and educational research methods, from Old Dominion University in 2012.

Allen E. Ivey, EdD, is a distinguished professor (emeritus) at the University of Massachusetts, Amherst. He is a fellow of the American Counseling Association. Board certified by the American Board of Professional Psychology, he is also a Fellow of the American Psychological Association.

Mary Bradford Ivey, EdD, is former vice president of Microtraining Associates, an educational publishing firm, and an independent consultant. She is a fellow of the American Counseling Association.

Chad Luke, PhD, is an associate professor in the Department of Counseling and Psychology at Tennessee Technological University. His most recent book is titled *Neuroscience for Counselors and Therapists: Integrating the Sciences of Brain and Mind,* published by Sage.

Justin Russotti, MSW, is a PhD student at the University of Rochester and leads a research lab examining the sequelae of childhood trauma.

Christopher Rybak, PhD, is a professor in the Department of Leadership in Education, Nonprofits, and Counseling at Bradley University, where he has taught graduate courses in brain-based counseling interventions.

Nancy Sherman, PhD, is a professor in the Department of Leadership in Education, Nonprofits, and Counseling at Bradley University.

Kiera D. Walker is a graduate student at the University of Alabama at Birmingham in the clinical mental health counseling track. Kiera has a BS in biology and a double minor in chemistry and psychology. Her current research includes Stage 4 brain cancer, known as glioblastoma, and she desires to further pursue research in the area of trauma.

Carlos P. Zalaquett, PhD, is a professor in the Department of Educational Psychology, Counseling, and Special Education in the College of Education at The Pennsylvania State University. He currently coleads the neurofeedback laboratory at Penn State's College of Education.

Part I
FOUNDATIONS OF CASE CONCEPTUALIZATION

The first section of the text reviews foundational knowledge needed to conceptualize client cases from a neurophysiological perspective. You will first be introduced to basic brain anatomy and systems before learning about neurophysiological development across the life cycle and the impact of neurophysiological marginality and traumatic stress on psychological health. This knowledge is considered fundamental to understanding the client's presenting problem from a neurophysiological perspective, leading to more effective counseling relationships, assessments, and interventions.

■ ■ ■

Chapter 1

Anatomy and Brain Development

Laura K. Jones

Learning about brain anatomy and the functioning of related systems may not be the first thing that comes to mind when you think about counselor education and training. Three facial expressions tend to emerge on counselors' faces when anatomy is mentioned: utter terror, complete boredom, or a smaller but growing contingency of expressions akin to fascination. If you are currently making one of the initial two expressions, perhaps you will find yourself, as you begin reading this and later chapters, becoming more engrossed and fascinated by the many wonders of the brain and how this information affects your work as a counselor.

Interest in the application of neuroanatomy to mental health has been long-standing. Sigmund Freud suggested in his classic 1914/2012 paper *On Narcissism* that "we must recollect that all of our provisional ideas in psychology will presumably one day be based on an organic substructure" (p. 78). Since Freud's early conjecture, limitations in technology have hampered understanding of the impact of the workings of the brain on mental health functioning. On April 2, 2013, a paradigm shift in mental health research began with the launch of the National Institute of Health's Brain Research through Advancing Innovative Neurotechnologies (BRAIN) initiative. The mission of this initiative is to understand "the circuits and patterns of neural activity that give rise to mental experience and behavior" (National Institutes of Health, 2014, p. 12) and, in doing so, to cultivate an integrative understanding of brain–behavior processes. This chapter is a first step to introducing you to the inner workings of the brain in an effort to inform your case conceptualizations, treatment plans, and ultimately clinical effectiveness with clients.

2016 CACREP Standards

This chapter addresses sections of the 2016 Council for Accreditation of Counseling and Related Educational Programs (CACREP) Standards pertinent to the common core area of Human Growth and Development (Standard II.F.3.):

- Theories of learning (Standard II.F.3.b.)
- Biological, neurological, and physiological factors that affect human development, functioning, and behavior (Standard II.F.3.e.)

This chapter also addresses the following Specialization Standard:

- Impact of biological and neurological mechanisms on mental health (Clinical Mental Health Counseling, Standard V.C.2.g.)

■ ■ ■

 ## Clinical Case Study: Rein

Rein is a 12-year-old female preadolescent of Native American descent. Her home environment is intact; she lives with both parents and a brother. Rein describes it as an attentive but conservative home with limited communication regarding emotions, physiological changes to the body, or interpersonal relationships. Her parents scheduled an appointment because of a marked decrease in Rein's grades at school—Rein previously having been a straight-A student—and a noticeable withdrawal from group activities during class. Rein reports feeling very sad and lonely and indicates that she has been feeling increasingly more distant from friends in the past 6 months. Rein denies feeling bullied or victimized, but she does not feel that anyone likes or understands her and has a hard time connecting with others. Her mother confirms that Rein often cries a lot and isolates herself from her family as well. Her mother also shared that Rein recently reached menarche and was concerned that Rein may feel embarrassed about this.

The Brain: Structure, Function, and Systems

Despite incredible advances in science, the human brain in many ways remains a mystery. Part of its enigmatic nature rests in its complexity.

Not only are there various internal and external structures of the brain specified for certain functions, but those parts directly and indirectly influence one another by way of various chemical messengers. Further still, several areas of the brain can work in concert to govern other aspects of people's mental and physical functioning. Something seemingly as simple as reading the word *counselor* requires a remarkable succession of processes that involve virtually the entire brain.

In addition, researchers are now discovering more and more about how people's physical health and even the nature of the microbes in their gut influence the functioning of the brain. Some of the paradigms of mental health are now shifting as researchers begin to further investigate the reciprocal functioning of the body and brain, such as the role of inflammation (the process by which white blood cells help to protect people from infection) in depression (Miller & Raison, 2016). As such, I want to share some of what is known about the various parts and coordinated systems of the brain and body.

External Structures

What is your first thought when you hear the word *brain*? Most people think of a gray folded mass that sits inside the skull. This folded mass is the outer layer or lateral part of the brain, called the *cerebral cortex*, or *cortex* for short. You may also know that in the interior of this folded cortex, or more medial (toward the midline) and ventral (toward the base of the brain), are other exceedingly important parts of the brain. These internal and external structures control virtually everything about you. They allow you to think, feel, behave, breathe, and ultimately survive.

The cerebral cortex, or outermost part of the brain, is actually a 2- to 4.5-mm-thick mass of gelatinous tissue (Fischl & Dale, 2000). Even though it is often thought of as gray (and parts of it are called *gray matter*), it is actually pink when it is healthy living tissue, much like other tissue in the body. This folded mass includes the ridges of cortex known as *gyri* (singular, *gyrus*) and the shallower grooves between the gyri known as *sulci* (singular, *sulcus*). *Fissures* are similar to sulci but are deeper and more clearly divide regions of the brain. The gyri, sulci, and fissures help to demarcate different regions of the brain.

Hemispheres

The cortex is made up of two hemispheres, one on the left and one on the right. Connecting these two hemispheres is a thick band of nerve fibers known as the corpus callosum. It is the largest collection of nerve fibers in the entire nervous system, containing roughly 200 million interhemispheric connections (Luders, Thompson, & Toga, 2010). This band of fibers allows the two hemispheres to communicate back and forth and integrate the information being processed on either side of the brain. A common misperception in popular culture is that individuals are either left brained or right brained. It is accurate that certain functions may be predominantly controlled by brain regions in one hemisphere or another; for example, the area of the brain responsible for language production is typically located in the left hemisphere. However, the notion that a person can be either left brained or right brained is an overgeneralization and a misrepresentation of brain functioning. More often than not, both sides of the brain are working in coordinated action to allow people to more fully perceive, respond, and adapt to their internal and external environments.

Lobes

The cerebral cortex is further divided into four sets of primary lobes, with analogous lobes in each hemisphere. Each lobe is specialized for certain functions, such as sight, somesthesis (e.g., skin senses and proprioception), hearing and language comprehension, motor control, and executive functioning. The four lobes are as follows: occipital lobe, parietal lobe, temporal lobe, and frontal lobe. Figure 1.1 depicts the general location of the four lobes.

Occipital lobe. At the very back of the brain sits the occipital lobe, which is the smallest of the four lobes. This is the visual center of the brain. The occipital lobes piece together the visual components of the surrounding world. This allows people to interpret and understand what their eyes are seeing, such as shape, color, size, depth, and

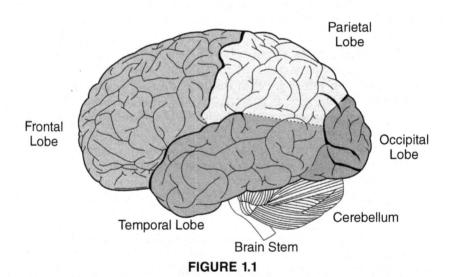

FIGURE 1.1

Lobes of the Brain

Note. From *Anatomy of the Human Body* (20th ed., Plate 728), by H. V. Carter, 1918, New York, NY: Lea & Febriger. In the public domain. Vectorized by Mysid, 2008, via Wikimedia Commons.

motion. However, visual processing is limited, meaning that people cannot process everything in the world around them. Visual perception is determined by several factors, including how many objects are present, how long the objects are in the visual field, and to which objects people allocate their attention.

Parietal lobe. The parietal lobe is located approximately halfway between the frontal lobe and the occipital lobe. This part of the brain contains the primary somatosensory cortex, which regulates the sensations that are perceived by the physical body, such as touch (e.g., temperature, pressure, pain), and the awareness of bodily movement and the orientation of the body in space (i.e., proprioception). The most anterior (i.e., toward the front) gyrus of this cortex (i.e., the postcentral gyrus) extends across both hemispheres and contains a map of one's entire body. For example, regions of this gyrus represent the thumb, tongue, arm, stomach, and even pinky toe. Every part of the body that one can feel is allocated a certain area of cortex on this gyrus, with the number of sensory receptors on the skin of that area governing how much of the cortex it represents. For example, the hands, face, and tongue are all represented by very large areas of cortex because people need to have very refined sensations of touch for these areas. The body maps are also contralateral (as opposed to ipsilateral), meaning that the right side of the body is mapped onto the left postcentral gyrus and vice versa.

Temporal lobe. The temporal lobe is located just behind the ears, below the parietal lobe and between the frontal lobe and the occipital lobe. The primary function of the temporal lobe is hearing and language comprehension. This region of the brain allows people to put together and comprehend all of the various sounds that are coming into their ears. Wernicke's area is the region of the temporal lobe that allows people to process spoken language. The temporal lobes are also involved in memory. The hippocampus is located in the medial (i.e., interior) region of the temporal lobes and is responsible for the formation of long-term memories.

Frontal lobe. The front section of the brain consists of the largest cortical lobe—and the largest of any mammal—which covers nearly half of the entire cortex. Aptly named the frontal lobe, this area is also the most extensive in terms of the functions that it controls. The most posterior (i.e., toward the back) gyrus of the frontal cortex (neighboring the parietal lobe) contains the primary motor cortex. Like the postcentral gyrus, this area contralaterally maps out the entire body, not for the purpose of feeling those parts but for the purpose of moving them. So, as you reach to turn the page of this book, neurons in the upper left side of this gyrus (right side if you are using your left hand) are firing. At the base of this primary motor cortex, extending down and forward and typically in the left hemisphere, is an area called *Broca's area,* which is responsible for language production. Note that the area for language comprehension is different from that for language production. Broca's area is located at the base of the primary motor cortex because that is the area of the cortex responsible for the movement of the face and mouth. The functioning of this area can actually be affected by experiences of extreme traumatic stress, which is further discussed in Chapter 4. Given that counseling most often consists of "talk therapy," especially with adults, any altered functioning of Broca's area may have notable clinical implications.

Beyond these functions, the frontal lobe is involved in problem solving, decision making, planning, moral reasoning, attention, emotion regulation, and even priming in memory. The frontal lobe also plays a role in one's personality. This was famously demonstrated by the case of Phineas Gage, a railroad worker who experienced significant damage to the most anterior region of his frontal lobe. An explosion sent a metal spike diagonally through his skull, from around his ear up to the opposite top side of his skull. He not only survived the accident but was walking around and talking minutes later. The most striking consequence of this accident was his change in personality and behavior. Before the accident, Phineas was seen as a friendly, polite, and even-tempered fellow. Afterward, he was reported to be angry, cantankerous, and even violent, often using considerable profanity and lacking in impulse control (Macmillan, 2002). The portion of his frontal lobe that was most notably affected was a region called the *prefrontal cortex*. The prefrontal cortex serves as the "executive control" center of the brain and is in charge of rational thinking. Much like a corporate executive, the prefrontal cortex helps people decide or judge what is best for them, plan for the future, work toward goals, and discriminate between varying options. It also regulates their emotions, attention, and social functioning. Put simply, it allows people to think through situations and behave in a deliberate, goal-directed manner.

Just underneath the outer surface of cortex in the frontal lobe, near the confluence of the frontal, parietal, and temporal lobes, lies an area of cortex called the *insula* (insular cortex). This area helps people translate the emotions that they feel in their body into their cognitive understanding of those emotions, or what is known as feelings. Yes, emotions and feelings are actually different things, processed by different areas of the brain (Damasio, 2001). The insula is the area of the brain that acts as a bridge between these two, converting emotions into feelings, or helping people to understand and put words to their bodily sensations. This sense of having an awareness of one's internal bodily state is known as *interoception*. Given the ability of the insula to facilitate awareness of one's emotional state, it is also a key brain region involved in consciousness and empathy (Craig, 2009; Decety & Lamm, 2006).

The cingulate cortex also lies underneath the outer surface of the cortex. This band of cortex extends lengthwise from the frontal to the occipital lobes of the brain, following the shape and curve of the corpus callosum. The job of the cingulate cortex is quite varied, given its role in learning, memory, reward, and social and emotional processing, with the anterior (frontal) and posterior (back) sections controlling different functions. The anterior cingulate cortex (ACC) is responsible for emotional processing and regulation, empathic responding, and socially driven interactions, with the dorsal (top) ACC (what is also called the *middle cingulate cortex*) participating in more cognitive aspects and the rostral (front) ACC participating in more affective aspects of such processes (Lavin et al., 2013; Stevens, Hurley, & Taber, 2011). The functioning of the posterior cingulate cortex (PCC), however, is a bit more elusive. Recent research has determined that it appears to play a role in internally directed cognition, retrieval of autobiographical memories, and planning for the future (Buckner, Andrews-Hanna, & Schacter, 2008; Leech & Sharp, 2014; Raichle et al., 2001). Such research has also identified the PCC as a central node of the default mode network, a system of functionally connected brain regions that become engaged when the brain is in a resting state and not involved in a specific attention-demanding, goal-oriented task.

Cerebellum and brain stem. In addition to these four primary lobes, two other key features of the exterior portion of the brain are the cerebellum and brain stem. The cerebellum, meaning "little brain," is the cauliflower-shaped structure at the back base of the brain. Like the cerebral cortex, the cerebellum is also divided into two hemispheres. It contains more neurons than the cortex—nearly 3.6 times as many (Herculano-Houzel, 2010). The cerebellum was originally thought to govern only motor control, such as posture and balance; fine-tuned motor learning (i.e., riding a bike); and the coordination of the fluid movements of multiple muscle groups. Researchers have more recently begun to recognize the integral role of the cerebellum in a range of functions related to cognition, emotion, sensory perception, attention, threat, and pleasure (Strick, Dum, & Fiez, 2009; Turner et al., 2007).

The brain stem is the structure of the brain that extends from the base of the brain to the spinal cord. It consists of the midbrain, the pons, and the medulla oblongata. The brain stem connects the brain to the rest of the body and is vital to survival. It regulates many of the nonconscious (not consciously directed) processes that keep people alive, such as breathing, heart rate, blood pressure, and circadian rhythms, including the sleep cycle.

Cranial Nerves

Extending directly from the brain out to various organs, muscles, and sensory systems are the 12 pairs

Reflective Question

Which cortical areas seem related to Rein's symptoms?

of cranial nerves (CNs). These nerves function in sensory, motor, and parasympathetic control, with most of the nerves controlling muscles of the face and neck or regulating the visual, olfactory, and auditory sensations. These allow people to, among other functions, chew, swallow, blink reflexively (corneal reflex), constrict or dilate the pupils, and vocalize. CNs also connect to organs that help people to regulate or calm their autonomic nervous system, thus helping to control nonconscious bodily functions such as heart rate, breathing, and digestion. For example, the facial cranial nerve (CN VII) controls the salivary glands. Among these nerves is the 10th cranial (CN X), or vagus, nerve, which extends down the trunk to connect with the heart, lungs, and gastrointestinal tract. It provides input to help slow breathing and heart rate, and it stimulates activity of the stomach and intestines, and thus digestion. The vagus nerve has been hypothesized to play a very important role in social connection, attachment, and internal experiences of safety (Porges & Furman, 2011).

Internal (Subcortical) Structures

Underneath the large outer cortex of the brain are a number of vitally important subcortical (below the cortex) brain structures. It is beyond the scope of this chapter to discuss every subcortical structure; however, several of the most notable are discussed later in this book. Figure 1.2 provides a useful diagram of some of these structures.

The most central of the subcortical structures is the thalamus. This is the primary relay station of the brain—all of the messages from the senses and the body that move out to the cortex, or vice versa, are sent through the thalamus. In this way, the thalamus ensures that

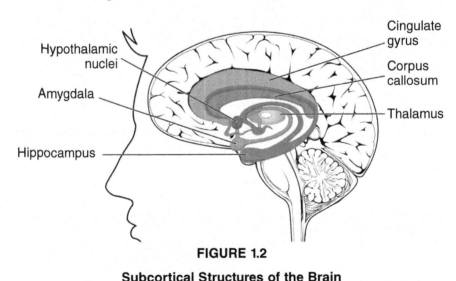

FIGURE 1.2

Subcortical Structures of the Brain

Note. From OpenStax College, 2013, via Wikimedia Commons. Used under Creative Commons Attribution 3.0 Unported License.

those messages are directed to the correct place. It can be thought of as the Grand Central Station of the brain, where all the trains (i.e., signals) to and from the cerebral cortex pass through to get to their final destinations (Taber, Wen, Khan, & Hurley, 2004).

Wrapping around the thalamus is a coordinated set of subcortical nuclei known as the basal ganglia. This set consists of the caudate nucleus and putamen (together known as the striatum), nucleus accumbens, globus pallidus, substantia nigra, and subthalamic nucleus. These structures play a considerable role in learning and memory, particularly implicit (i.e., outside of awareness) learning of automatized responses (Graybiel, 2000). The basal ganglia also contribute to motor functions, including both inhibiting and motivating movement. Over- or underactivity of this region is seen in motor disorders such as Parkinson's disease (Graybiel, 2000). Disrupted functioning of the basal ganglia area also occurs in addictions, obsessive–compulsive disorder, Tourette's disorder, and even schizophrenia (Graybiel, 2000). Closely associated with the basal ganglia and located at roughly the bottom center of the brain is a group of neurons called the ventral tegmental area. It is the source of a significant number of dopamine (a neurotransmitter related to pleasure) projections and is the primary source for the prefrontal cortex and nucleus accumbens. As a result, the ventral tegmental area functions in reward and motivation and has thus been implicated in addiction and other mental health disorders (Lammel et al., 2012).

Anterior and ventral (i.e., below, toward the base of the skull) to the thalamus and basal ganglia lies the hypothalamus. This almond-sized structure links the endocrine (collection of glands that secrete hormones) and nervous systems in the body. It also assists the body in maintaining a state of internal balance or equilibrium known as homeostasis; for example, it controls body temperature, food intake, and water intake. The hypothalamus is also responsible for the release of various key hormones in the body, for sexual development and physiology, and the ability to respond to stress.

Closely connected to the hypothalamus, located approximately behind the bridge of the nose, is the pituitary gland. This pea-sized structure is the master gland of the body, both producing and regulating the functioning of numerous hormones. It also controls other glands throughout the body, such as the thyroid and adrenal glands. The pituitary gland is highly active in the production of sex hormones and is vital to the body's ability to respond and adapt to stress.

Another central subcortical brain structure is the amygdala. You may previously have heard the conceptualization of the amygdala as the part of the brain responsible for making people angry or afraid. This understanding is limited and misrepresents the amygdala's role in overall functioning. LeDoux (2013) emphasized that fear and, similarly, anger are cognitive constructs that have no inherent meaning. They are evolutionarily advanced words and concepts, so to say that the amygdala is the source of specific feelings is erroneous. Instead, think of the amygdala as the principal brain region involved in detecting and responding to both innate and learned threats in the environment (LeDoux, 2012). The amygdala also plays a role in classical conditioning related to emotional responses and nondeclarative (i.e., implicit, not consciously retrievable) memories, and it can regulate the strength of both declarative and nondeclarative memories (Squire, 2004).

Just posterior to the amygdala is a seahorse-shaped structure called the hippocampus. The hippocampus is the area of the brain important for the consolidation (i.e., formation and storage) of long-term declarative (i.e., explicit, consciously retrievable) memories. Explicit memory—what is typically thought of as memory—is memory for facts and events that can be recalled.

Last, stemming from underneath the frontal and prefrontal cortices on either side are the olfactory bulbs. These structures are the sensory organs for the sense of smell. They are the only sensory organs that are directly connected to the subcortical areas of the brain, most notably the limbic system.

Coordinated Systems of the Brain and Body

Several key systems in the brain and body are essential to any discussion of neurophysiology. Each of these systems represents a set of functionally or anatomically interconnected structures that play a crucial role in mental health and healthy functioning in general. The first two systems are brain-based systems, and the remaining three are systems involving the brain and body.

Limbic System

Coined the *limbic system* by Paul MacLean in the 1950s, this set of functionally connected structures was first thought to include the cingulate cortex and select subcortical nuclei and was considered the emotional center of the brain (Nakano, 1998; Rajmohan & Mohandas, 2007). Since that time, researchers have come to understand that the functioning of the limbic system extends well beyond emotion. Not only does the limbic system allows people to respond to emotionally salient cues and threats in their environment, but it also plays a role in memory, social processing, sleep, appetite, motivation, addiction, and even sexual behavior (Nakano, 1998; Rajmohan & Mohandas, 2007). Some debate also remains about which structures comprise this functional system. Subcortical structures such as the amygdala, hippocampus, hypothalamus, and olfactory bulb have long been accepted to be part of the limbic system. However, the thalamus and basal ganglia are also occasionally included. With regard to cortical structures, the limbic system also includes the surrounding cingulate cortex.

> **Reflective Question**
>
> Which subcortical areas seem related to Rein's symptoms?

Default Mode Network

The next functional system or network in the brain is the default mode network (DMN), which serves as the default or resting state of the brain. The brain regions involved in the DMN include the prefrontal cortex, posterior cingulate cortex, and regions of the parietal and temporal lobes (Buckner, Andrews-Hanna, & Schacter, 2008; Raichle et al., 2001). Even when not actively directed toward some task, the brain is not simply inactive. It is in a sort of idle state, ready to engage. For example, the DMN is active during self-generated thought, such as when a person is daydreaming, passively reminiscing, or getting lost in thought. These areas deactivate when one engages in active cognitive tasks. The functioning of the DMN is disrupted in disorders such as attention-deficit/hyperactivity disorder, schizophrenia, autism spectrum disorder, depression, and posttraumatic stress disorder and can be disrupted by substance use as well (Andrews-Hanna, Smallwood, & Spreng, 2014).

Autonomic Nervous System

The autonomic nervous system is the part of the peripheral nervous system that innervates the tissues and organs of the body, such as the heart, lungs, stomach, and intestines, over which people have little to no conscious awareness. The autonomic nervous system consists of two different divisions, the sympathetic and parasympathetic branches, which act as complementary systems. The sympathetic nervous system functions to engage or excite the organs of the body, including in preparation for protective action. In this way, it activates the fight-or-flight system. The heart starts beating faster, the bronchi in the lungs dilate to allow one to take in more oxygen, the pupils dilate, the stomach and intestines slow down, and the liver makes more glucose. The opposite is true for the parasympathetic nervous system. The heartbeat slows, the bronchi constrict, and the stomach and intestines begin to function more regularly. In short, the parasympathetic nervous system helps people to regulate autonomic arousal and relax. It is also thought to have two branches, namely, the dorsal and ventral branches of the vagus nerve (Porges, 2011). According to Steven Porges's (2011) polyvagal theory, the dorsal branch is associated with the "freeze" response to threat. The ventral branch is associated more with relaxed communication and social engagement (Porges, 2011).

Hypothalamic–Pituitary–Adrenal Axis

The hypothalamic–pituitary–adrenal axis is the functional connection between three endocrine glands. This axis, along with the sympathetic–adrenal–medullary axis, allows people to adapt to both emotional and physical stress. The hypothalamus releases corticotropin-releasing hormone to the pituitary gland. This hormone stimulates the pituitary gland to release adrenocorticotropic hormone (ACTH). ACTH then travels down to the adrenal glands, which sit on top of the kidneys. The ACTH activates the adrenal cortex (outside of the adrenal glands, not to be confused with the cortex in the brain) to release glucocorticoids, in particular cortisol. The function of cortisol is to help restore homeostasis after stress, and it is essential to life. It also helps to control the reaction to stress by initiating what is called a *negative-feedback loop* that turns off the production of ACTH. The role of the sympathetic–adrenal–medullary axis and what happens when the feedback process of the hypothalamic–pituitary–adrenal axis breaks down is further discussed in Chapter 4 when traumatic stress is explored.

Microbiota–Gut–Brain Axis

Did you know that microbes in your gut can have a direct impact on your mental health? A growing body of research has substantiated the direct connection between the gut and the brain, a connection termed the *microbiota–gut–brain axis.* The gastrointestinal tract has its own nervous system, called the *enteric nervous system,* which contains as many as 600 million neurons. The gut also has the highest concentration of immune cells in the body and is filled with trillions of bacteria, fungi, and viruses (Forsythe, Kunze, & Bienenstock, 2016). It is controlled in part by the vagus nerve, which is one of the mechanisms of the direct bidirectional connection between the gut and the brain (Cryan & Dinan, 2012). Not only has the microbiota–gut–brain axis been linked to memory, pain, concentrations of brain-derived neurotrophic factor helpful in the development of brain cells and intercellular connections, and immune functioning, but recent research has linked aberrations in gut microbiota with disorders such as depression, anxiety, stress responses, and posttraumatic stress disorder (Cryan & Dinan, 2012; Cryan & O'Mahony, 2011; Forsythe et al., 2016; Leclercq, Forsythe, & Bienenstock, 2016).

How the Brain Communicates

You may be asking yourself how all of these various parts of the brain and body communicate with one another. For example, how does the prefrontal cortex help to regulate the amygdala and associated limbic regions of the brain? How does the thalamus transmit messages from one area to another?

Neurons

Communication in the brain is carried out by electrochemical messages transmitted between specialized cells called *neurons.* In addition to neurons, neuroglia or glial

Reflective Question

Which systems seem related to Rein's symptoms?

cells are a second type of cell that exists in the nervous system. These cells help neurons by providing insulation, nourishment, repair, and structural support. They also remove waste from the nervous system.

Neurons are cell bodies that have extensions on either side that allow them to connect to neighboring neurons and are composed of four primary parts, namely the cell body (soma), dendrites, axon, and the presynaptic or axon terminal (see Figure 1.3). The soma or cell body is the core part of the neuron, containing the nucleus and other cellular structures such as mitochondria used in energy production. Connected to the cell body are the dendrites, which are branches extending out from the cell body. These branches bring chemical messages or information into the cell body from neighboring neurons. Extending from the other side of the neuron is the axon, a long hairlike projection that carries chemical messages away from the cell body to neurons, glands, or muscles on the other side. Some axons are covered in a myelin sheath through a process called *myelination*. This fatty sheath, made out of fatty glial cells, helps electrochemical messages be transmitted faster down the axon. Rapid transmission is incredibly important to the functioning of the nervous system in general, such as when messages must be carried long distances or be transmitted very quickly. Disruptions and deterioration in myelin are a central feature of the autoimmune disorder multiple sclerosis (Steinman, 1996). This impairment can lead to neurological symptoms such as vision loss, pain, involuntary muscle movements, muscle paralysis, tingling and burning sensations, and impaired coordination.

The axon terminal is the area at the end of the axon where the axon branches and extends to come in close proximity to the neighboring structure (e.g., other neurons, muscles, glands). This is also the area where the chemical messages are released. Finally, the small space (tens

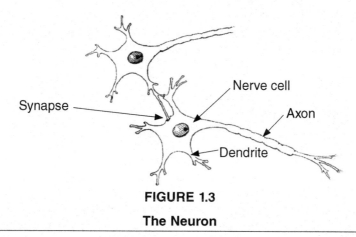

FIGURE 1.3

The Neuron

Note. From Olga Lednichenko, 2011 (Flikr), via Wikimedia Commons. Used under Creative Commons Attribution 2.0 Generic License.

of nanometers in width) between two neurons is called the *synaptic cleft*. The axon terminal, the synaptic cleft, and the dendrites compose what is called the *synapse*. There are nearly 1 billion neurons in the adult brain, and each one of these neurons connects to 10,000 others through these synapses. This means that adults have more than 100,000 trillion synaptic connections (Kolb & Gibb, 2011).

Often, the terms *gray matter* and *white matter* are used to describe certain visually distinct areas of the brain. For example, if you look at an image of the brain generated by an MRI machine, you will see areas of the brain that distinctly look gray and some areas that distinctly look white. The gray areas are the neuronal cell bodies and the white areas are the axons, in particular myelinated axons. The myelin is what gives the white matter its characteristic white color.

Neurotransmission and Action Potentials

So how do neurons communicate with each other? *Neurotransmission* is the communication of electrical or chemical signals from one neuron to another. During neurotransmission, a molecule, such as a hormone or neurotransmitter, binds to receptors on a cell's surface and relays external information into and along the neuron and then out to neighboring neurons on the other side. Neurons are said to "fire" when they begin transmitting these electrochemical messages via an action potential. This process starts when an external agent—for example, a neurotransmitter—approaches the dendrites of a neuron. These electrically charged chemicals bind to receptors on the dendrites and change the configuration of the ion channels, which control the flow of ions through the membrane. This binding, depending on the combination and concentration of the chemical messengers, initiates an action potential in the postsynaptic neuron. The transmission of this action potential down the axon leads to the opening of calcium channels. The calcium ions then cause the release of neurotransmitters into the synaptic cleft at the end of the axon. The neurotransmitters that are released into the synaptic cleft and do not bind to the postsynaptic neuron are either then recycled back into the presynaptic neuron through a process known as *reuptake* or metabolized by enzymes. Psychotropic drugs, such as selective serotonin reuptake inhibitors, work by influencing this process of communication between neurons.

Neurotransmitters and Hormones

Neurotransmitters are the chemical messengers that relay information across a synapse between two neurons. There are two basic categories of neurotransmitters, excitatory and inhibitory. Excitatory neurotransmitters enhance or increase the functioning of postsynaptic neurons, whereas inhibitory neurotransmitters inhibit or downregulate (decrease) the functioning of the postsynaptic neuron. Basically, they shift the likelihood of whether or not the postsynaptic neuron will fire or create an action potential. Some neurotransmitters can actually have both excitatory and inhibitory properties. Neurotransmitters act quickly across very short distances between neurons. Hormones, however, are secreted by the endocrine system into the bloodstream and can travel longer distances to act on target cells farther away from the endocrine gland. Interestingly, some chemicals can function as both. Some key hormones and neurotransmitters are presented in Table 1.1.

TABLE 1.1

Key Neurotransmitters, Peptides, and Hormones and Their Related Functioning

Name	Abbreviations/ Other Names	Structure	Type	Function
Acetylcholine	Ach	Amine neurotransmitter	Mostly excitatory	Often excitatory with muscles; involved in muscle movement; essential in memory; also important in attention, learning, neuroplasticity, arousal, and reward
Dopamine	DA	Monoamine/ catecholamine neurotransmitter	Both inhibitory and excitatory	Motivation, reward, addiction; feelings of pleasure, and voluntary muscle movement
Epinephrine	Epi; adrenaline	Monoamine/ catecholamine; neurotransmitter; hormone	Excitatory	Involved in fight or flight responses to increase heart rate and blood flow and enhance awareness
Gamma-aminobutyric acid	GABA	Amino acid neurotransmitter	Inhibitory	Primary inhibitory neurotransmitter; reduces neuronal excitability; helps to reduce anxiety. As an interesting side note, it is primarily excitatory in the developing brain.
Glucocorticoids	Cortisol (one example)	Steroid hormone		Essential for life, regulates stress, assists in homeostasis and immune functioning
Glutamate		Amino acid neurotransmitter	Excitatory	Primary excitatory neurotransmitter; essential in learning and memory; important in long-term potentiation (action potential) and long-term depression
Norepinephrine	NE; noradrenaline	Monoamine/ catecholamine neurotransmitter; hormone	Mostly excitatory	Prepare the brain and body to act; fight or flight; increases restlessness and anxiety; enhances attention, vigilance, and arousal; enhances memory formation and retrieval
Oxytocin		Neuropeptide; hormone		Social recognition, bonding and attachment, trust, and reproductive behaviors
Serotonin	5-HT	Monoamine neurotransmitter	Inhibitory	Mood, sleep cycles, appetite, and temperature

Neuroplasticity

The communication process just described can be modified by internal and external experiences. Neuroplasticity is the ability of the brain to alter its structure and function in response to develop-

Reflective Question

Which neurotransmitters and hormones seem related to Rein's symptoms?

ment, learning, memory, brain injury, and disease (Tardif et al., 2016). It occurs in response to sustained changes in the pattern of neural activity, which in turn alters one's neural connections and thus how one responds (Lillard & Erisir, 2011).

These new patterns of firing can result from several different sources. One can develop new neurons (neurogenesis), develop new connections between neurons (synaptogenesis), enhance or strengthen the connection between neurons, weaken the connections between neurons, and altogether prune connections between neurons (extinction). *Long-term potentiation* (LTP) refers to stable increases in neuronal sensitivity to stimulation and thus enhancement of the synaptic connection (Bliss & Cooke, 2011; Collingridge, Peineau, Howland, & Wang, 2010). Brain-derived neurotrophic factor is one class of proteins in the brain that is integral to neuronal and synaptic development and thus the process of LTP. As a complementary process, *long-term depression* (LTD) is the reduction in the synaptic transmission or a decrease in neuronal sensitivity to a repeated stimulus (Bliss & Cooke, 2011; Collingridge et al., 2010). LTP and LTD have been hypothesized to be the basis of learning and memory. In fact, a study by Nabavi et al. (2014) demonstrated that memories for fear could be inactivated or reactivated by altering the processes of LTD and LTP, respectively.

Neurogenesis, or the birth of new neurons, was historically thought to occur only during brain development and at later critical periods such as during adolescence and until age 20 years. In 1998, Eriksson et al. found for the first time that neurogenesis can occur in adult humans, particularly in the olfactory bulb (smell sensory organ) and the dentate gyrus of the hippocampus (Lillard & Erisir, 2011; Lledo, Alonso, & Grubb, 2006). Impairments in neuroplasticity are thought to underlie numerous mental health disorders, such as depression, bipolar disorder, autism, schizophrenia, and drug addiction (Collingridge et al., 2010) as well as degenerative diseases, such as Alzheimer's (Oberman & Pascual-Leone, 2013), and diseases of the central nervous system, such as Parkinson's disease (Bliss & Cooke, 2011). The brain is always adapting

Reflective Question

Imagine you are sitting in session with Rein. Practice the following:

In your own words, talk about neuroplasticity in a manner that empowers Rein.

and changing to the world around you, as well as to your internal world. This means that change is always possible. Counselors can use this understanding of neuroplasticity to empower their clients and enhance their clinical practice.

How the Brain Evolved Over Time

Understanding how and why the brain functions as it does requires examination of how the brain evolved over time. The core functional components of the brain, meaning the proteins that produce the electrical communication signals controlling behavior and thus survival, date back hundreds of millions of years to single-cell eukaryotes called *Choanoflagellates* (Burkhardt et al., 2011). Choanoflagellates existed before animals and are considered animals' closest ancestor. Their basic protein structure may be the raw material that gave rise to the more complex protein structures that function in the release of neurotransmitters in animals. Some of the first mammal and mammal-like creatures that existed nearly 200 million years ago seem to have had a prominent olfactory system, the system that governs the sense of smell. This growth in the olfactory region of the brain, followed closely by regions that control tactical sensations (i.e., touch) and muscular coordination or motor control, seems to have driven the development of the mammalian brain in terms of size and specificity (Rowe, Macrini, & Luo, 2011).

During evolution, the brain and the nervous system seem to have become more refined from the inside out, or from the brain stem to the cortex. Research examining the development of the vertebrate brain has suggested that nearly all vertebrate species have the same number of brain divisions (Northcutt, 2002). The divisions constitute three core areas: the rhombencephalon, or hindbrain (myelencephalon and metencephalon; brain stem); mesencephalon or midbrain; and the prosencephalon, or forebrain (telencephalon and diencephalon). However, both the size of the brain compared with the body and the size of the various divisions in relation to one another are different among the different classes of vertebrates. For example, the hindbrain in fish and amphibians, which includes the medulla oblongata, pons, and cerebellum, is much larger in comparison with the other divisions. Mammals, however, have a much larger cerebral cortex (telencephalon) than do other vertebrates, which is also the largest division within their brains. For vertebrates, the first brain region to become specialized consists of the areas that keep them alive (rhombencephalon), namely, the spinal cord and brain regions closer to the spinal cord that govern survival functions such as breathing, heart rate, and sleep. The last to specialize (the telencephalon of the forebrain) controls such processes as advanced learning and memory, sensory perception, decision making, speech, empathy, and social functioning. The size and complexity of the prefrontal cortex in particular appears to be what most notably differentiates humans from any other organism (Johnson et al., 2009).

Figure 1.4 depicts Siegel's (2010) hand model of the human brain, which can be used with clients. Although this model is not comprehensive, so to speak, it is a very useful way to understand and show others how the brain was formed evolutionarily and developmentally.

Polyvagal Theory

Stephen Porges (2011) asserted that evolution has led to a functional neural organization of the brain that regulates autonomic states to best support social behavior. This burgeoning theory, termed the *polyvagal theory*, describes the development and function of two branches of the parasympathetic nervous system, as mentioned earlier. Porges contended that, when in a balanced state of autonomic arousal, relaxed and engaged, an individual functions from the social engagement system, known as the ventral vagal system. This system promotes behaviors that enhance social

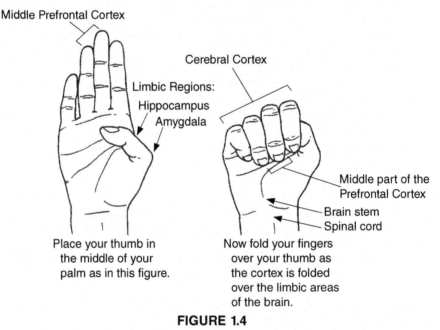

FIGURE 1.4

The Brain in the Palm of the Hand

Note. The hand model depicts the major regions of the brain: cerebral cortex in the fingers, limbic area in the thumb, and brain stem in the palm. The spinal cord is represented by the wrist. From Daniel J. Siegel, MD, *Mindsight: The New Science of Personal Transformation*, copyright © 2010 by Mind Your Brain, Inc.

bonds by regulating the ready control of muscles that function in eye gaze, facial expressions, voice tone, social gestures, and even the ability to extract the human voice from background noises. Porges also suggested that people have a physiological sensation of safety only when they are functioning within this zone of ventral vagal autonomic responding (Geller & Porges, 2014). This has considerable implications not only for social interactions but also for the counseling relationship.

My Brain-Based Approach to the Case of Rein

When working with Rein, I would consider what is going on just below the surface in her brain and body. For example, Rein's feelings of loneliness and withdrawal from social supports immediately make me consider polyvagal theory and the functioning of her autonomic nervous system. I might talk with her about feelings of safety and markers of autonomic reactivity (e.g., rapid heart rate or breathing, feelings of detachment). I would also speak with her about the difference between emotions and feelings and help her to talk through some of what she has been experiencing in her body (i.e., emotions) and what language she is using to understand those sensations (i.e., feelings). In turn, I would discuss how this interpretation of her sensations is affecting her. I would then intentionally blend aspects of gestalt and narrative approaches to help Rein gain further insight into her emotional and interpersonal experiences. In addition, I would also want to better understand her stage of brain development, which is explored further in the following chapter. Understanding brain development during adolescence will provide considerably more insight into how best to work with Rein.

Conclusion

To better understand the process of integrating neuroscience into professional counseling, you must first understand the physiology of the brain and body. This foundational knowledge in neuroscience serves as a metatheory of counseling because the functioning of the brain and body underlies everything counselors do. Understanding how brain structures, systems, and related connections function and change in response to internal and external events helps counselors understand symptom development and how clients can change over time. The foundational knowledge you have gained from this chapter will help you to better understand how the brain and related systems change over the life cycle. This chapter covered a vast amount of important terminology and concepts, and I recommend ensuring that you understand those terms before proceeding to subsequent chapters.

Quiz

1. Which of the following lobes of the brain is in charge of executive functioning?
   a. Frontal.
   b. Parietal.
   c. Temporal.
   d. Occipital.

2. Which functional system of the brain is primarily known for helping people to respond to emotionally salient cues and threats in their environment but also plays a role in memory, social processing, motivation, addiction, and sexual behavior?
   a. Default mode network.
   b. Hypothalamic–pituitary–adrenal axis.
   c. Limbic system.
   d. Autonomic nervous system.

3. The theory detailing the social engagement system suggests that which of the following nerves evolved in such a way as to optimize interpersonal functioning?
   a. Cranial nerve.
   b. Vagus nerve.
   c. Sensorimotor nerve.
   d. Thalamic nerve.

References

Andrews-Hanna, J. R., Smallwood, J., & Spreng, R. N. (2014). The default network and self-generated thought: Component processes, dynamic control, and clinical relevance. *Annals of the New York Academy of Sciences, 1316*, 29–52.

Bliss, T. V., & Cooke, S. F. (2011). Long-term potentiation and long-term depression: A clinical perspective. *Clinics, 66*, 3–17.

Buckner, R. L., Andrews-Hanna, J. R., & Schacter, D. L. (2008). The brain's default network: Anatomy, function, and relevance to disease. *Annals of the New York Academy of Sciences, 1124*, 1–38.

Burkhardt, P., Stegmann, C. M., Cooper, B., Kloepper, T. H., Imig, C., Varoqueaux, F., . . . Fasshauer, D. (2011). Primordial neurosecretory apparatus identified in the choanoflagellate *Monosiga brevicollis*. *Proceedings of the National Academy of Sciences, 108*, 15264–15269.

Carter, H. V. (Illus.). (1918). *Principal fissures and lobes of the cerebrum viewed laterally* [Digital image]. In W. H. Lewis (Ed.), *Anatomy of the human body* (20th ed., Plate 728). Philadelphia, PA: Lea & Febiger. Retrieved from https://commons.wikimedia.org/wiki/File:Gray728.svg

Collingridge, G. L., Peineau, S., Howland, J. G., & Wang, Y. T. (2010). Long-term depression in the CNS. *Nature Reviews Neuroscience, 11*, 459–473.

Council for the Accreditation of Counseling and Related Educational Programs. (2015). *2016 CACREP standards.* Retrieved from http://www.cacrep.org/wp-content/uploads/2012/10/2016-CACREP-Standards.pdf

Craig, A. (2009). How do you feel—Now? The anterior insula and human awareness. *Nature Reviews Neuroscience, 10*, 59–70.

Cryan, J. F., & Dinan, T. G. (2012). Mind-altering microorganisms: The impact of the gut microbiota on brain and behaviour. *Nature Reviews Neuroscience, 13*, 701–712.

Cryan, J. F., & O'Mahony, S. M. (2011). The microbiome-gut-brain axis: from bowel to behavior. *Neurogastroenterology & Motility, 23*, 187–192.

Damasio, A. (2001). Fundamental feelings. *Nature, 413*, 781–781. http://dx.doi.org/10.1038/35101669.

Decety, J., & Lamm, C. (2006). Human empathy through the lens of social neuroscience. *Scientific World Journal, 6*, 1146–1163.

Eriksson, P. S., Perfilieva, E., Björk-Eriksson, T., Alborn, A. M., Nordborg, C., Peterson, D. A., & Gage, F. H. (1998). Neurogenesis in the adult human hippocampus. *Nature Medicine, 4*, 1313–1317.

Fischl, B., & Dale, A. M. (2000). Measuring the thickness of the human cerebral cortex from magnetic resonance images. *Proceedings of the National Academy of Sciences of the United States of America, 97*, 11050–11055.

Forsythe, P., Kunze, W., & Bienenstock, J. (2016). Moody microbes or fecal phrenology: What do we know about the microbiota-gut-brain axis?. *BMC Medicine, 14*(1), 58. http://dx.doi.org/10.1186/s12916-016-0604-8

Freud, S. (2012). *On narcissism: An introduction.* London, England: Kandel Books. (Original work published 1914)

Geller, S. M., & Porges, S. W. (2014). Therapeutic presence: Neurophysiological mechanisms mediating feeling safe in therapeutic relationships. *Journal of Psychotherapy Integration, 24*, 178–192.

Graybiel, A. M. (2000). The basal ganglia. *Current Biology, 10*, R509–R511.

Herculano-Houzel, S. (2010). Coordinated scaling of cortical and cerebellar numbers of neurons. *Frontiers in Neuroanatomy, 4*, 12. http://dx.doi.org/10.3389/fnana.2010.00012

Johnson, M. B., Kawasawa, Y. I., Mason, C. E., Krsnik, Ž., Coppola, G., Bogdanović, D., . . . Šestan, N. (2009). Functional and evolutionary insights into human brain development through global transcriptome analysis. *Neuron, 62*, 494–509.

Kolb, B., & Gibb, R. (2011). Brain plasticity and behaviour in the developing brain. *Journal of Canadian Academy of Child and Adolescent Psychiatry/Académie canadienne de psychiatrie de l'enfant et de l'adolescent, 20*, 265–276.

Lammel, S., Lim, B. K., Ran, C., Huang, K. W., Betley, M. J., Tye, K. M., . . . Malenka, R. C. (2012). Input-specific control of reward and aversion in the ventral tegmental area. *Nature, 491*, 212–217.

Lavin, C., Melis, C., Mikulan, E. P., Gelormini, C., Huepe, D., & Ibanez, A. (2013). The anterior cingulate cortex: An integrative hub for human socially-driven interactions. *Frontiers in Neuroscience, 7*, 64.

Leclercq, S., Forsythe, P., & Bienenstock, J. (2016). Posttraumatic stress disorder: Does the gut microbiome hold the key? *Canadian Journal of Psychiatry, 61*, 204–213. http://dx.doi.org/10.1177/0706743716635535.

Lednichenko, O. (Ill.). (2011). *How does the brain work?* [Digital image]. Retrieved from https://www.flickr.com/photos/olga-ledichenko-photos-images-albums/6418954775/in/photolist-aMdPC4-aMdPw8-aMdPr4-aMdPmk-aMdPy4

LeDoux, J. (2012). Rethinking the emotional brain. *Neuron, 73*, 653–676.

LeDoux, J. E. (2013). The slippery slope of fear. *Trends in Cognitive Sciences, 17*, 155–156.

Leech, R., & Sharp, D. J. (2014). The role of the posterior cingulate cortex in cognition and disease. *Brain, 137*, 12–32.

Lillard, A. S., & Erisir, A. (2011). Old dogs learning new tricks: Neuroplasticity beyond the juvenile period. *Developmental Review, 31*, 207–239.

Lledo, P. M., Alonso, M., & Grubb, M. S. (2006). Adult neurogenesis and functional plasticity in neuronal circuits. *Nature Reviews Neuroscience, 7*, 179–193.

Luders, E., Thompson, P. M., & Toga, A. W. (2010). The development of the corpus callosum in the healthy human brain. *Journal of Neuroscience, 30*, 10985–10990.

Macmillan, M. (2002). An odd kind of fame: Stories of Phineas Gage. Cambridge, MA: MIT Press.

Miller, A. H., & Raison, C. L. (2016). The role of inflammation in depression: From evolutionary imperative to modern treatment target. *Nature Reviews Immunology, 16*, 22–34.

Nabavi, S., Fox, R., Prolux, C. D., Lin, J., Tsien, R. Y., & Malinow, R. (2014). Engineering a memory with LTD and LTP. *Nature, 511*, 348–352. http://dx.doi.org/10.1038/nature13294.

Nakano, I. (1998). The limbic system: An outline and brief history of its concept. *Neuropathology, 18*, 211–214.

National Institutes of Health. (2014). *Brain 2025: A specific vision.* Retrieved from http://braininitiative.nih.gov/pdf/BRAIN2025_508C.pdf

Northcutt, R. G. (2002). Understanding vertebrate evolution. *Integrative and Comparative Biology, 42,* 743–756.

Oberman, L., & Pascual-Leone, A. (2013). Changes in plasticity across the lifespan: Cause of disease and target for intervention. *Progress in Brain Research, 207,* 91–120.

OpenStax College. (Ill.). (2013). *The limbic lobe* [Digital image]. Retrieved from https://commons.wikimedia.org/wiki/File:1511_The_Limbic_Lobe.jpg

Porges, S. W. (2011). *The polyvagal theory: Neurophysiological foundations of emotions, attachment, communication, and self-regulation.* New York, NY: W. W. Norton.

Porges, S. W., & Furman, S. A. (2011). The early development of the autonomic nervous system provides a neural platform for social behaviour: A polyvagal perspective. *Infant and Child Development, 20,* 106–118.

Raichle, M. E., MacLeod, A. M., Snyder, A. Z., Powers, W. J., Gusnard, D. A., & Shulman, G. L. (2001). A default mode of brain function. *Proceedings of the National Academy of Sciences of the United States of America, 98,* 676–682.

Rajmohan, V., & Mohandas, E. (2007). The limbic system. *Indian Journal of Psychiatry, 49,* 132–139.

Rowe, T. B., Macrini, T. E., & Luo, Z. X. (2011). Fossil evidence on origin of the mammalian brain. *Science, 332,* 955–957.

Siegel, D. J. (2010). *Mindsight: The new science of personal transformation.* New York, NY: Bantam Books.

Squire, L. R. (2004). Memory systems of the brain: A brief history and current perspective. *Neurobiology of Learning and Memory, 82,* 171–177.

Steinman, L. (1996). Multiple sclerosis: A coordinated immunological attack against myelin in the central nervous system. *Cell, 85,* 299–302.

Stevens, F. L., Hurley, R. A., & Taber, K. H. (2011). Anterior cingulate cortex: Unique role in cognition and emotion. *Journal of Neuropsychiatry and Clinical Neurosciences, 23,* 120–125.

Strick, P. L., Dum, R. P., & Fiez, J. A. (2009). Cerebellum and nonmotor function. *Annual Review of Neuroscience, 32,* 413–434.

Taber, K. H., Wen, C., Khan, A., & Hurley, R. A. (2004). The limbic thalamus. *Journal of Neuropsychiatry and Clinical Neurosciences, 16,* 127–132.

Tardif, C., Gauthier, C., Steele, C., Bazin, P.-L., Schäfer, A., Schäfer, A., et al. (2016). Advanced MRI techniques to improve our understanding of experience-induced neuroplasticity. *NeuroImage, 131,* 55–72. doi:10.1016/j.neuroimage.2015.08.047

Turner, B. M., Paradiso, S., Marvel, C. L., Pierson, R., Ponto, L. L. B., Hichwa, R. D., & Robinson, R. G. (2007). The cerebellum and emotional experience. *Neuropsychologia, 45,* 1331–1341.

Chapter 2

Neurophysiological Development Across the Life Span

Laura K. Jones

Understanding and appreciating the client's developmental stage is a core tenet of the counseling profession. With the rapid expansion of technology and associated research in neuroscience and neurophysiology, our understanding of development is now being revolutionized. This chapter builds on Chapter 1 (Anatomy and Brain Development) to provide an overview of individual human growth and development with an emphasis on the neurophysiological changes that occur across the life span. This chapter discusses not only the unobstructed development of the brain and body across significant life stages but also touches on difficulties that can arise during these sensitive periods in brain development. The implications of such knowledge for case conceptualization, treatment planning, and the intentional selection of effective clinical interventions are also discussed and illustrated using the case example of Rein from Chapter 1.

 ## 2016 CACREP Standards

This chapter addresses sections of the 2016 Council for Accreditation of Counseling and Related Educational Programs (CACREP) Standards pertinent to the common core area of Human Growth and Development (Standard II.F.3.):

- Theories of learning (Standard II.F.3.b.)
- Theories of normal and abnormal personality development (Standard II.F.3.c.)
- Biological, neurological, and physiological factors that affect human development, functioning, and behavior (Standard II.F.3.e.)

The chapter also addresses the following Specialization Standards:

- Impact of biological and neurological mechanisms on mental health (Clinical Mental Health Counseling; Standard V.C.2.g.)
- Aging and intergenerational issues and related family concerns (Marriage, Couple, and Family Counseling; Standard V.F.2.f.)

■ ■ ■

Brain Development Over the Life Span

Each individual brain follows a sequence similar to the evolutionary course of development discussed in Chapter 1. As with evolution, the individual brain develops from the inside out, or from the brain stem to the prefrontal cortex. This process of brain development is slow and gradual. Although the base structure of the brain is formed prenatally, starting during the third week of gestation, the brain continues to become more refined, both in structure and function, into the late teens and early 20s. Let us look at this process in detail.

Prenatal Brain Development

First Trimester

The brain starts to develop during the third week of gestation with such development and changes lasting virtually across the life span (Stiles & Jernigan, 2010). Around Day 17 to Day 20, the embryo develops a neural plate, or the structure that will eventually become the nervous system, including the brain and spinal cord. Then during the third gestational week, a groove begins to form on the neural plate. This is the neural groove, which will later become the brain. Soon thereafter, the two sides of the groove begin to curl, folding in on themselves and becoming a tubelike structure known as the neural tube. Neural stem cells line the neural tube and eventually give rise to the many specialized cells in the nervous system, including neurons and glia. The cranial nerves begin to develop around Week 5 or 6 postconception. Soon thereafter, at around 50 days of gestation, neurogenesis begins. At its peak, neurons develop at the astonishing rate of 250,000 new neurons per minute (Cowan, 1979). This equates to more than 4,000 new neurons per second. This process of neurogenesis lasts until around the 5th month of gestation.

Researchers are trying to understand what drives stem cells to become neurons rather than glia or vice versa. Proteins called neurotrophic factors constitute one such mechanism for differentiation. Neurotrophic factors support the growth and survival of neurons. Brain-derived neurotrophic factor (BDNF) is one class of neurotrophic factor proteins that specifically supports the growth, survival, and differentiation of neurons in the central and peripheral nervous systems. BDNF also supports the development and strength of synapses between neurons. Events such as sustained or traumatic stress, head trauma, drug use, hypoglycemia, and even the microbes in the gut can influence the activity of BDNF, which may have mental health implications (Pitts, Taylor, & Gourley, 2016; Tapia-Arancibia, Rage, Givalois, & Arancibia, 2004; Zhang et al., 2006).

At approximately 60 days postconception, the presence of sex hormones, notably androgens (i.e., testosterone), or the absence thereof, initiates sexual differentiation of both the body and the brain. Exposure to sex hormones during development can also affect the functioning of the brain postnatally and throughout life. The importance of sex hormones in the brain and associated development are further discussed later in the chapter.

Second Trimester

By approximately the start of the second trimester, at 3 months postconception, the telencephalon, or cerebral cortex, becomes the largest structure of the prenatal brain. The cerebellum follows a similar process of regionalized development beginning in the second trimester (Liu et al., 2011). Neurogenesis starts to slow by the fifth month of gestation but continues until early postnatal stages (Urbán & Guillemot, 2013). Neurogenesis was historically thought not to extend beyond this period of early development, meaning that the neurons that were developed during prenatal and early postnatal development constituted all of the neurons that one had in life. However, groundbreaking research in the late 1990s found that the human brain continues to produce new neurons throughout adulthood (Eriksson et al., 1998).

Third Trimester

During the third trimester, synapses begin developing between neurons at a rate of approximately 40,000 per minute (Bourgeois, 1997). This also means that the brain is increasing in size, almost tripling in volume, during this last prenatal period. Consequently, during the seventh month of development, the gyri (folds) and sulci (grooves) of the cerebral cortex, which give it its characteristic wrinkled look, begin to emerge. Myelin begins to form around axons at about the seventh month of gestation and continues until around 9 months postnatally, with this process generally moving from the back to the front of the brain. The frontal region of the brain is the last to become myelinated. This means that basic survival functions (e.g., crying for food) precede rational thinking, planning, decision making, and emotional regulation. The cerebellum also increases dramatically in surface area. Given this rapid and expansive development of the brain during the third trimester, this period is also the most vulnerable to injury by both internal and external factors.

Brain Development During Infancy and Childhood

The prenatal period is only the first step in brain development, which is a long and extensive process that lasts through late adolescence and into early adulthood (Stiles & Jernigan, 2010). Development progresses from the bottom to the top and from the back to the front, meaning that the prefrontal cortex, maturing in the early to mid-20s, is one of the last areas to develop. However, it has been argued that the architecture of the brain continues to change throughout life and that the last areas to develop are some of the first to experience decline with increasing age. These developmental stages of the brain and the changes occurring during each stage may have marked influences on the counseling process.

After birth, the brain continues to rapidly grow and becomes more tailored in its functioning, increasing fourfold and reaching nearly 90% of adult brain volume by age 6 years (Stiles & Jernigan, 2010). However, this does not always happen in a smooth and gradual process. People experience growth spurts in brain development when their brain rapidly undergoes changes. These sensitive or optimum periods of development occur in the brain but are represented as periods of behavior change, when children (and, later, adolescents) are able to take on new tasks and regulate their emotions and behaviors accordingly. Unlike what are traditionally considered critical periods with definitive end points, sensitive or optimal periods are thought to be dependent on the learning process and are not inherently limited by time (Johnson, 2005; Werker & Tees, 2005).

The first rapid period of development, which starts during the third trimester and encompasses rapid neuronal growth and myelination of axons, continues until roughly the third year of life (Jernigan, Baaré, Stiles, & Madsen, 2011). Changes to the brain during this time are more clearly seen on structural scans than are changes that occur later in childhood and adulthood (Jernigan et al., 2011). Gray matter increases nearly 150% during the first year of life, with the cerebellum growing a whopping 240% (Knickmeyer et al., 2008). By age 3 years, a child has twice as many neuronal connections as he or she does as an adult. This may seem counterintuitive at first, given that the brain and head continue to grow in size well beyond age 3. However, during this early period the brain produces many more neuronal connections than one could ever actually use. This abundant growth in neurons and connections primes the child for rapid learning. Through learning (i.e., both structured and experiences), certain connections become reinforced, and others that are not used are pruned. This synaptic pruning, or thinning process, actually represents a fine-tuning of cerebral functioning that occurs in later childhood and through adolescence. It is a process of refining and engaging higher order cortical areas over the more evolutionarily primitive subcortical regions. This process of refinement, which may actually represent an increased myelination of axons, is generally first seen in the primary sensory and sensorimotor cortex and then moves out to multimodal areas (Jernigan et al., 2011; Sowell et al., 2004).

These first few years are considered the most critical to development and can have a marked impact on development later in life (Knickmeyer et al., 2008). To use an analogy, the first few years are similar to constructing the scaffolding on which later learning will build. During the first few years, humans move from primarily using motor reflexes that are key to survival (e.g., crying and the rooting–sucking reflex) to using their senses and vocalizations to communicate (e.g., head turning, cooing, and reaching for objects). They begin to crawl and then walk. They learn how to communicate through a symbolic system, most often language. Humans form interpersonal attachments with a primary caregiver and later learn social cognitive skills useful in cooperative play. These developments are rooted in changes taking place in the brain.

Attachment

Infants' survival and primary well-being are contingent on their attachment to a primary caregiver. Classic attachment theory (Bowlby, 1982) suggests that through these early relationships, people develop internal working models of human bonding that set the stage for later neurological and socioemotional development. These relationships help people to feel safe and accepted (Porges, 2011; Sullivan, 2003). However, finding a neurological system for attachment has been elusive. Eloquently paraphrasing Wittgenstein, Coan (2008) likened trying to find a functional system of attachment to "trying to find the real artichoke by peeling away all its leaves" (p. 3). In other words, attachment is a complex neurological system made up of a delicate balance of myriad intricate parts.

Much of the early research on infant attachment was in the area of imprinting, or the formation of an enduring cognitive representation of and behavioral response to a caregiver or caregiver-like figure soon after birth (Insel & Young, 2001). This process involves a predominance of different sensory systems in varying species. In birds, for example, imprinting is largely facilitated using more visual and auditory cues, whereas mammals (e.g., rats) use more olfactory cues (Insel & Young, 2001). In humans, the neurophysiological process of attachment seems to involve all three sensory systems, olfactory, auditory, and visual. The neuropeptide oxytocin seems to facilitate attachment bonding (Insel & Young, 2001). Oxytocin, developed in the hypothalamus, enhances learning and emotional memory and is thought to be transmitted from mother to child during early infant attachment experiences (Feldman, Gordon, & Zagoory-Sharon, 2010). Strong correlations have been found between salivary (spit) concentrations of oxytocin between rat mothers and offspring both before and after social intervening (e.g., grooming behaviors), with the higher oxytocin levels being associated with higher emotional synchrony and social engagement in infants (Feldman et al., 2010). In addition, the functioning of the amygdala helps humans to understand emotions on faces, and concentrations of both dopamine from the nucleus accumbens and norepinephrine from the locus coeruleus facilitate reward-driven behavior toward attachment figures (Coan, 2008). These attachment relationships support brain development.

31

For example, physical touch and connection appear to attenuate the stress response. In other words, attachment relationships help humans to regulate their autonomic nervous systems and the hypothalamic–pituitary–adrenal (HPA) axis (Coan, 2008; Porges, 2011).

Language

The ability to form a representative form of communication is a remarkable feat and one that unfolds over the first few years of life. At around 6 to 8 months of age, a baby can vocalize by canonical babbling or repeated consonant vowel sounds (Bates & Dick, 2002). As the child reaches toddlerhood, strings of meaningful words are juxtaposed to interact with adults and other children. Social interaction is essential for language development, yet children follow the same developmental course for language learning regardless of culture (Kuhl & Rivera-Gaxiola, 2008). Children acquire language in part through imitating or mirroring adults in the production of speech. Language development is thought to be assisted by mirror neurons (Bates & Dick, 2002; Kuhl & Rivera-Gaxiola, 2008). Located in the premotor and primary motor cortex, frontal lobe, Broca's area, and inferior parietal lobe (Kilner & Lemon, 2013), mirror neurons fire in the same way when one is perceiving the action of another as when one is conducting the action oneself. Some researchers consider mirror neurons to also be associated with emotional contagion, a rudimentary form of empathy.

Memory

The hippocampus and prefrontal cortex do not fully develop until adolescence and early adulthood, respectively. This protracted development has marked implications for children's memory systems. According to Squire (2004), the brain has two primary memory systems. Declarative or explicit memories are conscious, language-based memories of events that rely on the hippocampus and frontal lobes. Nondeclarative or implicit memories are memories largely outside of conscious awareness (i.e., preconscious), such as conditioned emotional and sensory learning, reflexes, and procedural learning. Implicit memories are formed with the aid of the amygdala and cerebellum (Squire, 2004). Research has suggested that children younger than age 18 months have not yet developed their declarative memory system (Fishbane, 2007) and that this system is still being solidified through the first 5 years of life (Siegel, 2006). Counselors should consider these limitations when working with young children.

Reflective Questions

Recall Rein's presenting concerns and broader context.

Given her current age, what milestones has Rein encountered with respect to her brain development?

How might Rein's environment have affected her brain development in childhood?

Brain Development During Adolescence

Spanning from roughly age 11 years to the mid-20s, adolescence represents a second, notable sensitive period of brain development and is considered by some to be perhaps the most critical period in development (Paus, Keshavan, & Giedd, 2008). It is also a period during which the onset of numerous mental health disorders is seen. A number of factors may contribute to this vulnerability and have implications for clinical practice, as summarized in Jones (2015).

During this time, individuals experience volumetric changes in both gray matter and white matter in the brain that represent an increased refinement in brain functioning (Casey, Jones, & Hare, 2008). For example, following a bell-shaped curve, the volume of gray matter in the frontal cortex, and particularly the prefrontal cortex, peaks in early adolescence and gradually decreases into late adolescence. Along with such alterations in gray matter, the volume of white matter follows a linear course of development, increasing across adolescence. Such changes in the prefrontal cortex parallel improvements in cognitive abilities and logical reasoning skills.

Emotional Regulation

Along with these changes in cortical structures, concurrent changes are also taking place in the limbic and paralimbic regions of the brain. The amygdala, hippocampus, anterior cingulate cortex, and nucleus accumbens also demonstrate progressive synaptic pruning during adolescence. In general, the limbic structures of the brain mature earlier than the prefrontal cortex (Casey et al., 2008). This asymmetrical development in part explains the emotional lability, self-consciousness, impulsiveness, and risk-taking behavior often seen during adolescence. The limbic, or more emotionally responsive and instinctual, parts of the brain are in overdrive, but the more cognitive, decision-making, and problem-solving areas of the brain have not yet caught up. Consequently, adolescents are not yet able to optimally regulate their limbic regions in emotionally charged situations. Adolescents appear to demonstrate a capacity for self-control and impulse regulation in nonemotional situations similar to that of adults (Casey & Caudle, 2013). As the adolescent ages and the volume of white matter increases between the prefrontal cortex and limbic regions, top-down control of limbic cortices will become more firmly established, and the individual will become better able to self-regulate in emotional contexts. In this way, adolescence also presents an opportunity to optimize brain development and functioning, potentially leading to enhanced cognitive, social, and emotional function and overall mental health in adulthood.

The HPA axis similarly goes through a second sensitive period of development during adolescence (Gunnar, Wewerka, Frenn, Long, & Griggs, 2009; Spear, 2000). Adolescents, on average, experience higher levels of cortisol in their systems in response to both psychological and social stressors. As such, chronic or acute stress during adolescence may have pronounced effects on the emergence of mental health disorders during adolescence as well as an individual's ability to self-regulate and cope with stress as an adult. During adolescence, the body also experiences an influx of neurotransmitters and hormones. Dopamine levels are particularly high during adolescence, and increased dopaminergic activity can help to explain why adolescents engage in increased sensation-seeking and risking-taking behaviors, including substance use (Sturman & Moghaddam, 2011).

The microbiota–gut–brain axis follows a similar developmental time course as that of the brain. Adolescence represents one of the most dynamic periods of change for gut microbiota (Borre et al., 2014). Such changes in the microbiota–gut–brain axis during adolescence may even influence the development of anxiety (Foster & Neufeld, 2013). Also, Hoban et al. (2016) found that a lack of proper colonialization of microbes in the gut could influence development of the prefrontal cortex through the overproduction of myelin. These findings and the growing interest in the gut–brain access may have significant implications for the development of mental health disorders, such as schizophrenia and mood disorders, that present during this time.

Social Development

Adolescence is a period of differentiating from parents and developing stronger interpersonal connections with friends. It is also, in many cultures, the onset of developing amorous interests and relationships with potential partners. Blakemore and Mills (2014) emphasized that adolescence is a decisive period in the development of social cognition. Social cognition, or the ability to "recognize others, and to evaluate our own and others' mental states" (Blakemore & Mills, 2014, p. 134), is governed by a set of brain structures including the medial prefrontal cortex, anterior cingulate cortex, inferior frontal gyrus, posterior superior temporal sulcus, temporo-parietal junction, amygdala, and anterior insula (Sebastian, Viding, Williams, & Blakemore, 2010). Changes going on in these regions underlie the process of theory of mind, or the ability to attribute mental states to others, and can lead adolescents to be more sensitive to social cues, especially facial expressions (L. A. Thomas, De Bellis, Graham, & LaBar, 2007). Adolescents can thus become more sensitive to bullying and social ostracization, feeling more emotional effects than adults (Sebastian et al., 2010). K. M. Thomas et al. (2001) examined how adolescents and adults perceive facial expressions differently, examining the brain activity underlying behavioral responses. The adolescents in their study frequently perceived more emotions incorrectly. Their amygdalae were also more active than those of adults, even to neutral faces. This pattern of brain development in adolescence may help to explain why individuals feel increasingly self-conscious during this time. Just as they start to develop the capacity to grasp the perspective of another (theory of mind), adolescents' emotional response may be exaggerated and more negative than adults. However, during early and mid-adolescence, they may not yet have the cortical capacity to optimally regulate that emotional response.

The reciprocal importance of social functioning and brain development during this time also leads to questions of what impact a reliance on technology during this time has on the brain. Although research is ongoing in this area and many questions remain to be answered, one study has suggested the potential effects of technology on empathy. Uhls et al. (2014) found that tweens who abstained from television, computer, and smartphone use for 5 days significantly improved their ability to read nonverbal emotion cues compared with peers with technology access.

Influence of Sex Hormones

As reviewed in Jones (2016), nearly every change in the brain that occurs during adolescence is in some manner influenced by the deluge of sex hormones initiated during this period. This is also when more of the broad sex-related differences in mental health begin to emerge in terms of the prevalence of certain disorders. Cerebral blood flow, HPA axis functioning, and levels of neurotransmitters are all regulated by levels of gonadal steroids, such as estrogen and testosterone. Estrogen not only enhances cerebral blood flow but also influences levels of serotonin, dopamine, and oxytocin. Increased levels of both estrogen and testosterone enhance the functioning of the HPA axis and related corticosterone release and negative-feedback loops. During the menstrual cycle, levels of gonadal hormones fluctuate. Early evidence has suggested that this may affect susceptibility to addiction, relapse, posttrauma pathology, and even suicidality. For example, Baca-Garcia et al. (2010) found that female suicide attempts increased when levels of estrogen and progesterone were low (early follicular phase), that these attempts were more severe, and that suicidal ideation increased in female adolescents when progesterone levels were low. The influx of hormones furthermore leads to a sex differentiation in the gut microbiome, which again influences mental health (Jašarević, Morrison, & Bale, 2016). Researchers such as Sisk and Zehr (2005) have suggested that it is this influx of hormones coupled with rapid brain development that increases the risk for psychopathology during adolescence.

The Aging Brain

The percentage of adults older than age 65 is expected to exceed 30% in many countries by 2050 (Wright & Díaz, 2014). Nearly one in five older adults experience mental health challenges such as depression, dementia, and Alzheimer's disease. However, those mental health needs are not currently being met (Karel, Gatz, & Smyer, 2012). Various aspects of cognitive functioning, including processing speed, executive functioning, and difficulty with episodic declarative memory, which is conscious memory of events, have also been found to decline with age (Grady, 2012). However, other cognitive functions, such as emotional regulation and crystallized tasks such as vocabulary, appear to stay intact (Wright & Díaz, 2014). Understanding the neuroscience of aging will be helpful in elucidating how counselors can best support older adult clients.

Reflective Questions

Reflect back on the case of Rein and consider the following questions:

How might adolescent brain development be influencing Rein's symptoms?

What other factors might you want to consider in addition to these influences?

Gray Matter

As individuals age, they often experience a loss of brain volume, with different brain areas displaying different aging trajectories. Generally speaking, the last brain areas to develop are often the first to experience age-related declines (Tamnes et al., 2013). The most notable volumetric loss has been reported in the frontal and prefrontal cortices, temporal lobes and hippocampus, thalamus, and nucleus accumbens (Fjell & Walhovd, 2010). Rather than the result of necrosis (neuronal death), gray matter changes appear to be related to the shrinkage of neurons, reduction of synaptic spines, decrease in the number of synapses, and loss of glial cells (Fjell & Walhovd, 2010).

White Matter

Changes in the volume and integrity of white matter are also seen in the healthy aging brain. After the increase and peak in white matter during adolescence and subsequent volumetric plateau, declines in white matter volume seem to start gradually around age 50 and decline more steeply after age 70 (Fjell & Walhovd, 2010). The majority of this decline is seen in the frontal lobe, with notable loss also occurring in the corpus callosum (Geerligs, Renken, Saliasi, Maurits, & Lorist, 2015; Gunning-Dixon, Brickman, Cheng, & Alexopoulos, 2009). Decreases in myelinated axons within and across various brain regions may underscore much of this volumetric change, with a reduction in the length of myelinated axons by nearly 50% (Fjell & Welhovd, 2010). This is also thought to be indicative of decreased connectivity between brain regions. For example, functional connectivity of the default mode network declines with age, which may have implications for working memory (Tomasi & Volkow, 2012).

Increased Bilateral Brain Activity

One other interesting phenomenon documented in healthy aging brains is an increase in bilateral activation of the frontal and prefrontal cortices during tasks that used to be unilateral in young adults (Grady, 2012). Researchers have provided several explanations for such seemingly counterintuitive changes. Initially, such increased activation was thought to represent compensatory activity in the brain. In other words, greater activation and more brain regions are needed to perform the same task. Another possible explanation is a concept called *dedifferentiation*. Dedifferentiation can be defined as "a process by which structures . . . that were specialized for a given function lose their specialization and become simplified, less distinct or common to different functions" (Baltes & Lindenberger, 1997, as cited in Sleimen-Malkoun, Temprado, & Hong, 2014, p. 2). As such, multiple different tasks can now activate similar brain regions. For example, brain regions that support sensory, motor, and cognitive tasks are more correlated in older adults, as are different types of visual processing and memory functions (Sleimen-Malkoun, Temprado, & Hong, 2014).

Alzheimer's Disease

Significant research has also examined changes in the brain related to various degenerative disorders, such as dementia and Alzheimer's disease. Such disorders have a prevalence rate of around 11% among adults older than age 65 in the United States (Alzheimer's Association, 2013). Alzheimer's disease is the most common form of dementia that progressively affects memory, thought processes, and, consequently, behavior. The characteristic markers of Alzheimer's disease include reduced brain weight, cortical atrophy, and associated ventricular enlargements, in addition to neurofibrillary tangles of tau protein filaments typically occurring in the hippocampus and related limbic structures and amyloid plaques typically found throughout the cortex (Rossini, Rossi, Babiloni, & Polich, 2007).These changes can be associated with synapse elimination and necrosis. Alzheimer's-related impairments in episodic memory have also been documented as being noticeable more than 6 years before diagnosis was made (Bäckman, Small, & Fratiglioni, 2001). Grady (2012) suggested that, given this window, providers should be assessing aging clients for Alzheimer's disease risk factors, such as mild cognitive impairment.

Developmentally Informed Interventions

Understanding brain development over the life span enriches case conceptualization and treatment planning. In clinical work, child and adolescent clients are often grouped together into a single special population. From this review of brain development, it is clear that children and adolescents are two separate groups, each warranting a unique approach. Best practices for working with children, such as play therapy, honor the neurodevelopmental stage of young clients by providing a symbolic framework that does not rely on linguistic production and declarative memory systems. The child does not have to tell a story in words but symbolically represents the feelings of the body and the implicit memory of events in an environment that is safe and secure, fostering relationship and attachment. According to Gaskill and Perry (2014), the somatosensory experiences involved in play can help to create the necessary neurological foundations for "advanced mental skills, such as creativity, abstract thought, prosocial behavior, and expressive language" (p. 180). However, best practices for adolescents alone are not as well established.

In addition to assessing for mild cognitive impairment, research is examining the rehabilitative effects of training on the aging brain. Older adults who practiced active tasks lasting from 2.5 to 10 hours related to divided attention, episodic memory, and working memory had cortical activation similar to that of younger adults in their prefrontal, frontal, and temporal cortices (Grady, 2012). Wright and Díaz (2014) also emphasized the importance of assessing for depression in aging clients, because depression coupled with volumetric changes in the hippocampus can lead to more rapid cognitive decline (Sawyer, Corsentino, Sachs-Ericsson, & Steffens, 2012).

My Brain-Based Approach to the Case of Rein

Rein's developmental stage of early adolescence is central to understanding her presenting symptoms. During this period, the subcortical and limbic regions of her brain and associated HPA axis are developing at a faster rate than the cortical regions of her brain such as the prefrontal cortex. When emotional or under stress, she is likely to have limited cognitive control and may respond in an impulsive and emotionally driven manner. Rein is beginning to develop the capacity for theory of mind and mentalizing, and thus she may be more self-conscious about how others view her. Because Rein is just starting to develop these cognitive aspects of empathy, she is likely more sensitive to social cues, particularly facial expressions. She recently initiated menarche, and the considerable influx of gonadal hormones such as estrogen is altering the functioning of neurotransmitters, hormones, and the HPA axis, all of which can have significant implications for her mental health.

In working with Rein, I would first provide psychoeducation about how the changes she is experiencing in her brain and body affect how she is currently feeling. I would explore with Rein the emotions and physical sensations she is experiencing in her body. Verbally labeling an emotional stimulus can assist Rein with emotional regulation by decreasing cerebral blood flow (i.e., activity) in the amygdala and increasing activation of the prefrontal cortex (Hariri, Bookheimer, & Mazziotta, 2000). Grounding and breathing exercises, mindfulness practices, biofeedback, and neurofeedback have all been used to enhance optimal brain development among adolescents. Brain-based guidance curriculums are also available for school settings. Last, I would work collaboratively with a primary care provider or nutritionist to develop a nutrition and exercise program. Among a host of other advantages, exercise promotes the release of BDNF from the hippocampus and cortex (Rasmussen et al., 2009).

Conclusion

The principle of working from a developmental perspective represents one of the pillars of the counseling profession. Understanding brain development across the life span enriches the ability to conceptualize client concerns within a developmental context and address clients' developmental needs. This chapter provided a brief overview of notable milestones, sensitive periods, and considerations in the development of the human brain over the life span as related to cognitive, emotional, behavioral, and interpersonal functioning. As research in this area continues to burgeon, especially research examining the nuances of neurophysiological functioning and shifts in adolescent and aging populations, the importance of considering clients' developmental stage will become even more clear, and counselors will be better equipped to support the cognitive, behavioral, emotional, interpersonal, and neurophysiological needs of their clients.

Quiz

1. During which stage of development do synapses begin developing at a rate of approximately 40,000 per minute?
   a. First trimester.
   b. Second trimester.
   c. Third trimester.
   d. First 3 months of postnatal development.
2. During adolescent brain development, which of the following is true?
   a. Subcortical limbic regions of the brain develop before the prefrontal cortical areas.
   b. The HPA axis no longer changes.
   c. Neurotransmitter expression is the lowest than at any other point in development.
   d. Prefrontal cortical areas of the brain develop before subcortical limbic regions.
3. In older adults, which of the following *do not* seem to be impaired by healthy aging?
   a. Memory.
   b. Emotion regulation.
   c. Processing speed.
   d. All of the above.

References

Alzheimer's Association. (2013). Alzheimer's disease facts and figures. *Alzheimer's & Dementia, 9*, 208–245. doi:10.1016/j.jalz.2013.02.003

Baca-Garcia, E., Diaz-Sastre, C., Ceverino, A., Perez-Rodriguez, M. M., Navarro-Jimenez, R., Lopez-Castroman, J., . . . Oquendo, M. A. (2010). Suicide attempts among women during low estradiol/low progesterone states. *Journal of Psychiatric Research, 44*, 209–214.

Bäckman, L., Small, B. J., & Fratiglioni, L. (2001). Stability of the preclinical episodic memory deficit in Alzheimer's disease. *Brain, 124*, 96–102.

Bates, E., & Dick, F. (2002). Language, gesture, and the developing brain. *Developmental Psychobiology, 40*, 293–310.

Blakemore, S. J., & Mills, K. L. (2014). Is adolescence a sensitive period for sociocultural processing? *Annual Review of Psychology, 65*, 187–207. doi: 10.1146/annurev-psych-010213-115202

Borre, Y. E., O'Keeffe, G. W., Clarke, G., Stanton, C., Dinan, T. G., & Cryan, J. F. (2014). Microbiota and neurodevelopmental windows: Implications for brain disorders. *Trends in Molecular Medicine, 20*, 509–518.

Bourgeois, J. P. (1997). Synaptogenesis, heterochrony and epigenesis in the mammalian neocortex. *Acta Paediatrica, 86*, 27–33.

Bowlby, J. (1982). *Attachment and loss* (Vol. 1). New York, NY: Basic Books.

Casey, B. J., & Caudle, K. (2013). The teenage brain: Self control. *Current Directions in Psychological Science, 22*, 82–87.

Casey, B. J., Jones, R. M., & Hare, T. A. (2008). The adolescent brain. *Annals of the New York Academy of Sciences, 1124*, 111–126. http://dx.doi.org/10.1196/annals.1440.010

Coan, J. A. (2008). Toward a neuroscience of attachment. In J. Cassidy & P. R. Shaver (Eds.), *Handbook of attachment: Theory, research, and clinical applications* (2nd ed., pp. 241–265). New York, NY: Guilford Press.

Council for the Accreditation of Counseling and Related Educational Programs. (2015). *2016 CACREP standards*. Retrieved from http://www.cacrep.org/wp-content/uploads/2012/10/2016-CACREP-Standards.pdf

Cowan, W. M. (1979). The development of the brain. *Scientific American, 241*, 113–133.

Eriksson, P. S., Perfilieva, E., Björk-Eriksson, T., Alborn, A. M., Nordborg, C., Peterson, D. A., & Gage, F. H. (1998). Neurogenesis in the adult human hippocampus. *Nature Medicine, 4*, 1313–1317.

Feldman, R., Gordon, I., & Zagoory-Sharon, O. (2010). The cross-generation transmission of oxytocin in humans. *Hormones and Behavior, 58*, 669–676.

Fishbane, M. D. (2007). Wired to connect: Neuroscience, relationships, and therapy. *Family Process, 46,* 395–412.

Fjell, A. M., & Walhovd, K. B. (2010). Structural brain changes in aging: Courses, causes and cognitive consequences. *Reviews in the Neurosciences, 21,* 187–222.

Foster, J. A., & Neufeld, K. A. M. (2013). Gut–brain axis: How the microbiome influences anxiety and depression. *Trends in Neurosciences, 36,* 305–312.

Gaskill, R. L., & Perry, B. D. (2014). The neurobiological power of play. In C. A. Malchiodi & D. A. Crenshaw (Eds.), *Creative arts and play therapy for attachment problems* (pp. 178–194). New York, NY: Guilford Press.

Geerligs, L., Renken, R. J., Saliasi, E., Maurits, N. M., & Lorist, M. M. (2015). A brain-wide study of age-related changes in functional connectivity. *Cerebral Cortex, 25,* 1987–1999.

Grady, C. (2012). The cognitive neuroscience of ageing. *Nature Reviews Neuroscience, 13,* 491–505.

Gunnar, M. R., Wewerka, S., Frenn, K., Long, J. D., & Griggs, C. (2009). Developmental changes in hypothalamus–pituitary–adrenal activity over the transition to adolescence: Normative changes and associations with puberty. *Development and Psychopathology, 21,* 69–85.

Gunning-Dixon, F. M., Brickman, A. M., Cheng, J. C., & Alexopoulos, G. S. (2009). Aging of cerebral white matter: A review of MRI findings. *International Journal of Geriatric Psychiatry, 24,* 109–117.

Hariri, A. R., Bookheimer, S. Y., & Mazziotta, J. C. (2000). Modulating emotional responses: Effects of a neocortical network on the limbic system. *NeuroReport, 11,* 43–48.

Hoban, A. E., Stilling, R. M., Ryan, F. J., Shanahan, F., Dinan, T. G., Claesson, M. J., . . . Cryan, J. F. (2016). Regulation of prefrontal cortex myelination by the microbiota. *Translational Psychiatry, 6,* e774

Insel, T. R., & Young, L. J. (2001). The neurobiology of attachment. *Nature Reviews Neuroscience, 2,* 129–136.

Jašarević, E., Morrison, K. E., & Bale, T. L. (2016). Sex differences in the gut microbiome–brain axis across the lifespan. *Philosophical Transactions of the Royal Society B, 371,* 20150122.

Jernigan, T. L., Baaré, W. F., Stiles, J., & Madsen, K. S. (2011). Postnatal brain development: Structural imaging of dynamic neurodevelopmental processes. *Progress in Brain Research, 189,* 77–92.

Johnson, M. H. (2005). Sensitive periods in functional brain development: Problems and prospects. *Developmental Psychobiology, 46,* 287–292.

Jones, L. K. (2015). The evolving adolescent brain. *Counseling Today, 57*(7), 14–17.

Jones, L. K. (2016). Sex-related variations in neuroscience and endocrinology and their effects on mental health. *Counseling Today, 58*(10), 16–19.

Karel, M. J., Gatz, M., & Smyer, M. A. (2012). Aging and mental health in the decade ahead: What psychologists need to know. *American Psychologist, 67,* 184–198.

Kilner, J. M., & Lemon, R. N. (2013). What we know currently about mirror neurons. *Current Biology, 23,* 1057–1062.

Knickmeyer, R. C., Gouttard, S., Kang, C., Evans, D., Wilber, K., Smith, J. K., . . . Gilmore, J. H. (2008). A structural MRI study of human brain development from birth to 2 years. *Journal of Neuroscience, 28,* 12176–12182.

Kuhl, P., & Rivera-Gaxiola, M. (2008). Neural substrates of language acquisition. *Annual Review of Neuroscience, 31,* 511–534.

Liu, F., Zhang, Z., Lin, X., Teng, G., Meng, H., Yu, T., . . . Liu, S. (2011). Development of the human fetal cerebellum in the second trimester: A post mortem magnetic resonance imaging evaluation. *Journal of Anatomy, 219,* 582–588.

Paus, T., Keshavan, M., & Giedd, J. N. (2008). Why do many psychiatric disorders emerge during adolescence? *Nature Reviews Neuroscience, 9,* 947–957.

Pitts, E. G., Taylor, J. R., & Gourley, S. L. (2016). Prefrontal cortical BDNF: A regulatory key in cocaine- and food-reinforced behaviors. *Neurobiology of Disease, 91,* 326–335.

Porges, S. W. (2011). *The polyvagal theory: Neurophysiological foundations of emotions, attachment, communication, and self-regulation.* New York, NY: W. W. Norton.

Rasmussen, P., Brassard, P., Adser, H., Pedersen, M. V., Leick, L., Hart, E., . . . Pilegaard, H. (2009). Evidence for a release of brain-derived neurotrophic factor from the brain during exercise. *Experimental Physiology, 94,* 1062–1069.

Rossini, P. M., Rossi, S., Babiloni, C., & Polich, J. (2007). Clinical neurophysiology of aging brain: From normal aging to neurodegeneration. *Progress in Neurobiology, 83,* 375–400.

Sawyer, K., Corsentino, E., Sachs-Ericsson, N., & Steffens, D. C. (2012). Depression, hippocampal volume changes, and cognitive decline in a clinical sample of older depressed outpatients and non-depressed controls. *Aging & Mental Health, 16,* 753–762.

Sebastian, C., Viding, E., Williams, K. D., & Blakemore, S. J. (2010). Social brain development and the affective consequences of ostracism in adolescence. *Brain and Cognition, 72,* 134–145.

Siegel, D. J. (2006). An interpersonal neurobiology approach to psychotherapy. *Psychiatric Annals, 36,* 248–256.

Sisk, C. L., & Zehr, J. L. (2005). Pubertal hormones organize the adolescent brain and behavior. *Frontiers in Neuroendocrinology, 26,* 163–174.

Sleimen-Malkoun, R., Temprado, J. J., & Hong, S. L. (2014). Aging induced loss of complexity and dedifferentiation: Consequences for coordination dynamics within and between brain, muscular and behavioral levels. *Frontiers in Aging Neuroscience, 6,* 140.

Sowell, E. R., Thompson, P. M., Leonard, C. M., Welcome, S. E., Kan, E., & Toga, A. W. (2004). Longitudinal mapping of cortical thickness and brain growth in normal children. *Journal of Neuroscience, 24,* 8223–8231.

Spear, L. P. (2000). The adolescent brain and age-related behavioral manifestations. *Neuroscience and Biobehavioral Reviews, 24,* 417–463.

Squire, L. R. (2004). Memory systems of the brain: A brief history and current perspective. *Neurobiology of Learning and Memory, 82,* 171–177.

Stiles, J., & Jernigan, T. L. (2010). The basics of brain development. *Neuropsychology Review, 20,* 327–348.

Sturman, D. A., & Moghaddam, B. (2011). The neurobiology of adolescence: Changes in brain architecture, functional dynamics, and behavioral tendencies. *Neuroscience and Biobehavioral Reviews, 35,* 1704–1712.

Sullivan, R. M. (2003). Developing a sense of safety. *Annals of the New York Academy of Sciences, 1008,* 122–131.

Tamnes, C. K., Walhovd, K. B., Dale, A. M., Østby, Y., Grydeland, H., Richardson, G., . . . Holland, D. (2013). Brain development and aging: Overlapping and unique patterns of change. *NeuroImage, 68,* 63–74.

Tapia-Arancibia, L., Rage, F., Givalois, L., & Arancibia, S. (2004). Physiology of BDNF: Focus on hypothalamic function. *Frontiers in Neuroendocrinology, 25,* 77–107.

Thomas, K. M., Drevets, W. C., Whalen, P. J., Eccard, C. H., Dahl, R. E., Ryan, N. D., & Casey, B. J. (2001). Amygdala response to facial expressions in children and adults. *Biological Psychiatry, 49,* 309–316.

Thomas, L. A., De Bellis, M. D., Graham, R., & LaBar, K. S. (2007). Development of emotional facial recognition in late childhood and adolescence. *Developmental Science, 10,* 547–558.

Tomasi, D., & Volkow, N. D. (2012). Aging and functional brain networks. *Molecular Psychiatry, 17,* 549–558.

Uhls, Y. T., Michikyan, M., Morris, J., Garcia, D., Small, G. W., Zgourou, E., & Greenfield, P. M. (2014). Five days at outdoor education camp without screens improves preteen skills with nonverbal emotion cues. *Computers in Human Behavior, 39,* 387–392.

Urbán, N., & Guillemot, F. (2013). Neurogenesis in the embryonic and adult brain: Same regulators, different roles. *Frontiers in Cellular Neuroscience, 8,* 396–396.

Werker, J. F., & Tees, R. C. (2005). Speech perception as a window for understanding plasticity and commitment in language systems of the brain. *Developmental Psychobiology, 46,* 233–251.

Wright, S. L., & Díaz, F. (2014). Neuroscience research on aging and implications for counseling psychology. *Journal of Counseling Psychology, 61,* 534–540.

Zhang, H., Ozbay, F., Lappalainen, J., Kranzler, H. R., van Dyck, C. H., Charney, D. S., . . . Gelernter, J. (2006). Brain derived neurotrophic factor (BDNF) gene variants and Alzheimer's disease, affective disorders, posttraumatic stress disorder, schizophrenia, and substance dependence. *American Journal of Medical Genetics Part B: Neuropsychiatric Genetics, 141,* 387–393.

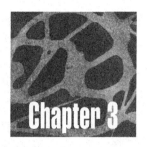

Chapter 3

Biology of Marginality: A Neurophysiological Exploration of the Social and Cultural Foundations of Psychological Health

Kathryn Z. Douthit and Justin Russotti

Honoring social and cultural diversity in counseling practice has been a cornerstone of the profession for the past half century. The profession has long grasped the ethical imperative in honoring how culture and ethnicity provide a framework for the ways in which clients make meaning of their world. With an eye toward social justice, the profession is also deeply concerned about the suffering incurred by those whose social or cultural status places them in the margins of the social world. This chapter challenges counselors to expand their understanding of those living in the margins by grappling with some of the biological mechanisms that are affected by a life of marginality. The implications of the biological literature related to marginality are profound—injustices in the social world become imprinted in flesh-and-blood realities that have an impact on mental and physical health. Whether it is the chronic stress wrought by bigotry, dehumanization, and disdain or the environmental scars of poverty that deprive whole communities of quality food, uncontaminated water, safe housing, green spaces, and satisfactory educational experiences, marginality leaves in its wake psychological suffering, life-threatening diseases, and, for some, premature death.

Multiple dimensions of human biology inform the understanding of the physiological responses to social injustice. This chapter focuses on two of these dimensions, one being psychoneuroimmunology (PNI) and the other being epigenetics. These two dimensions are spotlighted primarily because of their dramatic association with the biologically driven mental health struggles of marginalized clients and their potential for counseling prevention and intervention. These counseling approaches to prevention and intervention are pivotal in navigating the case of Henrietta, the client portrayed in this chapter's case study.

 ## 2016 CACREP Standards

This chapter addresses sections of the 2016 Council for Accreditation of Counseling and Related Educational Programs (CACREP) Standards pertinent to the common core areas of Social and Cultural Diversity (Standard II.F.2.) and Human Growth and Development (Standard II.F.3.):

- The impact of heritage, attitudes, beliefs, understandings, and acculturative experiences on an individual's views of others (Standard II.F.2.d.)
- Systemic and environmental factors that affect human development, functioning, and behavior (Standard II.F.3.f.)

■ ■ ■

 ## Clinical Case Study: Henrietta

Henrietta is a 48-year-old African American woman who looks many years older than her actual age. She is living in a Rust Belt city and has had diabetes and high blood pressure for the past decade. Subsisting on an income that she pieces together from two physically taxing jobs, she resides in the second-floor unit of a poorly maintained 1940s house situated in a section of a medium-sized city that has gained national recognition for its deep and enduring poverty. In addition to her daily struggle to keep a roof over her head, pay for her medications, and put food on the table, Henrietta assumes much of the responsibility for raising her three male grandchildren, ages 11, 12, and 14. The children are all enrolled in the notoriously troubled city school system and are at an age at which they are lured by the local gang culture. The boys' mother is currently serving time.

Henrietta, who has had lifelong struggles with anxiety and has relied heavily on her faith to give her the strength to meet the environmental challenges she encounters on a daily basis, feels like she is losing her battle. As her grandchildren have gotten older and more defiant and the infrastructure in her neighborhood has steadily declined, her anxiety has become more pervasive and intense, and she finds herself plagued by an accompanying sense of despair, isolation, and worthlessness. Taking two long bus rides in frigid weather and absorbing the lost income from the time that it takes to make the trip, Henrietta seeks counseling services in the behavioral health clinic of a large, urban teaching hospital. Prompted by her counselor, Henrietta describes the overwhelmingness of trying to cope with the immense odds that she faces:

> I always thought that if I prayed hard enough that the Lord would see me through. But I think the Lord has grown weary of listening to me. I worry all day and all night—I worry that the boys are going to turn bad. I worry that I won't be able to feed them. I worry that my health is going to get worse and I won't be able to take care of them.

In inquiring about Henrietta's psychological history, the counselor learns about her growing struggle with depression.

> I could always rely on Jesus to take my hand when things got real bad—He helped me dig deep inside and feel strong. But Jesus doesn't seem to hear me any more. I feel so alone, and when I look in the mirror I feel like I am looking at a ghost. I see someone who is old and tired who hasn't done nothin' good in their life. If I were a better person, Jesus would have shown me the way. But I don't deserve His love and I don't have the strength to carry on.

Henrietta's Case Through a "Social Determinants of Health" Lens

Many of the chronic conditions plaguing Henrietta are conditions that take a disproportionate toll on marginalized communities, such as those in which poor African American and Latino/Latina populations often reside. Obesity, diabetes, hypertension, heart disease, stroke, dementia, certain cancers, depression, and anxiety are a few of the physical and psychological challenges that have a higher incidence among individuals who live at the intersection of racial and economic marginality (Marmot & Wilkerson, 2005). Much of what is known about the biology of marginality emerged from two seminal British studies that set the course for several generations of transformational research on what became known more broadly as "the social determinants of health" (Marmot & Wilkerson, 2005). The now-famous Whitehall I and Whitehall II studies, launched by Sir Michael Marmot and a large team of researchers, opened a window into the close relationship between human health and the surrounding social world. The alarming message emerging from these studies was that lack of status, authority, and control affects physical and mental health in ways that can have life-or-death consequences (Marmot et al., 1991; Marmot & Wilkerson, 2005).

Although the Whitehall studies focused primarily on social class, other major studies in the social determinants of health literature have focused specifically on issues of health and mental health in relation to racial discrimination. A groundbreaking meta-analysis targeting research on discrimination against adult Black Americans included 66 of these studies and showed a compelling link between the experience of race among Black Americans and anxiety, depression, and a variety of other psychiatric conditions (Pieterse, Todd, Neville, & Carter, 2012).

For counselors working in the mental health field with a client base that consists of individuals struggling with the daily assaults of a marginal status or a multiplicity of intersecting marginal statuses, understanding how the daily experience of marginality can become a flesh-and-blood reality that compromises the health of mind and body can help to foster an informed intervention strategy targeting psychological struggles at their source. In this spirit, the remainder of this chapter aims first to clarify some of the main biological mechanisms that are catalyzed by experiences of marginality and foster processes injurious to psychological and physical health and second to suggest intervention strategies that disrupt the cycles of harm fueled by the day-to-day experiences of marginality.

Chronic Stress: Multiple Pathways to Harm

For clients living in the margins, the barrage of assaults they experience translates into a relentless exposure to stress. Whether it is the fear of becoming the next crime victim, the inability to access adequate health care, perpetual fear of being racially profiled by law enforcement, or chronic unemployment, repeated exposure to stress-inducing events is a reality when one is marginalized and a springboard for an array of pathways that lead to mental and physical injury.

Being able to mount the occasional stress response in the face of impending harm is an important survival tool. It is the body's way of garnering peak physical performance and sharpened senses when one is confronted with life-threatening conditions. Situations in which the body needs to pull out all the stops in the interests of survival are not difficult to imagine. Relying on primitive instincts, the amygdala, a part of the brain that perceives threat, sounds an alarm that puts into motion a neuroendocrine cascade that helps the body either stand its ground and enter into a battle or, alternatively, flee to a secure safe space (Sapolsky, 2004). Chapter 4 has an extended discussion of this fight-or-flight acute stress response and the related functions of the cortisol-producing hypothalamic–pituitary–adrenal (HPA) axis and the epinephrine-producing sympathetic–adrenal–medullary axis (Sapolsky, 2004)

As Chapter 4 details, a key to maintaining physical and psychological health rests on one's ability to return, by way of a negative-feedback system, to an unactivated state (McEwen, 2007; Sapolsky, 2004). What happens, however, in an environment in which threats to psychological and physical safety and security are an everyday affair—in which feelings of aggression and anger are repeatedly triggered by despair, defeat, insult, and a lack of fairness, respect, or dignity? In short, the feedback systems that normally function to return cortisol to normal levels become increasingly less efficient, doing less and less to keep the cortisol at a healthy concentration. The acute stress response that can be so lifesaving is thus transformed into a state of chronic stress, which is a threat to mental and physical well-being and can ultimately be life threatening (McEwen, 2007).

Since the publication of Whitehall I in 1978, countless studies have underscored the toxicity of chronic stress (see, e.g., Juster, McEwen, & Lupien, 2010). The myriad physical health outcomes from chronic stress include diabetes, heart disease, stroke, asthma, cancers, and dementia, and the psychological outcomes can include depression, anxiety, and exacerbation of a long list of psychiatric problems, including bipolar disorder, schizophrenia, and posttraumatic stress disorder (Juster et al., 2010; McEwen, 2003; Wilson, Finch, & Cohen, 2002). Although numerous biological pathways threaten wellness under conditions of chronic stress, two particularly salient and interrelated pathways to ill health can be found in the fields of PNI and epigenetics.

PNI Pipeline

The PNI pipeline involves a complex array of biological mechanisms that collectively comprise some of the most startling evidence that humans are inextricably one with their social world. The field of PNI emerged in the 1970s and, by bringing into sharp relief how nonmaterial perceptions of one's social context can be transformed into material flesh-and-blood realities, shed light on the ways in which the work of counselors can have an impact on both mental and physical health (Ader & Cohen, 1993).

More broadly, PNI describes the complex associations between the psychological state of a given individual, the neurological and hormonal processes that respond to that state, and the immunological mechanisms that communicate with those neurological and hormonal processes (Ader, Cohen, & Felten, 1995). Although these systems can work in perfect harmony to maintain health, certain challenges can wreak havoc on how the systems interrelate, thus resulting in threats to health and well-being. To understand how the immune system, which is so vital in protecting people from potentially harmful invaders, such as bacteria, viruses, and cancer cells, can threaten physical and psychological wellness, it is helpful to start with some basic information on the immune system more generally.

Immune function is generally divided into two types, one termed *acquired* and the other *innate*. Acquired immunity refers to the ability to target and destroy specific disease-producing microorganisms (e.g., specific bacteria or specific viruses; Janeway, Travers, Walport, & Shlomchik, 2001). *Specificity* in this case means that an acquired immune response to a cold virus does not help one's ability to fight salmonella from contaminated food or a staph infection from an injury.

In contrast to the very targeted mechanism of acquired immunity, innate immunity, which is more commonly known as *inflammation,* mounts a defense that is nonspecific (Janeway et al., 2001). Innate immunity involves a generalized rallying of cells (i.e., leukocytes or white blood cells) that travel to a site of tissue damage; regardless of how the tissue became injured, the damage signals a generalized response that attempts to destroy and clear any invading microorganisms and foreign debris and initiates tissue repair (Janeway et al., 2001).

This introduction to immunology, though brief, provides a window into the deeply rooted relationship between people's perceptions of the world around them and the health of their minds and bodies. For those who, like Henrietta, live under conditions of chronic stress, the life-sustaining mechanisms of acquired and innate immunity are each compromised in distinctive ways. The dysregulation of the stress response that occurs with chronic stress causes the neuroendocrine system to communicate with the immune system in a manner that suppresses the cells responsible for acquired immune mechanisms and activates the cells responsible for innate immunity (Kendall-Tackett, 2009; Marshall, 2011). The consequences of this ill-fated neuroendocrine–immune dialogue are twofold. In the case of a dampened acquired immune response, one sees increased susceptibility to infections and various cancers, and the problems related to intensification of the innate immune response, that is, inflammation, are connected to a multitude of physical and psychological challenges, including heart disease, cerebrovascular disease, dementia, arthritis, autoimmune diseases, chronic fatigue, and fibromyalgia (Hänsel, Hong, Cámara, & Von Kaenel, 2010; Kendall-Tackett, 2009; Marshall, 2011; Kiecolt-Glaser et al., 2005; Wilson et al., 2002).

What is most relevant for counselors to understand from this description of the chronic stress–immune dysregulation relationship is that within this mind–body communication there are two major ways through which mental health is affected. Both pathways can be understood through a concept that is well known to many counselors, namely, a diathesis–stress model (D-SM) of mental health. This model draws the logical conclusion that the mental health of any given individual is determined by his or her degree of predispositional vulnerability and the environmental stresses to which he or she is subjected (Zuckerman, 1999). In the D-SM, individuals have a threshold for managing environmental stress, after which they no longer have the capacity to bounce back, thus generating the conditions for psychological suffering.

In the context of PNI, both the environmental stress and the level of predispositional vulnerability components of the D-SM are affected. It is not difficult to see how environmental stress might be intensified when PNI mechanisms are left unchecked. Individuals such as Henrietta are faced with the prospect of living with pain and disability in a neighborhood in which good medical care is nonexistent and transportation to geographic locations with available health care is dismal. When one considers the inherent vulnerability component of the D-SM, the role of PNI in translating chronic environmental stress into physiological susceptibility is quite clear. Strong evidence exists for a distinct connection between inflammation and depression, which occurs by way of two different but related pathways (Glassman & Miller, 2007; Surtees et al., 2008). Chemicals called *proinflammatory cytokines*, which are released by cells of the immune system and promote inflammation, mediate both of these pathways. In one pathway, the cytokines trigger a series of reactions that end in a disruption of the production of the neurotransmitter serotonin, which has an important role in mood (Dantzer, O'Connor, Lawson, & Kelley, 2011). In the other pathway, a cytokine participates in a series of reactions that slow the production of brain-derived neurotrophic factor (BDNF), which in turn suppresses neuroplasticity and results in neuron death and brain tissue shrinkage, leading to depression, anxiety, anhedonia, and social withdrawal (Brunoni, Lopes, & Fregni, 2008; Dowlati et al., 2010). Thus, there is a "a vicious cycle in which chronic stress begets immunologically mediated mood disturbance, which then compromises resilience and further fuels the chronic stress condition" (Douthit, 2015b, p. 14). Figure 3.1 depicts the complex dynamic relationship between stress and illness through the lens of marginality, mediated by several variables that include PNI, epigenetics, and mental health challenges.

Reflective Question

As a counselor with an understanding of the relationship between the stresses of extreme poverty and immunologically mediated changes in mental health, how might you help Henrietta to reframe her fears that God has grown weary of her need for support and has consequently abandoned her?

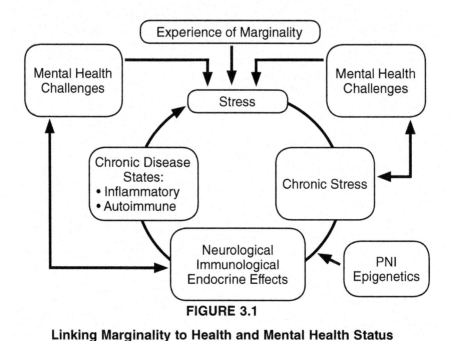

FIGURE 3.1

Linking Marginality to Health and Mental Health Status

Note. PNI = psychoneuroimmunology.

If one returns to the D-SM and looks more closely at the notion of predispositional vulnerability, the biology of marginality becomes even more complex than just discussed. The science of vulnerability now shows that social forces can insert themselves at the level of gene function to actually shape predispositional vulnerability. In particular, work in the field of epigenetics has done much to elucidate the mechanisms that allow contextual hardships to genetically reconfigure people's capacity for resilience. Although we focus on epigenetics in relation to chronic stress, suffice it to say that epigenetics can intersect with marginality in other injurious ways beyond the scope of this chapter.

Epigenetics

The term *epigenetics* is used to describe an array of mechanisms in which aspects of the environment are able to control how genes are expressed. Genes are composed of DNA that carries the instructions or codes that direct the synthesis of proteins needed for growth, development, and other life-sustaining functions (McGowan & Szyf, 2010). Epigenetics shows that environmental forces, including those related to structural inequality, can alter the way genes are expressed both quantitatively and qualitatively without altering the code embedded in the gene. The most widely studied epigenetic mechanism in human research is called *methylation*. In the process of methylation, tiny molecules called *methyl groups* attach to various parts of the gene and through this attachment have the ability to physically control gene output and guide qualitative changes in the final gene product (Jones & Takai, 2001). In some cases, these epigenetic changes allow organisms (including humans) to rapidly adapt to new and challenging environments. Often, these adaptations are life sustaining, but in some cases, as in the case of chronic stress, they can also be toxic (McGowan & Szyf, 2010; Nestler, 2014).

So, how do epigenetic mechanisms relate to the D-SM and predispositional vulnerability? To answer this question, we need to return to chronic stress and see how epigenetic mechanisms, as a response to chronic stress, can actually create biological outcomes that promote a lower threshold for stress reactivity—that is, make individuals more reactive to stress, thus increasing predispositional vulnerability. Several studies have suggested that fetal exposure to poverty-related prenatal stressors including poor nutrition, smoking, maternal depression, maternal anxiety, and violence are associated with epigenetic changes to genes involved in the regulation of the stress response of the neonate, which then result in increased stress reactivity that feeds the cycle of chronic stress not only in the newborn child but also across the life course (Conradt, Lester, Appleton, Armstrong, & Marsit, 2013; Knopik, Maccani, Francazio, & McGeary, 2012; Lester, Conradt, & Marsit, 2016; Oberlander et al., 2008). This epigenetic programming can continue during the early postnatal environment because stressful early caretaking experiences such as poor maternal sensitivity and maternal separations have also been shown to result in increased stress reactivity through epigenetic modifications of HPA axis genes (Conradt et al., 2016). This bolstered reactivity to stress in essence creates a greater predispositional vulnerability to the psychological outcomes of chronic stress such as anxiety, depression, and manifestation of preexisting psychiatric conditions (McEwen, 2003; Walker & Diforio, 1997).

Another type of epigenetic change that occurs in the face of the extreme childhood stress often associated with poverty results in decreased production of BDNF. A detailed description of the emotional and cognitive outcomes of dampened BDNF production (Radtke et al., 2015) can be found in Chapter 4. Suffice it to say that the decrease in BDNF resulting from epigenetic changes wrought by early childhood trauma is suspect in the etiology of emotional, behavioral,

Reflective Question

Based on what you have learned thus far about the impact of extreme stress on body function, what kinds of prevention and intervention strategies do you think would be helpful for Henrietta's current mental health concerns?

and cognitive challenges experienced across the life course, including mood disorders, suicidality, disruptive behavioral and attention problems, and struggles with learning (McClelland, Korosi, Cope, Ivy, & Baram, 2011; McGowan & Szyf, 2010; Mill & Petronis, 2008; Nestler, 2014; Szyf, 2011).

Our Brain-Based Approach to the Case of Henrietta

Working with the case of Henrietta as a central reference point, this section demonstrates how knowledge of PNI and epigenetics can inform intervention. When one views Henrietta's physiological, psychological, and spiritual health as inextricably intertwined, an integrative intervention strategy is called for that addresses the multiple factors contributing to her distress. Learning and practicing techniques that foster a sympathetic–parasympathetic shift could address physiological concerns, and the many sociocultural dimensions of her current circumstances could be addressed through culturally informed, multitargeted counseling. The progress that is made through these two counseling approaches could be reinforced through preventive wellness counseling. "These interventions, taken as a whole, provide an ecological approach to intervention that includes individual biology, the self-in-context, and social-structural affordances" (Douthit, 2015b, p. 14).

Sympathetic–Parasympathetic Shift

Although whether Henrietta has endured epigenetic changes that affected her stress reactivity cannot be known with certainty, an intervention targeting her current reactive state is key to addressing her compromised immunological, cardiovascular, and mental health. Henrietta would benefit from tools enabling her to foster a sympathetic–parasympathetic shift, achievable through techniques that support a shift away from a state in which the sympathetic nervous system is dominant to one in which the parasympathetic nervous system prevails (Benson, 2011). The sympathetic nervous system, a major player in the stress response, increases heart rate, promotes high blood pressure, disrupts sleep, causes digestive problems such as irritable bowel, fuels anxiety, and plays a role in dysregulation of the immune response (Sapolsky, 2004). In stark contrast, the parasympathetic nervous system lowers heart rate and blood pressure, creates a sense of calm, and supports healthy immune function. Techniques that could be used to achieve a sympathetic–parasympathetic shift for Henrietta include mindfulness and other meditation modalities, breath work, neurofeedback, biofeedback, guided imagery, sand tray work, and creative arts (Benson, 2011; McEwen, 2016). Outside of counseling, Henrietta could be encouraged to engage in low-cost, parasympathetic nervous system–promoting activities such as crossword puzzles, Sudoku, yoga, tai chi, progressive muscle relaxation, and needlework such as knitting and crocheting (Benson, 2011). There is actually growing evidence that a shift to a parasympathetic nervous system–dominant state might reverse epigenetic effects that favor stress reactivity (Kaliman et al., 2014).

Culturally Informed, Multitargeted Counseling

Culturally informed, multitargeted counseling can be fruitfully designed to focus on the long-term, psychological effects of challenging environmental conditions while attending to cultural sensitivities, internalized oppression, and the need for a range of community and governmental resources (Douthit, 2015a, 2015b). In many cases, the psychological sequelae of conditions of marginality can be successfully targeted by empirically supported treatments such as trauma-focused cognitive behavior therapy for intensely aversive experiences (Ponniah & Hollon, 2009) and cognitive behavior therapy for anxiety and depression (Butler, Chapman, Forman, & Beck, 2006). Counselors can also use therapeutic interventions, such as interpersonal psychotherapy, that emphasize client education and would aim to inform clients such as Henrietta about potential epigenetic mechanisms related to marginality (Swartz, 1999).

An intervention with an eye toward social justice such as narrative therapy is particularly well designed to address experiences of marginality by helping clients to challenge their own experiences of internalized oppression and to re-create or, in the language of narrative therapy, re-story their identities, thus developing narratives that transcend self-injurious identities and construct a sound base for bolstering personal empowerment (Akinyela, 2002)

Cultural congruence is the cornerstone of successful intervention with marginalized clients (Sue & Sue, 2016). Any intervention strategy that fails to attend to cultural sensitivities has the potential to revictimize clients, thus reinforcing perceptions of marginality and exacerbating the stress cycle (Ridley, 2005). In cases in which poverty intersects with ethnicity, gender, ability, and other categories of cultural difference, it is important for counselors to familiarize themselves with community and governmental resources that will help them to address their clients' most fundamental and urgent material needs (Douthit, 2015b; Summers, 2016).

Preventive Wellness Counseling and Early Interventions

In the face of chronic stress, PNI, and epigenetic challenges, Henrietta would want to engage in healthy lifestyle practices that disrupt cycles of chronic stress from taking hold. The Wheel of Wellness model (Myers, Sweeney, & Witmer, 2000), discussed in Chapter 4, addresses many dimensions of wellness including spirituality, a centrally important aspect of Henrietta's counseling, that would intervene in her disconnection from her internal spiritual resources. Many of the

Drawing on both your understanding of the biology of marginality and the many sociocultural and psychological challenges that Henrietta faces, how might you construct a multifaceted model explaining her current depressed mood?

On the basis of the model constructed in Question 1, how might you conceptualize a comprehensive intervention strategy to address Henrietta's depressed mood?

Argue for or against the following statement: "The most effective interventions for addressing the psychological outcomes of epigenetic and PNI mechanisms must necessarily involve psychopharmacological or other medical interventions."

elements of this model favor a parasympathetic state and could bolster resiliency in the face of sociocultural adversity.

Considering the critical importance of the early prenatal and postnatal environments in epigenetic changes to stress reactivity, prevention and early interventions targeting prenatal experiences and early parent–child interaction patterns are vital. Several of these interventions are described in Chapter 4.

Conclusion

As science progresses, we will likely have a clearer understanding about the impact of conditions of oppression on emotional and physical well-being. Animal and human research has opened vistas of intervention to address the toxic outcomes of chronic stress, giving counselors new tools to provide aid for victims of social injustice. Such research is very promising for those who are putting their hope in the future of neurocounseling and the ways in which it can inform intervention by building on an understanding of the relationships among mind, body, and the social world. Most important in the context of this chapter is the notion that emerging mind–body science affirms the belief, central to the counseling profession, that intervention that addresses social justice issues ultimately has the power to transform (Douthit, 2015a).

Quiz

1. Which of the following statements does not accurately characterize what is known about PNI?
   a. Chronic stress can affect both innate and acquired immunity.
   b. Chronic stress causes inflammatory shutdown.
   c. Inflammatory pathways can lead to depression, anxiety, and social withdrawal.
   d. Chronic stress can lead to numerous debilitating chronic illnesses.

2. Which of the following statements is not a characteristic of chronic stress?
   a. It can exacerbate existing psychiatric conditions.
   b. It causes physical problems, generating additional chronic stress.
   c. It can result in psychological struggles that reduce resilience.
   d. It initiates negative-feedback systems to control cortisol.

3. Epigenetic changes can explain which of the following?
   a. A decrease in neuroplasticity.
   b. The decreased stress reactivity seen in chronic stress.
   c. Enhanced cognitive and emotional development.
   d. All of the above.

4. Which of the following best describes the notion of predispositional vulnerability?
   a. People's level of vulnerability remains constant throughout their lifetime.
   b. It is determined by inheritance alone.
   c. It can change over time as a result of the impact of environmental forces.
   d. People are all born with the same basic vulnerability.

References

Ader, R., & Cohen, N. (1993). Psychoneuroimmunology: Conditioning and stress. *Annual Review of Psychology, 44,* 53–85.

Ader, R., Cohen, N., & Felten, D. (1995). Psychoneuroimmunology: Interactions between the nervous system and the immune system. *Lancet, 345,* 99–103.

Akinyela, M. (2002). De-colonizing our lives: Divining a post-colonial therapy. *International Journal of Narrative Therapy and Community Work, 2,* 32–43.

Benson, H. (2011). *The relaxation revolution: The science and genetics of mind–body healing.* New York, NY: Scribner.

Brunoni, A. R., Lopes, M., & Fregni, F. (2008). A systematic review and meta-analysis of clinical studies on major depression and BDNF levels: Implications for the role of neuroplasticity in depression. *International Journal of Neuropsychopharmacology, 11,* 1169–1180.

Butler, A. C., Chapman, J. E., Forman, E. M., & Beck, A. T. (2006). The empirical status of cognitive-behavioral therapy: A review of meta-analyses. *Clinical Psychology Review, 26,* 17–31.

Conradt, E., Hawes, K., Guerin, D., Armstrong, D. A., Marsit, C. J., Tronick, E., & Lester, B. M. (2016). The contributions of maternal sensitivity and maternal depressive symptoms to epigenetic processes and neuroendocrine functioning. *Child Development, 87,* 73–85.

Conradt, E., Lester, B. M., Appleton, A. A., Armstrong, D. A., & Marsit, C. J. (2013). The roles of DNA methylation of NR3C1 and 11β-HSD2 and exposure to maternal mood disorder in utero on newborn neurobehavior. *Epigenetics, 8,* 1321–1329. http://dx.doi.org/10.4161/epi.26634

Council for Accreditation of Counseling and Related Educational Programs. (2015). *2016 CACREP standards.* Retrieved from http://www.cacrep.org/wp-content/uploads/2012/10/2016-CACREP-Standards.pdf

Dantzer, R., O'Connor, J. C., Lawson, M. A., & Kelley, K. W. (2011). Inflammation-associated depression: From serotonin to kynurenine. *Psychoneuroendocrinology, 36,* 426–436.

Douthit, K. (2015a). Bringing the laboratory into the office: How epigenetics can inform counseling practice. *Counseling Today, 58*(3), 18–23.

Douthit, K. (2015b). Psychoneuroimmunology: Tapping the potential of counseling to heal the mind-body. *Counseling Today, 57*(9), 12–15.

Dowlati, Y., Herrmann, N., Swardfager, W., Liu, H., Sham, L., Reim, E. K., & Lanctôt, K. L. (2010). A meta-analysis of cytokines in major depression. *Biological Psychiatry, 67,* 446–457.

Glassman, A. H., & Miller, G. E. (2007). Where there is depression, there is inflammation . . . sometimes! *Biological Psychiatry, 62,* 280–281.

Hänsel, A., Hong, S., Cámara, R. J., & Von Kaenel, R. (2010). Inflammation as a psychophysiological biomarker in chronic psychosocial stress. *Neuroscience and Biobehavioral Reviews, 35,* 115–121.

Janeway, C. A., Travers, P., Walport, M., & Shlomchik, M. (2001). *Immunobiology: The immune system in health and disease* (5th ed.). New York, NY: Garland Science.

Jones, P. A., & Takai, D. (2001). The role of DNA methylation in mammalian epigenetics. *Science, 293,* 1068–1070.

Juster, R. P., McEwen, B. S., & Lupien, S. J. (2010). Allostatic load biomarkers of chronic stress and impact on health and cognition. *Neuroscience and Biobehavioral Reviews, 35,* 2–16.

Kaliman, P., Álvarez-López, M. J., Cosín-Tomás, M., Rosenkranz, M. A., Lutz, A., & Davidson, R. J. (2014). Rapid changes in histone deacetylases and inflammatory gene expression in expert meditators. *Psychoneuroendocrinology, 40,* 96–107.

Kendall-Tackett, K. (2009). Psychological trauma and physical health: A psychoneuroimmunology approach to etiology of negative health effects and possible interventions. *Psychological Trauma: Theory, Research, Practice, and Policy, 1,* 35–48.

Kiecolt-Glaser, J. K., Loving, T. J., Stowell, J. R., Malarky, W. B., Lemeshow, S., Dickinson, S. L., & Glaser, R. (2005). Hostile marital interactions, proinflammatory cytokine production, and wound healing. *Archives of General Psychiatry, 62,* 1377–1384.

Knopik, V. S., Maccani, M. A., Francazio, S., & McGeary, J. E. (2012). The epigenetics of maternal cigarette smoking during pregnancy and effects on child development. *Developmental Psychopathology, 24,* 1377–1390.

Lester, B. M., Conradt, E., & Marsit, C. (2016). Introduction to the special section on epigenetics. *Child Development, 87,* 29–37.

Marmot, M. G., Smith, G. D., Stansfeld, S., Patel, C., North, F., Head, J., . . . Feeney, A. (1991). Health inequalities among British civil servants: The Whitehall II study. *Lancet, 337,* 1387–1393.

Marmot, M., & Wilkerson, R. (Eds.). (2005). *Social determinants of health.* Oxford, England: Oxford University Press.

Marshall, G. D. (2011). The adverse effects of psychological stress on immunoregulatory balance: Applications to human inflammatory diseases. *Immunology and Allergy Clinics of North America, 31,* 133–140.

McClelland, S., Korosi, A., Cope, J., Ivy, A., & Baram, T. Z. (2011). Emerging roles of epigenetic mechanisms in the enduring effects of neonatal stress and experience on learning and memory. *Neurobiology of Learning and Memory, 96,* 79–88.

McEwen, B. S. (2003). Mood disorders and allostatic load. *Biological Psychiatry, 54,* 200–207.

McEwen, B. S. (2007). Biology and physiology of stress and adaptation. *Physiological Reviews, 87,* 873–904.

McEwen, B. S. (2016). In pursuit of resilience: Stress, epigenetics, and brain plasticity. *Annals of the New York Academy of Sciences, 1373,* 56–64. http://dx.doi.org/10.1111/nyas.13020

McGowan, P. O., & Szyf, M. (2010). The epigenetics of social adversity in early life: Implications for mental health outcomes. *Neurobiology of Disease, 39,* 66–72.

Mill, J., & Petronis, A. (2008). Pre- and peri-natal environmental risks for attention-deficit hyperactivity disorder (ADHD): The potential role of epigenetic processes in mediating susceptibility. *Journal of Child Psychology and Psychiatry, 49,* 1020–1030. http://dx.doi.org/10.1111/j.1469-7610.2008.01909.x

Myers, J. E., Sweeney, T. J., & Witmer, J. M. (2000). The Wheel of Wellness counseling for wellness: A holistic model for treatment planning. *Journal of Counseling & Development, 78,* 251–266.

Nestler, E. J. (2014). Epigenetic mechanisms of depression. *JAMA Psychiatry, 71,* 454–456. http://dx.doi.org/10.1001/jamapsychiatry.2013.4291

Oberlander, T. F., Weinberg, J., Papsdorf, M., Grunau, R., Misri, S., & Devlin, A. M. (2008). Prenatal exposure to maternal depression, neonatal methylation of human glucocorticoid receptor gene (NR3C1) and infant cortisol stress responses. *Epigenetics, 3,* 97–106.

Pieterse, A. L., Todd, N. R., Neville, H. A., & Carter, R. T. (2012). Perceived racism and mental health among Black American adults: A meta-analytic review. *Journal of Counseling Psychology, 59,* 1–9.

Ponniah, K., & Hollon, S. D. (2009). Empirically supported psychological treatments for adult acute stress disorder and posttraumatic stress disorder: A review. *Depression and Anxiety, 26,* 1086–1109.

Radtke, K. M., Schauer, M., Gunter, H. M., Ruf-Leuschner, M., Sill, J., Meyer, A., & Elbert, T. (2015). Epigenetic modifications of the glucocorticoid receptor gene are associated with the vulnerability to psychopathology in childhood maltreatment. *Translational Psychiatry, 5,* e571.

Ridley, C. R. (2005). *Overcoming unintentional racism in counseling and therapy: A practitioner's guide to intentional intervention* (2nd ed.). Thousand Oaks, CA: Sage.

Sapolsky, R. M. (2004). *Why zebras don't get ulcers.* New York, NY: Holt.

Sue, D. W., & Sue, D. (2016). *Counseling the culturally diverse: Theory and practice* (7th ed.). Hoboken, NJ: Wiley.

Summers, N. (2016). *Fundamentals of case management practice: Skills for the human services* (5th ed.). Boston, MA: Cengage.

Surtees, P. G., Wainwright, N. W. J., Bockholdt, S. M., Luben, R. N., Wareham, N. J., & Khaw, K. T. (2008). Major depression, C-reactive protein, and incident ischemic heart disease in healthy men and women. *Psychosomatic Medicine, 70,* 850–855.

Swartz, H. A. (1999). Interpersonal psychotherapy. In M. E. Hersen & A. S. Bellack (Eds.), *Handbook of comparative interventions for adult disorders* (pp. 139–155). Hoboken, NJ: Wiley.

Szyf, M. (2011). DNA methylation, the early-life social environment, and behavior disorders. *Neurodevelopmental Disorders, 3,* 238–249.

Walker, E. F., & Diforio, D. (1997). Schizophrenia: A neural diathesis-stress model. *Psychological Review, 104,* 667–685.

Wilson, C. J., Finch, C. E., & Cohen, H. J. (2002). Cytokines and cognition: The case for a head-to-toe inflammatory paradigm. *Journal of the American Geriatrics Society, 50,* 2041–2056.

Zuckerman, M. (1999). *Vulnerability to psychopathology: A biosocial model.* Washington, DC: American Psychological Association.

Chapter 4

Neurophysiology of Traumatic Stress

Laura K. Jones, Christopher Rybak,
and Lori A. Russell-Chapin

Psychological trauma is pervasive in the United States. An estimated 89.7% of clients seen in community mental health clinics have experienced at least one incident of trauma during their lifetime (Kilpatrick et al., 2013). Research has further indicated that most people experience not just one but multiple experiences of trauma over the course of their life (Kessler, 2000). It is almost inevitable that counselors will work with a trauma survivor at some point in their career. Trauma survivors are a unique population of clients that warrant a unique skill set (Briere & Scott, 2013). Unprepared counselors can unknowingly retraumatize clients, predominantly by pushing them into processing traumatic memories before they are emotionally or physiologically prepared (Wells, Trad, & Alves, 2003). It is essential for counselors working with trauma survivors to take a trauma-informed approach that considers these unique sensitivities and is informed by an understanding of how the brain and body respond to traumatic experiences. This chapter examines not only the neurophysiological responses to stress and traumatic stress but also the implications of this knowledge for how counselors interact with clients after traumatic events. These concepts are illustrated through the story of Julian.

 ## 2016 CACREP Standards

This chapter addresses a section of the 2016 Council for Accreditation of Counseling and Related Educational Programs (CACREP) Standards pertinent to the common core area of Human Growth and Development (Standard II.F.3.):

- Effects of crisis, disasters, and trauma on diverse individuals across the life span (Standard II.F.3.g.)

This chapter also addresses the following Specialization Standards:

- Impact of crisis and trauma on individuals with mental health diagnoses (Clinical Mental Health Counseling, Standard V.C.2.f.)
- Impact of crisis and trauma on marriages, couples, and families (Marriage, Couple, and Family Counseling, Standard V.F.2.g.)
- Impact of interpersonal violence on marriages, couples, and families (Marriage, Couple, and Family Counseling, Standard V.F.2.i.)

■ ■ ■

Clinical Case Study: Julian

Julian is a 22-year-old cisgender American woman of Eastern European heritage (second generation). She is a law student at a prestigious university in the southeastern United States and identifies as heterosexual. Julian was referred from the university counseling center after experiencing a panic attack after one of her classes. She reported that she has never experienced a panic attack before this situation but said that over the past 6 months she has experienced nightmares and difficulty sleeping, she has felt agitated and jumpy, and her grades have been dropping. She also reported that she has generally felt down and has increased her use of alcohol, suggesting that she drinks around two glasses of wine a night to relax and not be so "amped up" so she can sleep. She reported that, on the day of the panic attack, she had just been in a role-play scenario acting as a defense attorney for a hypothetical male client accused of rape. Julian stated that she thought she was just nervous during the trial. Julian reported very shallow, rapid breathing, racing heartbeat, profuse sweating, tense shoulders, and dry mouth. She made it through the scenario. After class, she sat alone in the library studying for a test and started thinking about the survivor's story in the scenario. At that point, she began to feel as though she could not breathe, and swallowing became challenging. Her heart was pounding, and she thought she was having a heart attack. One of her best friends passed by her and asked whether she was okay. She nodded yes, but the friend knew that something was wrong. Julian indicated that the friend put a hand on her back and sat down with her. She said that she instantly started feeling soothed as she felt her friend's hand and heard her voice, and the friend made eye contact with her.

Nature of Stress

To fully conceptualize the effects of traumatic stress on the body, a better understanding of the nature of stress in general is needed. The phrase "I'm just really stressed right now" is ubiquitous in counseling. Clients seem more comfortable discussing stress than many other complaints. It is socially acceptable, if not expected, to be stressed in this Western culture. However, the concept of stress is often misunderstood. Stress can be characterized as any pressure that is put on the system (i.e., body and brain) from a psychological, physical, or environmental source. It is often considered a detrimental experience, but that is not always the case. In small, contained doses, stress can be beneficial to people's attention, motivation, processing, and actually to their overall health, such as in immune responses. It helps people's bodies and minds to adapt and warns them that changes need to be made to their internal or external environments. Stress that has beneficial effects on the system is called *eustress* (Selye, 1975). However, the system can only be pushed so hard and for so long. Eventually, a person exceeds his or her ability to cope. At this point, stress can have deleterious effects. Even if a person experiences low-intensity stress, it can be harmful if it is chronic. Stress that leads to adverse responses is called *distress* (Selye, 1975). Between these two is an optimal level of arousal and associated bodily functioning that corresponds to optimal or peak performance. As such, one's goal should not be to get rid of stress entirely.

The body's response to stress is an adaptive process. This ability to exhibit resiliency and adaptively respond to life stressors is termed *allostasis*. It is a response by the whole organism in a changing and often challenging environment not only to present stressors but also in anticipation of future stressors (Raglan & Schulkin, 2014). *Allostatic load* refers to the wear and tear on the body in the face of chronic or extreme stress, those circumstances in which one tends to feel overwhelmed and more vulnerable to a range of physiological and psychological difficulties (Raglan & Schulkin, 2014). Thus, the goal is to learn to cope with stress in a healthy way or, to put it in terms of the brain and body, physiologically adapt and regulate one's autonomic response in the face of changing psychological, physical, or environmental pressures. Understanding this adaptive nature of the body in response to stress in general is essential in understanding the body's response to traumatic stress and the clinical implications of working with survivors. We now take a closer look at the effects that traumatic events can have on one's body, life, and relationships.

Posttraumatic Stress

Although the terms are often used interchangeably, *trauma* and *posttraumatic stress* represent different concepts. A trauma (i.e., traumatic event) is defined in the fifth edition of the *Diagnostic and Statistical Manual of Mental Disorders* (*DSM-5;* American Psychiatric Association, 2013) as the experience of actual or threatened death, serious injury, or sexual violation. According to *DSM-5,* a person could experience these three situations in four ways: personal exposure, direct observation, learning of an event occurring to a family member or friend, or repeated exposure to aversive details of the situation (with the exception of media, television, or movie exposure, unless work related). Traumatic events are often characterized as existing along a spectrum, from single-incident trauma (e.g., a car accident) to complex trauma, or chronic, ongoing traumatic experiences that occur within a specific context (e.g., child maltreatment, partner violence; Courtois, 2004).

As opposed to the actual event, traumatic and posttraumatic stress encompass the symptoms that arise as a result of the traumatic event. Whether behavioral, physical, emotional, or cognitive, these symptoms that counselors often see and hear result from the physiological responses of the body to that traumatic event. They are people's best efforts at processing (consciously or preconsciously) and staying safe in the midst or aftermath of the trauma. In this way, the body's response to a traumatic event is inherently an adaptive process. The body is trying to keep the person safe and protect him or her from future potential harm. However, for some individuals, this traumatic stress response lasts long after the threat for harm has dissipated and leads to a host of maladaptive social, emotional, cognitive, and physical outcomes, such as affective dysregulation, reexperiencing of the trauma, decreased self-monitoring, irritability, engagement in risky behaviors, and poor impulse control.

After exposure to a traumatic event, many adult survivors frequently experience a heightened state of vigilance (e.g., scanning the environment for perceived threats), an implicit or explicit desire to avoid reminders of the trauma, and affective responding (e.g., intense feelings of anxiety, fear related to the past trauma, or persistent negative mood). For many, such responses begin to dissipate over time. For others, however, the reexperiencing of the event becomes a debilitating state, precipitating multiple *DSM-5* diagnoses, most notably those that fall under trauma- and stressor-related disorders. Most commonly reported among survivors are symptoms of posttraumatic stress disorder, or PTSD (American Psychiatric Association, 2013). Nearly one in eight adult trauma survivors develops PTSD, a condition that encompasses interconnected neurological, physiological, psychological, and interpersonal consequences (American Psychiatric Association, 2013; Breslau & Kessler, 2001).

The *DSM-5* characterizes PTSD as a combination of symptoms that fall into one of the following four symptom clusters: (a) the intrusion of flashbacks, memories, nightmares, or reminders of the event; (b) avoidance of anything associated with the event; (c) negative alterations of mood and cognitions associated with anything related to the traumatic event, including an inability to remember aspects of the event, negative mood state and inability to experience positive emotions, and exaggerated beliefs about the self in relation to others;

Reflective Questions

Which symptoms of PTSD may Julian have been experiencing?

What aspects of these symptoms may play an adaptive or protective role for Julian??

and, last, (d) changes in autonomic arousal and reactivity, which can include hypervigilance, reckless behaviors, sleep disturbance, irritability and anger, and being easily startled.

Neurophysiology of Posttraumatic Stress

Underlying each of these symptoms is a host of aberrations in brain and body functioning. When exposed to traumatic stress, nearly every part of the brain and much of the body is affected. Just imagine this scenario:

Trigger Warning If you have experienced personal trauma, please be aware that envisioning the forthcoming scenario may be triggering. In other words, you may begin experiencing symptoms similar to what you experienced when you yourself were exposed.

Imagine that you are walking late at night down a dark city street. There is only one streetlight in the distance, and it begins flickering and then goes out. You are alone. You feel your senses becoming more acute. You are hyperaware of everything around you. You may begin to breathe a bit faster and feel your heart rate start to increase. As you begin to pick up your pace, a sound catches your attention, and you look over to your left. When you look back, you notice someone standing directly in front of you with what appears to be a knife.

Did you notice anything about your body when you were reading this story? Can you imagine what your body would be experiencing if you lived it? When you are awake and alert, information from the body (visceral sensations) and senses is constantly being brought into the brain, processed by the thalamus, and directed toward the appropriate subcortical or cortical areas used in optimally processing the information. When you are exposed to a trauma or acutely stressful experience, incoming sensory information is registered as threatening, and your body begins to sound its alarm system and adapt in such a way as to keep you safe. Your amygdala sends signals to the hypothalamus to release hormones that will initiate the fight-or-flight response. This response is a two-tiered system (Gunnar & Quevedo, 2007). The first tier, known as the sympathetic–adrenal–medullary axis, activates the sympathetic nervous system. The hypothalamus sends messages down to the adrenal glands and the adrenal medulla (i.e., inside of the adrenal glands) to release epinephrine and norepinephrine. These catecholamines initiate energy metabolism and activate the sympathetic nervous system, causing many of the classic symptoms that you experienced when reading the preceding story. This leads to an accelerated heart rate, increased pulse and blood pressure, increased breathing rate, stimulated glucose release by the liver, dilated pupils, and inhibited gut and intestinal functioning. Basically, the body is sending all of its energy and resources to the parts of the body that will help to keep you alive, to fight your way out of the situation or flee from it as quickly as you can. You are not stopping to make careful decisions and weigh options, functions that would recruit higher cortical areas of your brain. That would waste time and potentially threaten your survival. In this moment, you are functioning from the more primitive and instinctual areas of your brain.

The hypothalamic–pituitary–adrenal (HPA) axis is the second tier of the fight-or-flight response. As discussed in Chapter 1, the HPA axis is responsible for regulating the release of the stress hormone cortisol from the cortex (i.e., outer region) of the adrenal glands. Cortisol primarily helps to regulate the amount of glucose that is circulating through the bloodstream at any given time (see Figure 4.1). Under prolonged or chronic stress, it can also impede immune functioning and lead to atrophy of the hippocampus. During this process, endogenous opioids can also be released into the system (Sherin & Nemeroff, 2011). These opioids act as an analgesic, limiting sensitivity to emotional and physical pain (van der Kolk, Greenberg, Orr, & Pitman, 1989).

Once the threat is no longer pervasive and the secretion of cortisol has reached an optimal threshold, the adrenal glands send chemical signals back up to the hypothalamus to discontinue production of corticotropin-releasing factor. Thus, the supply of cortisol in the system diminishes (Sriram, Rodriguez-Fernandez, & Doyle, 2012). This is part of the process known as allostasis. The body is constantly responding to changes and perceived threats and has built-in mechanisms to reregulate itself. However, in the face of marked trauma or chronic unrelenting stress, this negative-feedback loop is one of the systems that becomes dysregulated.

Other parts of the brain also become dysregulated in response to traumatic stress. This process of chronic threat responding, namely the overactivation of the amygdala and resulting sympathetic nervous system and HPA responses, disrupts the functioning of the frontal and prefrontal cortices as well as the hippocampus. Within the prefrontal cortex is a region known as the orbitofrontal cortex that has marked effects on interpersonal functioning. Not only does this area of cortex regulate autonomic responses, it is also explicitly involved in the regu-

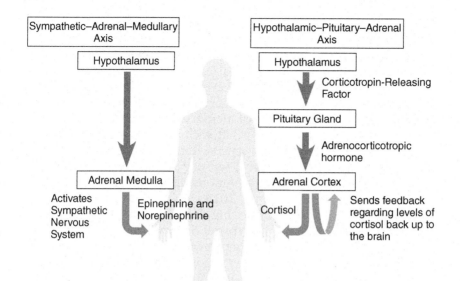

FIGURE 4.1

**Hypothalamic–Pituitary–Adrenal (HPA) and
Sympathetic–Adrenal–Medullary (SAM) Axis**

Note. Derivative work of human body silhouette, Mikael Häggström, 2009, made transparent by Frédéric Michel, via Wikimedia Commons. Public domain.

lation of emotion and attuned interpersonal communication involving eye contact, response flexibility, and social cognition (Cavada & Schultz, 2000). The dorsolateral prefrontal cortex also shows decreased activation. This area plays a role in controlling unwanted memories and gives a sense of time to experiences, thereby giving an individual a sense that the experience will come to an end (Anderson et al., 2004). The decreased activation in these areas impairs the ability of the prefrontal cortex to optimally regulate the limbic and autonomic nervous systems (i.e., top-down control). This, in turn, can contribute to a host of maladaptive social, emotional, cognitive, and physical outcomes, such as affective dysregulation, reexperiencing of the trauma, decreased self-monitoring, irritability, engagement in risky behaviors, and poor impulse control. The intense fear experienced in trauma can lead to decreased activation in the region of the frontal cortex, known as Broca's area, associated with language production (Shin et al., 1999). This may in turn affect survivors' ability to put words to experiences, particularly when reexperiencing the traumatic event.

PTSD can also disrupt declarative long-term memory consolidation in the hippocampus, leading to impaired integration of factual information with the emotional memory of the traumatic event (Hayes et al., 2011). Impeded functioning of the thalamus in response to trauma may also have an impact on memory of the event (van der Kolk, 2014). The thalamus helps to integrate one's sensory experiences with declarative or autobiographical components of memory. Because the functioning of the thalamus is impaired, one is left with a memory of the trauma that is trapped in one's body and senses. Rather than a fluid narrative of the event, survivors may describe sensory experiences of the event, such as sights, sounds, and bodily sensations, all accompanied by intense emotional reactions (van der Kolk, 2014).

The functioning of the anterior cingulate cortex and insula is also disrupted in traumatic stress. The rostral or forward part of the anterior cingulate shows a decrease in activation, which suggests a failure to appropriately weigh distracting emotional information and inhibit the functioning of the amygdala (Offringa et al., 2013). Conversely, the dorsal (top) anterior cingulate cortex increases in activation. Such functioning is related to the exaggerated fear response that is classic in PTSD (Shin et al., 2011). Furthermore, increased activation of the anterior insula in PTSD may be associated with a heightened awareness of internal bodily arousal during reexperiencing and hyperarousal symptoms (Hopper, Frewen, van der Kolk, & Lanius, 2007). Conversely, in states of hypoarousal, such as with emotional numbing and dissociative experiences, inverse patterns in the insula are seen, whereby the person has decreased activation and impaired awareness of bodily states (Hopper et al., 2007).

Although the sympathetic–adrenal–medullary and HPA axes, along with the allied effects of epinephrine, norepinephrine, and cortisol, have taken center stage in research detailing the physiological underpinnings of traumatic responses, researchers have more recently begun to investigate and recognize the pronounced role of gamma-aminobutyric acid (GABA) and oxytocin in PTSD symptomatology and recovery (Olff, 2012; Vaiva et al., 2006). GABA, the body's primary inhibitory neurotransmitter, plays a role in stress responses and the regulation of anxiety. Decreased levels of GABA have been demonstrated in PTSD and may serve a diagnostic role in the disorder (Vaiva et al., 2006).

Similarly to corticotropin-releasing factor in the HPA axis, oxytocin is also produced in the paraventricular nucleus of the hypothalamus, which extends neuronal projections directly to the amygdala, hippocampus, and brain stem (Campbell, 2010). Oxytocin is essential to the development and fostering of social and intimate bonds and has been found to play an integral role in deciphering the emotions of others (Hurlemann et al., 2010) and assessing interpersonal trustworthiness (Zak, Kurzban, & Matzner, 2004). In addition, oxytocin has been found to increase prefrontal cortex activity and decrease amygdala activity, which may improve emotion regulation and decrease avoidance behavior (Olff, Langeland, Witteveen, & Denys, 2010). Given the palliative effects of oxytocin on physiological stress responses, authors have proposed the use of pharmacological oxytocin to augment and enhance the efficacy of cognitive behavior therapy and exposure therapy with survivors (Olff, 2012).

Porges (2011) believes that the autonomic nervous system responds to trauma following a "phylogenetic hierarchy" (p. 155), whereby an individual typically first responds from the most evolutionarily recent cortical components. When this fails, more primitive structural defense systems are engaged. The autonomic nervous system is composed of three branches: (a) the sympathetic nervous system, (b) the dorsal vagal branch of the parasympathetic nervous system, and (c) the ventral vagal branch of the parasympathetic nervous system, each corresponding to a level of autonomic arousal, namely hyperarousal, hypoarousal, and optimal arousal, respectively. When hyperaroused, individuals experience emotional dysregulation, hypervigilance, and a reliance on survival mechanisms. In a hypoaroused state, individuals often experience dissociation, emotional numbing, and immobility, sometimes considered the freeze response.

The ventral vagal branch of the parasympathetic nervous system, also known as the social engagement system, represents a state of regulated arousal, generating feelings of safety and promoting behaviors that enhance social bonds (Fosha, Siegel, & Solomon, 2009; Porges, 2003). These behaviors are thought to include eye gaze, facial expressions, voice tone, social gestures, and even the ability to extract a human voice from background noises by modulating the function of a set of muscles of the inner ear. Individuals with PTSD often experience a dysregulated autonomic response and fluctuate between hypo- and hyperaroused states, and they are not functioning from the social engagement system. Steuwe et al. (2012) found that, compared with individuals without PTSD, survivors of trauma with PTSD experience threat-mediated arousal in areas of the brain associated with the autonomic nervous system when exposed to direct eye contact. Survivors of trauma also have difficulty with affective prosody, or the ability to properly interpret emotional cues in the rhythm, pitch, stress, and intonation of language (Freeman, Hart, Kimbrell, & Ross, 2009). This may be due to the dysregulation of the autonomic nervous system and an inability to effectively modulate muscles of the inner ear that detect such variations (Porges, 2011).

Sex Differences in Posttraumatic Stress Disorder

Notable differences exist in the prevalence, symptoms, and duration of posttraumatic stress between males and females. Males are more likely to experience traumatic events, yet females are more than twice as likely to develop PTSD, with PTSD symptomatology lasting as much as four times longer even when controlling for the extent of trauma exposure and type of trauma experienced (Blain, Galovski, & Robinson, 2010; Kessler, 2000; Olff, Langeland, Draijer, & Gersons, 2007; Tolin & Foa, 2006). Males tend to experience more anger and reexperiencing symptoms, whereas females experience greater degrees of emotional numbing, restricted affect, and avoidance responses as well as higher levels of psychological reactivity to traumatic stimuli than do males (Litz, Orsillo, Kaloupek, & Weathers, 2000; Orsillo, Batten, Plumb, Luterek, & Roessner, 2004; Spahic-Mihajlovic, Crayton, & Neafsey, 2005).

The role of sex hormones may be one factor contributing to such differences. Both testosterone and estrogen serve as protective factors against developing PTSD and anxiety disorders and enhance fear regulation (Daskalakis, McGill, Lehrner, & Yehuda, 2016; Glover et al., 2012). However, levels of estrogen are constantly cycling during a woman's menstrual cycle. This has led to innovative discussions about whether where in her menstrual cycle a woman is at the time of a trauma can potentially influence how likely she is to develop PTSD. In other words, would a woman who experienced a trauma just before ovulation, for example, when estrogen levels peak, be more psychologically resilient to it than if she experienced the trauma when estrogen levels are lower? In a provocative article, Ferree, Wheeler, and Cahill (2012) reported that the use of emergency contraception, namely Ogestrel (a combination of exogenous estradiol and progestin) after sexual assault was associated with decreased posttraumatic stress symptoms. More research is clearly needed to tease apart sex differences and role of sex hormones in responses to trauma.

Complex Posttraumatic Stress

Complex trauma, or ongoing experiences that entail exposure to multiple types of trauma, especially interpersonal traumas occurring during childhood, may lead to a distinct type of posttraumatic response distinct from PTSD (Cloitre et al., 2011; Courtois, 2004). In addition to symptoms of PTSD, individuals experiencing complex PTSD often demonstrate difficulties in the following five core areas: emotional regulation, relational capacities, attention and consciousness (e.g., dissociation), belief systems, and somatic distress (Cloitre et al., 2011). Furthermore, the younger

Reflective Questions

Consider the symptoms of PTSD identified earlier.

What might be the neurophysiological origins of Julian's PTSD symptoms?

How did these neurophysiological changes lead to maladaptive experiences?

the individual was at the age of the first trauma, the more likely that individual is to experience the symptoms of complex PTSD in addition to those of PTSD (van der Kolk, Roth, Pelcovitz, Sunday, & Spinazzola, 2005).

Unique patterns of brain and neuroendocrine changes are seen in complex trauma survivors, particularly those who experience child maltreatment (van der Kolk et al., 2005). As with symptom expression, both earlier age at onset and longer duration of the complex trauma lead to more pronounced structural and functional changes in the brain (Andersen et al., 2008). There may also be sensitive periods for the influence of early, complex traumatic stress on brain functioning and development (Teicher, Tomoda, & Andersen, 2006). Changes stemming from early child maltreatment in particular include decreases in the volume of and synaptic density in the amygdala, hippocampus, corpus callosum, and prefrontal cortex (Andersen et al., 2008; Teicher et al., 2006). Exposure to early life trauma may also lower morning cortisol levels and blunt the diurnal rhythm of cortisol, a marker for HPA dysregulation (Bevans, Cerbone, & Overstreet, 2008). Lower morning levels of cortisol are also linked to childhood aggression and difficulties with affect regulation (Cicchetti & Rogosch, 2007; Murray-Close, Han, Cicchetti, Crick, & Rogosch, 2008). As additional research is conducted on complex PTSD, a better understanding of the unique structural and functional neurophysiological changes that occur in the face of prolonged and repeated traumatic stress will begin to emerge.

Trauma-Focused Interventions

Multiple therapies have emerged and been refined, stemming from such knowledge of the brain. Cognitive behavior therapy interventions, such as prolonged exposure therapy (Foa, Hembree, & Rothbam, 2007), cognitive processing therapy (Resick & Schnicke, 1993), and trauma-focused cognitive behavior therapy (Ponniah & Hollon, 2009) are considered best practices in the field and have a solid research base. Additional therapies that honor the role of the body, nondeclarative memory, and bottom-up processing (initiating change in the body and subcortical areas of the brain that then affects the cortex, as opposed to top-down interventions that start by altering cognitive understandings that aim to influence the functioning of more subcortical and sensory structures) in conceptualizations of trauma are beginning to gain even more solid empirical evidence of their effectiveness. These therapies include eye movement desensitization and reprocessing (Shapiro & Solomon, 1995), neurofeedback (Chapin & Russell-Chapin, 2014), and sensorimotor psychotherapy (Ogden & Minton, 2000). These approaches work to help clients regulate the body's and brain's response to emotionally laden traumatic memories and in doing so allow survivors to develop a sense of agency and regain ownership of the body (van der Kolk, 2014).

Researchers have effectively demonstrated that of the interventions currently investigated, none are successful in addressing "the full range of clinical problems observed in trauma survivors" (McFarlane & Yehuda, 2000, p. 941). Tragically, somewhere between 20% and 50% of clients who are trauma survivors drop out of psychotherapy (Bryant et al., 2007; Schottenbauer, Glass, Arnkoff, Tendick, & Gray, 2008), with those higher in avoidance coping and numbing being more prone to discontinue counseling (Bryant et al., 2007). Not surprisingly, impairments in emotional regulation, a hallmark of PTSD, directly interfere with participation in psychotherapy (Freeman et al., 2009). Given these very real therapeutic challenges, what can counselors do to improve clinical outcomes with this population?

Briere and Scott (2013) suggested that regardless of theoretical underpinnings, effective trauma-informed therapy for PTSD can be broken down into several core principles that follow a phase-oriented approach to trauma treatment first cited by Herman (1992). The International Society for Traumatic Stress Studies's best practices for complex PTSD similarly recommend a sequenced and phase-based approach to working with survivors (Cloitre et al., 2011). Given the difficulties cited with regard to interpersonal trust and the posited importance of the ventral vagal social engagement system in autonomic arousal, the first consideration in trauma care is safety and security. The therapeutic relationship is recognized as the essential context in which healing from trauma can occur (Herman, 1992) and is strongly predictive of therapeutic outcomes (Roth & Fonagy, 2006). Providing and ensuring safety encompasses both physical and psychological safety. When clients do not perceive a sense of safety, disclosing and working through the trauma may actually be retraumatizing. Thus, counselors should take time to attend to the therapeutic relationship initially.

After the establishment of a trusting relationship, clients can benefit from knowledge about and skills to cope with their condition. Providing culturally, linguistically, and developmentally appropriate psychoeducation about what trauma does to the body and brain can empower clients. Psychoeducation can be augmented by visual brain models—either three-dimensional or the hand model presented in Figure 1.4—pictures, or metaphors. As with all psychoeducation, it is important that clients personally relate to the information and make it applicable to their understanding and experience. Psychoeducation may also lead to self-compassion regarding survivors' present experience. Developing self-compassion has been associated with reducing PTSD symptoms such as negative self-perceptions (Seligowski, Miron, & Orcutt, 2015).

Trauma survivors need to learn distress tolerance and affect regulation techniques before trauma is cognitively processed, because thinking and talking about the traumatic event may cause distress.

This is where biofeedback, mindfulness, and grounding exercises may be used. Deep breathing and yoga can also be helpful, although they should be approached with caution. Certain yoga poses and the sensation of filling the lungs with air during deep-breathing exercises can be triggering for some clients. For example, the sensations of deep breathing may, either implicitly or explicitly, remind the survivor of running away during the trauma. Identifying, discriminating, and labeling emotions may also be beneficial. As described in Chapter 2, the cognitive labeling of physiologically based emotions (feelings) can help to calm autonomic responses (Roth & Fonagy, 2006). This building of distress tolerance helps clients to develop coping skills to manage what distress may arise as the difficult trauma-related memories and sensations are encountered and later processed.

Subsequent phases of trauma treatment typically target the cognitive and emotional processing of the trauma (Briere & Scott, 2013). A central notion exists among many trauma theorists that the key to lasting treatment for PTSD resides in the successful integration of bifurcated memories of the traumatic event (the explicit and implicit experiences of the event), whereby the declarative memory of the traumatic event is reintegrated with the powerfully distressing implicit, emotional, and somatic traumatic memory (Foa & Rothbaum, 1998). This can be accomplished through any number of the aforementioned therapies, each with its own unique way of processing the trauma. Many of these therapies involve telling or writing out the trauma story. However, some approaches, such as eye movement desensitization and reprocessing, do not require an overt retelling of the story at all. In addition, Briere and Scott (2013) suggested that improving identity and relational functioning may also be a necessary treatment component for individuals who have experienced complex or attachment traumas early in life.

Our Brain-Based Approach to the Case of Julian

At first hearing Julian's story, I (Laura K. Jones) wondered whether Julian had experienced past trauma, especially interpersonal trauma given the nature of the trial that triggered her panic attack. Despite this hypothesis, I did not jump into asking her about past trauma. Instead, I held on to this information and recognized that the primary task with Julian would be to develop a strong therapeutic relationship, relying heavily on person-centered techniques of empathy and reflective listening. Slowly and consistently forming this strong, nonjudgmental environment helped to keep Julian feeling safe and accepted within that relationship.

As an established base was formed with Julian, she began to disclose more detail around events 6 months before the panic attack in which she experienced a sexual assault. I provided psychoeducation about how trauma can affect the body and the brain, as well as trust within interpersonal relationships. Discussing the adaptive nature of trauma responses and even the potential role of estrogen in this process is important. Next, I discussed the phases of general trauma therapy and the importance of self-regulation skills. Immediacy was used to help Julian identify moments when she starts to become hyper- or hypoaroused. We discussed what arousal feels like in her body and started to label some of those sensations. I used a feelings chart for Julian to begin applying a wider range of words to her sensations. Exercises that help her to maintain control over her arousal and emotions were located. In session, we practiced mindfulness, diaphragmatic breathing, and grounding exercises so that Julian could practice these outside of session as she became more comfortable. On those occasions when Julian began to disassociate or have flashbacks in session, I recognized that her Broca's area may not be fully functioning and she might have difficulty describing what she is experiencing in that moment.

This process of building a safe connection, understanding Julian's emotions, and finding effective means of regulating Julian's arousal and emotions was a long, slow process. I knew that until this was accomplished, working through Julian's traumatic memories would likely retraumatize her and have a negative impact on her ultimate recovery. When she felt safe and grounded enough to discuss her past trauma in detail, we discussed her optimal level of challenge and created a stress–fear exposure hierarchy. Together, we slowly worked through each level of that hierarchy, starting with the least challenging level and progressing to the most challenging. Julian was given full autonomy to determine when she was ready to take on the next level of the hierarchy. During this process, we eventually addressed the traumatic memories and associated triggers through imaginal exposure. Julian began to slowly retell her memories.

As she told her story, we regularly paused to reflect back on the material to establish a slow and steady pace to the story. Julian was taught to stop intermittently to discuss her emotions as she was telling her story. As she retold her narrative, Julian used her newly learned verbal feeling labels and her grounding skills to manage her level of arousal and stress. Throughout the course of her story, I closely watched her nonverbal expressions of emotion and provided feedback. I also intermittently reiterated that Julian was safe and in the counseling room as opposed to reliving the trauma. The slow pace of the therapy allowed Julian to maintain an optimal level of arousal, strengthening the connections between her prefrontal cortex and limbic system and allowing for greater executive control over her subcortical limbic structures and a reintegration of the trauma memory. Moreover, by stopping to discuss and put words to Julian's emotions, we began to integrate her implicit and explicit memories of the events. This process occurred repeatedly until Julian was able to get through the entire story and maintain her level of arousal. This can be a very protracted process.

During the final stage of therapy, Julian began to adapt to life without her traumatic response, learning how to function differently in her social environment given her enhanced corticolimbic connections, self- and emotional regulation, and improved neural and memory integration. At this point, I began to work with Julian on developing her interpersonal functioning and communication so that she could enhance her connections with others. Julian wanted to become involved in a support group for survivors to establish role models for healthy interpersonal interactions and build trust outside of the therapeutic relationship. I emphasized Julian's strengths throughout our work, empowering her to reach out and help others.

Conclusion

During and after exposure to a traumatic event, the brain and body undergo a cascade of neurophysiological changes. In the face of danger or life threat, these changes are adaptive and protective in nature. However, once the acute threat is no longer present, the persistence of such responses can become maladaptive and lead to unrelenting symptoms of mental and physical health distress. Trauma survivors are a unique population of clients who require counselors to have specialized knowledge of how trauma affects the body and brain to offer safe and effective care to clients.

This chapter provided an initial overview of the neurophysiology of stress and traumatic stress as well as how such knowledge has and is continuing to inform best-practice models. As new research emerges, therapeutic approaches to trauma will continue to strengthen and unfold, in hopes that counselors can deliver even more effective interventions for trauma survivors that increase therapeutic retention rates, lead to symptom reduction, and aid neurophysiological regulation and optimal functioning.

Quiz

1. In the face of extreme or chronic stress, which of the following statements regarding cortisol is true?
   a. A negative-feedback loop for the HPA axis is initiated, which impairs the body's ability to regulate levels of cortisol.
   b. Cortisol levels stay consistent.
   c. Cortisol is released from the cingulate cortex.
   d. The negative-feedback loop for the HPA axis is disrupted, which impairs the body's ability to regulate levels of cortisol.

2. Which of the following structures is not implicated in impaired traumatic memories?

   a. Amygdala.
   b. Pineal gland.
   c. Thalamus.
   d. Hippocampus.

References

American Psychiatric Association. (2013). *Diagnostic and statistical manual of mental disorders* (5th ed.). Arlington, VA: Author.

Andersen, S. L., Tomada, A., Vincow, E. S., Valente, E., Polcari, A., & Teicher, M. H. (2008). Preliminary evidence for sensitive periods in the effect of childhood sexual abuse on regional brain development. *Journal of Neuropsychiatry and Clinical Neurosciences, 203,* 292–301.

Anderson, M. C., Ochsner, K. N., Kuhl, B., Cooper, J., Robertson, E., Gabrieli, S. W., . . . Gabrieli, J. D. (2004). Neural systems underlying the suppression of unwanted memories. *Science, 303,* 232–235.

Bevans, K., Cerbone, A., & Overstreet, S. (2008). Relations between recurrent trauma exposure and recent life stress and salivary cortisol among children. *Development and Psychopathology, 20,* 257–272.

Blain, L. M., Galovski, T. E., & Robinson, T. (2010). Gender differences in recovery from posttraumatic stress disorder: A critical review. *Aggression and Violent Behavior, 15,* 463–474.

Breslau, N., & Kessler, R. C. (2001). The stressor criterion in *DSM-IV* posttraumatic stress disorder: An empirical investigation. *Biological Psychiatry, 50,* 699–704.

Briere, J., & Scott, C. (2013). *Principles of trauma therapy: A guide to symptoms, evaluation and treatment.* Thousand Oaks, CA: Sage.

Bryant, R. A., Moulds, M. L., Mastrodomenico, J., Hopwood, S., Felmingham, K., & Nixon, R. D. V. (2007). Who drops out of treatment for post-traumatic stress disorder? *Clinical Psychologist, 11,* 13–15. http://dx.doi.org/10.1080/13284200601178128

Campbell, A. (2010). Oxytocin and human social behavior. *Personality and Social Psychology Review, 14,* 281–295. http://dx.doi.org/10.1177/1088868310363594

Cavada, C., & Schultz, W. (2000). The mysterious orbitofrontal cortex. *Cerebral Cortex, 10,* 205.

Chapin, T., & Russell-Chapin, L. A. (2014). *Neurotherapy and neurofeedback: Brain-based treatments for psychological and behavioral problems.* New York, NY: Routledge.

Cicchetti, D., & Rogosch, F. A. (2007). Personality, adrenal steroid hormones, and resilience in maltreated children: A multilevel perspective. *Development and Psychopathology, 19,* 787–809.

Cloitre, M., Courtois, C. A., Charuvastra, A., Carapezza, R., Stolbach, B. C., & Green, B. L. (2011). Treatment of complex PTSD: Results of the ISTSS expert clinician survey on best practices. *Journal of Traumatic Stress, 24,* 615–627.

Council for Accreditation of Counseling and Related Educational Programs. (2015). *2016 CACREP standards.* Retrieved from http://www.cacrep.org/wp-content/uploads/2012/10/2016-CACREP-Standards.pdf

Courtois, C. A. (2004). Complex trauma, complex reactions: Assessment and treatment. *Psychotherapy: Theory, Research, Practice, Training, 41,* 412–425.

Daskalakis, N. P., McGill, M. A., Lehrner, A., & Yehuda, R. (2016). Endocrine aspects of PTSD: Hypothalamic-pituitary-adrenal (HPA) axis and beyond. In C. R. Martin, V. R. Preedy, & V. B. Patel (Eds.), *Comprehensive guide to post-traumatic stress disorder* (pp. 245–260). Cham, Switzerland: Springer International.

Ferree, N. K., Wheeler, M., & Cahill, L. (2012). The influence of emergency contraception on post-traumatic stress symptoms following sexual assault. *Journal of Forensic Nursing, 8,* 122–130.

Foa, E. B., Hembree, E. A., & Rothbaum, B. O. (2007). *Prolonged exposure therapy for PTSD: Emotional processing of traumatic experiences.* Oxford, England: Oxford University Press.

Foa, E. B., & Rothbaum, B. O. (1998). *Treating the trauma of rape: Cognitive-behavioral therapy for PTSD.* New York, NY: Guilford Press.

Fosha, D., Siegel, D. J., & Solomon, M. F. (2009). *The healing power of emotion: Affective neuroscience, development, and clinical practice.* New York, NY: W. W. Norton.

Freeman, T. W., Hart, J., Kimbrell, T., & Ross, E. D. (2009). Comprehension of affective prosody in veterans with chronic posttraumatic stress disorder. *Journal of Neuropsychiatry and Clinical Neurosciences, 21,* 52–58. http://dx.doi.org/10.1176/appi.neuropsych.21.1.52

Glover, E. M., Jovanovic, T., Mercer, K. B., Kerley, K., Bradley, B., Ressler, K. J., & Norrholm, S. D. (2012). Estrogen levels are associated with extinction deficits in women with posttraumatic stress disorder. *Biological Psychiatry, 72,* 19–24.

Gunnar, M., & Quevedo, K. (2007). The neurobiology of stress and development. *Annual Review of Psychology, 58,* 145–173.

Häggström, M. (Illus.). (2009). *Human body silhouette* [Digital image]. Retrieved from https://commons.wikimedia.org/wiki/File%3AHuman_body_silhouette.svg

Hayes, J. P., LaBar, K. S., McCarthy, G., Selgrade, E., Nasser, J., Dolcos, F., & Morey, R. A. (2011). Reduced hippocampal and amygdala activity predicts memory distortions for trauma reminders in combat-related PTSD. *Journal of Psychiatric Research, 45,* 660–669. http://dx.doi.org/10.1016/j.jpsychires.2010.10.007

Herman, J. L. (1992). *Trauma and recovery: The aftermath of violence from domestic abuse to political terror.* New York, NY: Basic Books.

Hopper, J. W, Frewen, P. A, van der Kolk, B. A, & Lanius, R. A. (2007). Neural correlates of reexperiencing, avoidance, and dissociation in PTSD: Symptom dimensions and emotion dysregulation in responses to script-driven trauma imagery. *Journal of Traumatic Stress, 20,* 713–725. http://dx.doi.org/10.1002/jts.20284

Hurlemann, R., Patin, A., Onur, O. A., Cohen, M. X., Baumgartner, T., Metzler, S., . . . Kendrick, K. M. (2010). Oxytocin enhances amygdala-dependent, socially reinforced learning and emotional empathy in humans. *Journal of Neuroscience, 30,* 4999–5007. http://dx.doi.org/10.1523/jneurosci.5538-09.2010

Kessler, R. C. (2000). Posttraumatic stress disorder: the burden to the individual and to society. *Journal of Clinical Psychiatry, 61*(Suppl. 5), 4–12.

Kilpatrick, D. G., Resnick, H. S., Milanak, M. E., Miller, M. W., Keyes, K. M., & Friedman, M. J. (2013). National estimates of exposure to traumatic events and PTSD prevalence using *DSM-IV* and *DSM-5* criteria. *Journal of Traumatic Stress, 26,* 537–547. http://dx.doi.org/10.1002/jts.21848

Litz, B. T., Orsillo, S. M., Kaloupek, D., & Weathers, F. (2000). Emotional processing in posttraumatic stress disorder. *Journal of Abnormal Psychology, 109,* 26–39.

McFarlane, A. C., & Yehuda, R. (2000). Clinical treatment of posttraumatic stress disorder: Conceptual challenges raised by recent research. *Australian and New Zealand Journal of Psychiatry, 34,* 940–953. http://dx.doi.org/10.1046/j.1440-1614.2000.00829.x

Murray-Close, D., Han, G., Cicchetti, D., Crick, N. R., & Rogosch, F. A. (2008). Neuroendocrine regulation and physical and relational aggression: the moderating roles of child maltreatment and gender. *Developmental Psychology, 44,* 1160–1176.

Offringa, R., Brohawn, K. H., Staples, L. K., Dubois, S. J., Hughes, K. C., Pfaff, D. L., . . . Haber, S. N. (2013). Diminished rostral anterior cingulate cortex activation during trauma-unrelated emotional interference in PTSD. *Biology of Mood & Anxiety Disorders, 3*(1), 10.

Ogden, P., & Minton, K. (2000). Sensorimotor psychotherapy: One method for processing traumatic memory. *Traumatology, 6*(3), Article 3.

Olff, M. (2012). Bonding after trauma: On the role of social support and the oxytocin system in traumatic stress. *European Journal of Psychotraumatology, 2012,* 3. http://dx.doi.org/10.3402/ejpt.v3i0.18597

Olff, M., Langeland, W., Draijer, N., & Gersons, B. P. R. (2007). Gender differences in posttraumatic stress disorder. *Psychological Bulletin, 133,* 183–204. http://dx.doi.org/10.1037/0033-2909.133.2.183

Olff, M., Langeland, W., Witteveen, A., & Denys, D. (2010). A psychobiological rationale for oxytocin in the treatment of posttraumatic stress disorder. *CNS Spectrums, 15,* 522–530.

Orsillo, S. M., Batten, S. V., Plumb, J. C., Luterek, J. A., & Roessner, B. M. (2004). An experimental study of emotional responding in women with posttraumatic stress disorder related to interpersonal violence. *Journal of Traumatic Stress, 17,* 241–248. http://dx.doi.org/10.1023/b:jots.0000029267.61240.94

Ponniah, K., & Hollon, S. D. (2006). Empirically supported psychological treatments for adults with acute stress disorder and posttraumatic stress disorder: A review. *Depression and Anxiety, 26,* 1086–1109.

Porges, S. W. (2003). Social engagement and attachment. *Annals of the New York Academy of Sciences, 1008,* 31–47. http://dx.doi.org/10.1196/annals.1301.004

Porges, S. W. (2011). *The polyvagal theory: Neurophysiological foundations of emotions, attachment, communication, and self-regulation.* New York, NY: W. W. Norton.

Raglan, G. B., & Schulkin, J. (2014). Introduction to allostasis and allostatic load. In M. Kent, M. Davis, & J. W. Reich (Eds.), *The resilience handbook: Approaches to stress and trauma* (pp. 44–52). New York, NY: Routledge/Taylor & Francis.

Resick, P. A., & Schnicke, M. (1993). *Cognitive processing therapy for rape victims: A treatment manual* (Vol. 4). Newberry Park, CA: Sage.

Roth, A., & Fonagy, P. (2006). *What works for whom: A critical review of psychotherapy research.* New York, NY: Guilford Press.

Schottenbauer, M. A., Glass, C. R., Arnkoff, D. B., Tendick, V., & Gray, S. H. (2008). Nonresponse and dropout rates in outcome studies on PTSD: Review and methodological considerations. *Psychiatry: Interpersonal and Biological Processes, 71,* 134–168. http://dx.doi.org/10.1521/psyc.2008.71.2.134

Seligowski, A. V., Miron, L. H., & Orcutt, H. K. (2015). Relations among self-compassion, PTSD symptoms, and psychological health in a trauma-exposed sample. *Mindfulness, 6,* 1033–1041. http://dx.doi.org/10.1007/s12671-014-0351-x

Selye, H. (1975). Confusion and controversy in the stress field. *Journal of Human Stress, 1*(2), 37–44.

Shapiro, F., & Solomon, R. M. (1995). *Eye movement desensitization and reprocessing.* New York, NY: Wiley.

Sherin, J. E., & Nemeroff, C. B. (2011). Post-traumatic stress disorder: The neurobiological impact of psychological trauma. *Dialogues in Clinical Neuroscience, 13,* 263–278.

Shin, L. M., Bush, G., Milad, M. R., Lasko, N. B., Brohawn, K. H., Hughes, K. C., . . . Orr, S. P. (2011). Exaggerated activation of dorsal anterior cingulate cortex during cognitive interference: A monozygotic twin study of posttraumatic stress disorder. *American Journal of Psychiatry, 168,* 979–985. doi:10.1176/appi.ajp.2011.09121812

Shin, L. M., McNally, R. J., Kosslyn, S. M., Thompson, W. L., Rauch, S. L., Alpert, N. M., . . . Pitman, R. K. (1999). Regional cerebral blood flow during script-driven imagery in childhood sexual abuse-related PTSD: A PET investigation. *American Journal of Psychiatry, 156,* 575–584.

Spahic-Mihajlovic, A., Crayton, J. W., & Neafsey, E. J. (2005). Selective numbing and hyperarousal in male and female Bosnian refugees with PTSD. *Journal of Anxiety Disorders, 19,* 383–402.

Sriram, K., Rodriguez-Fernandez, M., & Doyle, F. J., III. (2012). Modeling cortisol dynamics in the neuro-endocrine axis distinguishes normal, depression, and post-traumatic stress disorder (PTSD) in humans. *PLoS Computational Biology, 8,* e1002379.

Steuwe, C., Daniels, J., Frewen, P., Densmore, M., Pannasch, S., Beblo, T., . . . Lanius, R. (2012). Effect of direct eye contact in PTSD related to interpersonal trauma: An fMRI study of activation of an innate alarm system. *Social Cognitive and Affective Neuroscience, 9,* 88–97. http://dx.doi.org/10.1093/scan/nss105

Teicher, M. H., Tomoda, A., & Andersen, S. L. (2006). Neurobiological consequences of early stress and childhood maltreatment: Are results from human and animal studies comparable? *Annals of the New York Academy of Sciences, 1071,* 313–323.

Tolin, D. F., & Foa, E. B. (2006). Sex differences in trauma and posttraumatic stress disorder: A quantitative review of 25 years of research. *Psychological Bulletin, 132,* 959–992.

Vaiva, G., Boss, V., Ducrocq, F., Fontaine, M., Devos, P., Brunet, A., . . . Thomas, P. (2006). Relationship between posttrauma GABA plasma levels and PTSD at 1-year follow-up. *American Journal of Psychiatry, 163,* 1446–1448.

van der Kolk, B. A. (2014). *The body keeps the score: Brain, mind, and body in the healing of trauma.* New York, NY: Penguin.

van der Kolk, B. A., Greenberg, M. S., Orr, S. P., & Pitman, R. K. (1989). Endogenous opioids, stress induced analgesia, and post-traumatic stress disorder. *Psychopharmacology Bulletin, 25,* 417–421.

van der Kolk, B. A., Roth, S., Pelcovitz, D., Sunday, S., & Spinazzola, J. (2005). Disorders of extreme stress: The empirical foundation of a complex adaptation to trauma. *Journal of Traumatic Stress, 18,* 389–399.

Wells, M., Trad, A., & Alves, M. (2003). Training beginning supervisors working with new trauma therapists. *Journal of College Student Psychotherapy, 17,* 19–39. http://dx.doi.org/10.1300/J035v17n03_03

Zak, P. J., Kurzban, R., & Matzner, W. T. (2004). The neurobiology of trust. *Annals of the New York Academy of Sciences, 1032,* 224–227. doi: 10.1196/annals.1314.025

Part II
COUNSELING RELATIONSHIPS AND ASSESSMENTS

The second section of the text explicates how neuroscience both explains and informs counseling relationships and clinical assessment. These chapters build on the foundational knowledge presented in the first section by describing how to build and maintain rapport with the client in the counseling room from a neuroscience-informed perspective. We first introduce the neuroscience of attention and its implications for empathy and microskills, along with a neuroscience-informed approach to integrating counseling theories. We then present a neurocounseling approach to clinical assessment, along with assessing wellness and optimized performance.

■ ■ ■

Chapter 5

Neuroscience of Attention: Empathy and Counseling Skills

Allen E. Ivey, Thomas Daniels, Carlos P. Zalaquett,
and Mary Bradford Ivey

Counseling changes the brains of both client and counselor. Interpersonal interactions have the potential to strengthen existing neuronal connections, build new neural networks, and produce new neurons. Learning, practicing, or remembering activates the brain. When clients learn a new skill, repeatedly practice a new behavior, or access memories, their neural networks fire in concert, creating electrochemical routes that shape themselves into long-term memories and possible new patterns of behavior. This process is known as *neuroplasticity*—the selective organizing of connections among neurons in the brain. With practice, connections become stronger and more efficient, and they establish connections with other parts of the brain. The old view that brain cells are irreplaceable and that if a brain cell died you were out of luck has changed. Furthermore, the idea that people only lose neurons as they age is a myth. Older adults, through learning and new experiences, have the potential to increase the gray matter in their brains.

However, learning and memory are not possible without attention. Attentional processes, and the microskill of attending to behavior, make possible and enhance learning, memory, and change. Attention is essential for counseling and therapy. You cannot help clients cope with stress and change behavior without attending empathically to their stories and goals. Current research in neuroscience and neurobiology has reinforced and supported what counselors and therapists have done for years. It is time to draw on this new information and apply it further to counseling and clinical practice. Advances in both disciplines will enhance the mind–brain–body conceptualization and enable counselors to practice more effectively.

Divided into four main sections, this chapter summarizes how attention serves as a basis for counseling and therapy practice and establishes its neuroscientific foundation. "Neuroscience of Attention" focuses on key brain structures basic to attention—alerting, orienting, and executive functioning. "Attention, Empathic Understanding, and Microskills" discusses differential aspects of practical applied neuroscience in a review of cognitive and affective empathy as well as mentalizing (Theory of Mind). "Counseling Skills, Calming, and Activating" discusses microskills, and "Rewiring of Memories Into Positive Resilient Action" discusses the importance of memory and carrying changes forward through action planning. A real-life case study illustrates how neuroscience helps the counselor to both conceptualize and act in the counseling and therapy interview.[1]

 ## 2016 CACREP Standards

This chapter addresses a section of the 2016 Council for Accreditation of Counseling and Related Educational Programs (CACREP) Standards pertinent to the common core area of Counseling and Helping Relationships (Standard II.F.5.):

- Counselor characteristics and behaviors that influence the counseling process (Standard II.F.5.f.)

■ ■ ■

 ## Clinical Case Study: Nelida[1]

> Let us look at a counselor and client from a brain-based skills approach. The 22-year-old Cuban American client, Nelida, shares a story of a microaggression she experienced in her graduate program, which has left her fearing to speak up in class because of her "different accent." She participated actively in her first class, but afterward two students asked her, "Where are you from?" Nelida answered, "Miami." "No, where are you *from?*" continued the students. Not getting the information they wanted, they walked off, leaving Nelida standing there. This seemingly simple interaction distracts and disturbs many people and leaves them feeling that they do not belong in this country. The counselor, Allen Ivey, is faced with a new client.

---

[1]Nelida has given her written permission to use her name. This is from a recorded interview with Allen Ivey. Detailed transcripts including step-by-step neuroscientific analysis of the session are available in Ivey, Ivey, and Zalaquett (2017).

Before proceeding, consider that this is a microaggression in action. It seems mild to many of us and as though it should be ignored, but you see the immediate and powerful reaction it brought out in Nelida. Continued racist, sexist, or homophobic microaggressions gradually make the world feel unsafe and dangerous, alienating the recipient.

Can you think of microaggressions you and your clients may have received in the past? Bullying is one common example, as is sexist language, and even being ignored.

What is counselors' responsibility? How can they handle these events to facilitate client empowerment and resilience?

Neuroscience of Attention

Nelida is attending to a strong stimulus, that of a microaggression. Negative experiences such as these rapidly lock themselves into long-term memory and can change behavior. There can be no counseling and therapy without attention. The counselor needs to draw out Nelida's story, her thoughts and feelings. This chapter is designed to reveal how attentional processes, microskills, and neurobiological structures and mechanisms underlie counseling and the therapy process.

The nervous system and its main branches, the central nervous system and the peripheral nervous system, play a pivotal role in active attending. Impairments to the nervous system can reduce one's capacity to attend (e.g., toxins or diseases can reduce attention). What one attends to can be traumatic, leading to fight-or-flight reactions by the sympathetic nervous system, or it can be soothing ("rest and digest") through action in parasympathetic nervous system and its vagus nerve. In this case, the negative interaction has awakened the sympathetic nervous system, and there is a need for calming via the parasympathetic nervous system and the vagus nerve.

Both the sympathetic and the parasympathetic nervous systems are part of the autonomic nervous system, a branch of the peripheral nervous system. A balance between the sympathetic and parasympathetic systems is critical for both mental and physical health. Key to achieving balance are three basic networks identified by Petersen and Posner (2012): alerting, orienting, and executive attention.

Alerting

The wakeup call of the nervous system is a whole brain–body activity that starts with perceptions—visual, auditory, tactile, olfactory, and taste. One or more of these perceptions wakes up the brain stem to vigilance and arousal, producing norepinephrine. In turn, the spinal cord, thalamus, amygdala, hypothalamus, and prefrontal and parietal areas of the brain become involved. Maintaining vigilance after perception relies on the prefrontal cortex.

Alerting is most easily described as anything that draws one's immediate attention, such as a car horn, a shout, a thunderclap, or a microaggression such as that experienced by Nelida. Alerting can actually occur any time one's emotions are evoked or one has motivation—for example, when one sees a friend out of the corner of one's eye, is suddenly drawn to a brilliant sunset, senses danger, or feels one is not approved of. Alerting represents the focal point of the beginning of attention and the counseling relationship.

The process of alerting can take considerable brain energy, devouring glucose necessary for cell functioning. Maintaining vigilance and awareness appears to gradually wear down alerting and brain efficiency. For example, consider Transportation Security Administration staff, truck drivers, and prison guards—anyone with a stressful but important job. Reaction times vary throughout the day. Moreover, people of color can become weary and lose attention and alertness as a result of necessary vigilance in unwelcoming situations. Needless to say, alerting becomes an issue not only for clients but for counselors. A counselor's attention can decline during the day and even during a session, and as such, he or she may miss important things that clients say in the here and now. For counselors and therapists, the obvious point is that if they are to be with clients in the moment, they need to increase their efforts to be alert to them and discover what patterns alert clients both to danger (sympathetic nervous system) and to comfort (parasympathetic nervous system, vagus nerve).

Orienting

Once the counselor has been alerted to the client through the senses, the counselor must navigate all incoming information to the brain. The orienting network is involved in directing attention to a specific stimulus and location in space. The function of the orienting network can be stimulus driven (exogenous, automatic, or bottom-up) and goal directed (endogenous, voluntary, or top-down). So far, Allen and Nelida have been alerted, and both have oriented their attention to the classroom story. The next attentional issue occurs once the counselor has all the information. This action of the mind—executive functioning—is, somewhat surprisingly, what counseling is all about.

Executive Attention

Executive attention is more popularly known as self-regulation, executive functioning, emotional regulation, and self-efficacy. Counselors attend to clients; they listen for cognitions and underlying emotions. They try to understand what is going on in the client's mind. They make decisions. This is executive functioning in action.

A critical part of executive functioning is cognitive and emotional regulation. At the beginning of counseling, Allen discovers that Nelida's emotions have allowed her to take on the microaggression internally and that she believes that she is the one who is inadequate and should not speak up. Emotions often rule cognitions. Counselors need to have competence in controlling and regulating themselves because it is their goal to facilitate client executive functioning and emotional regulation and build resilience through appropriate attentional patterns. Executive functioning, as with alerting and orienting, requires widespread brain connections. The prefrontal cortex, insula, and anterior cingulate cortex are particularly important in balancing emotion and cognition.

Petersen and Posner (2012) discussed two executive attentional networks. The first monitors behavioral acts and was the original definition of executive control. This top-down regulation is also critical to maintaining focus on a topic or task. The second attention network operates differently, through monitoring, error detection, and correction. Every counselor makes mistakes in counseling, and the ability to self-reflect and correct them is essential. With Nelida, there is a need to strengthen her cognitive executive control but also to help her understand her emotional error in accepting false and disruptive behavior from others.

Executive functioning is also related to mentalizing, located primarily in the prefrontal cortex, anterior cingulate cortex, and temporal parietal junction (Mahy, Moses, & Pfeifer, 2014). Mentalizing, also termed *Theory of Mind* (ToM), is the process of making sense of others (clients) and oneself. It includes subjective processes, such as the thoughts occurring in others and one's own self-reflections. Mentalizing requires the counselor to enter the client's world, but with awareness that it is the client's world, not the counselor's. Given these many important functions, the understanding of executive func-

Reflective Questions

Consider a response to the following questions:

How do you work to balance emotion and cognition?

Does the concept of ToM make sense to you?

What is going on in Nelida's mind?

This section contains a lot of input on the importance of alerting, orienting, and executive attention, relatively new practical concepts for the field of counseling and therapy. As you think about a past client, can you identify these three aspects as they occurred in the interview?

What is the place of the nervous system in counseling work?

tioning, emotional regulation, and self-regulation is vital to becoming an effective counselor and therapist. ToM is basic to empathy, and an important part of Allen's task is to generate a theory of how Nelida is processing information in her mind.

Attention, Empathic Understanding, and Microskills

> By saying what the client said, known as reflecting, something new will occur. The client will soon say something new, and then we can respond to that. By featuring responsivity at every small and specific step . . . the therapist carries forward not only what the client has said, but also the client's experience. (Gendlin, 1970, p. 545)

Carl Rogers made empathy central to the helping field. Gendlin (Carl Rogers's central follower) commented that this process empowers the client to understand self and situation more fully. Neuroscience, however, has taken understanding the meaning and value of empathy to a new level. Extensive functional MRI (fMRI) studies of the brain have both theoretical and applied implications for the counseling field. The following discussion illustrates the complexity of understanding and experiencing the world of others. Spunt (2013) spoke to the importance of the brain's mirror system (specifically mirror neurons, discussed in Chapter 2) as basic to understanding empathy's place in the communication process. The basics of the mirror system are most easily understood in terms of observational learning. Think of an Australian Aboriginal youth who wants to learn how to throw a boomerang. Watching his or her parent throw the boomerang activates portions of the youth's brain.

The counseling relationship facilitates neurogenesis, and practice (homework and action plans) outside of the therapeutic relationship strengthens the development of new neural networks. The conversation in counseling helps rewire the brain for more effective living. Neurophysiology has shown that empathy is indeed a necessary (and sometimes sufficient) condition for the relationship, which can itself enable client change.

Empathy consists of various different components, such as cognitive empathy, affective empathy, and mentalizing. Affective empathy helps counselors understand the emotions experienced by others, and cognitive empathy enables them to understand client verbalizations, thought patterns, and behaviors. Advances in neuroscience have confirmed that empathy is a multicomponent construct, essential in navigating the social environment and developing deeper intellectual and emotional understanding. A meta-analysis conducted by Fan, Duncan, de Greck, and Northoff (2011) across 40 fMRI studies showed that affective empathy is associated with increased activity in the insula, whereas the right supramarginal gyrus recognizes a lack of empathy and autocorrects (Engen & Singer, 2013). Cognitive empathy is associated with higher activity in the midcingulate cortex and the dorsomedial prefrontal cortex.

On the importance of self-correction in listening, Tania Singer said,

> When assessing the world around us and our fellow humans, we use ourselves as a yardstick and tend to project our own emotional state onto others. While cognition research has already studied this phenomenon in detail, nothing is known about how it works on an emotional level. It was assumed that our own emotional state can distort our understanding of other people's emotions, in particular if these are completely different to our own. But this emotional egocentricity had not been measured before now. (as cited in Berglund, 2013)

Eres, Decety, and Molenberghs (2015) found greater gray matter density in both places. Neuroimaging studies by Lamm, Decety, and Singer (2011) have also shown that emotional components are shared vicariously. When people experience direct pain themselves (first-hand sensation), the somatosensory motor cortex, insula, and anterior cingulate cortex are activated. When they watch others experience pain (second-hand pain), the insula and anterior cingulate cortex are activated, but not the somatosensory cortex. The insula integrates visceral and autonomic information with salient stimuli, acting as an infrastructure for the representation of subjective bodily feelings of positive and negative emotions.

Listening is the building block of the relationship. The microskills approach has made the underlying behaviors of listening clear. New research using fMRI has revealed that listening literally lights up the brain. Kawamichi et al. (2015) found that the Rogerian microskills of attending to behavior, paraphrasing, reflecting feelings, and summarizing create the foundation for a strong therapeutic relationship and the benefits that stem from this alliance.

Counselors activate key brain structures when they listen. The ventral striatum becomes active when encountering abstract positive communication. Counselors think of Rogerian positive regard, authenticity, and being with the client as key aspects of listening. The microcounseling approach identified the concrete behaviors of listening in 1966 and developed the term *attending behavior.* The importance of culturally appropriate eye contact, body language, vocal tone, and verbal following has since become a standard basic counseling practice.

The right anterior insula has been identified as key in emotional appraisal. Ghahremani, Rastogi, and Lam (2015) pointed out that the insula identifies what is salient and has a close connection with the anterior cingulate cortex, which is concerned with empathy, emotion, and reward anticipation. Together, these structures are important in inhibitory control, a critical factor in dealing constructively with emotion. The superior temporal sulcus is involved in the perception of where others are gazing (joint attention) and thus is important in determining where others' emotions are being directed (Beauchamp, 2015).

Polyvagal Theory and Safety

Physiological needs and safety are the foundation of Maslow's (1943) Hierarchy of Needs (see Figure 5.1). Counselors too often focus on self-actualization in counseling and therapy with insufficient attention to Maslow's foundation of physiological and safety needs. In developing his Polyvagal Theory, Porges (2011) clarified the importance of Maslow's original ideas. He identified the vagus nerve and its connections as the physiological basis for safety. To conduct effective counseling and therapy, counselors need to provide a safe environment in an effective relationship.

Safety is a major issue for Nelida in the counseling relationship with Allen. A trusting relationship is necessary. Then the interview needs to address the lack of feelings of safety that Nelida experiences in the classroom. Yes, they are cognitive and emotional issues, but they are based on physiological foundations. Unless the client feels safe, cognition and even emotional recognition are not enough.

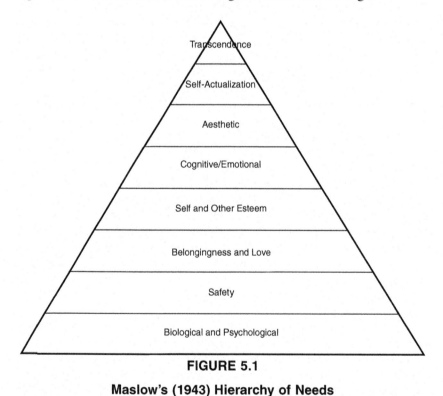

FIGURE 5.1

Maslow's (1943) Hierarchy of Needs

Notice that neuroscience brings us back to counseling's emphasis on relationship. Safety, both cognitive and physiological, is foundational to any relationship.

Think through the differential challenges in providing safety and compassion when you are culturally similar to your client. Now, change the client's gender to be different from yours. How might safety and relationship change?

Next, assume a cultural difference between you and your client such as race, ethnicity, sexual orientation, spirituality, or economic background. How prepared are you to provide a safe relationship?

Porges (2011) focused on four factors of compassionate relationship that will sound familiar to those who have worked with microskills. Porges gave considerable attention to prosodic vocal tone, facial expression and body language, and eye contact as key to building feelings of safety. He also spoke of socialization in which verbalizations provide content to these key nonverbal dimensions. Furthermore, he provided additional specifics that can help guide the client to a calming state (e.g., taking a deep breath). Attending, listening skills, and empathy help to substantiate the relationship and thus help to engender feelings of safety and trust between counselor and client. In this way, the relationship itself produces pleasurable dopamine in the client's brain, thus enabling the client to be more open to discussing his or her issues fully.

Counseling Skills, Calming, and Activating

The microskills framework first focused on listening skills and attending behavior from 1966 to 1968 (Ivey, Normington, Miller, Morrill, & Haase, 1968). At that time, the basics of attending behavior were identified through study of videotaped sessions—visuals, vocal tone, verbal following, body and facial language—basically parallel to Porges's (2011) physiological safety observations. Through an authentic and safe relationship and listening, counselors can encourage feelings in the body that support cognitive and emotional change. Counselors are not just counseling with words; they are working with the whole of the client's body, brain, and mind. An axiom of today is that microcounseling is the mind–brain–body axis operating in an atmosphere of people and the environment.

Listening skills provide a calming and safe foundation for relationship. If heard, clients can learn and develop in a compassionate counseling relationship and prepare to take risks. One way of fostering growth is through empathy. Listening microskills communicate to clients the three components of empathy (affective, cognitive, mentalizing). Deficits in empathic listening may lead to ineffective counselors, deficient counseling relationships, and damaging interventions. The microskill of reflection of feeling is central to affective empathy, the emotional dimension of empathy, which helps one experience, in a conscious way, the emotional state of the other person. At the same time, affective empathy will often enable one to feel at least some of the client's emotions in one's own body. Affective empathy implies a self–other distinction, as well as an understanding of the origin of the other person's emotional experience. Why is this important? Because it increases one's general sensitivity to the emotions of others, enhances one's capacity to fully understand their emotional experience, and facilitates helping behavior.

Paraphrasing and clarifying clients' language and thought processes are critical to the counselor's ability to understand the minds of others and predict their behavior without necessarily sharing their emotions. Cognitive empathy with minimal affective empathy could also facilitate competitive, antagonistic, and deceptive behavior.

The microskill of summarization is closely associated with ToM and mentalizing. Human behavior is based on fluid mental states, which makes understanding others difficult. Everyone's actions are driven by needs, feelings, desires, beliefs, or reasons. When people interact with another person, they automatically (often preconsciously) read their underlying mental states and base their responses on what underlies the other person's behavior. At times, people understand others quite inaccurately, often because they do not listen fully. Counselors make serious errors in mentalizing when they unconsciously mix up their own experiences with the thoughts and feelings of the client.

The basic listening sequence encompasses the empathic skills of active listening, using open and closed questions, encouraging, paraphrasing, reflecting feelings, and summarizing to help clients explore and find ways to address their issues (Ivey, Ivey, & Zalaquett, 2017). The purpose of the basic listening sequence is to not only draw out the client's cognitive and affective worlds but also to understand the client's internal mental state. Most summaries are primarily cognitive but include client emotional and feeling tone. Because emotions are often first reactions and may occur before cognition regulates them, counselors need to consistently think about (mentalize) the possible underlying unsaid emotions. Clients feel reassured when they sense that they are in tune with the counselor.

Through the basic listening sequence, Allen draws out Nelida's story, develops increased empathy, and begins to understand what is going on in Nelida's mind (ToM). Equally as important, perhaps even more so, is the basis of trust in the relationship that enables Nelida to explore issues more fully and move later to behavioral change and action.

Because this chapter focuses primarily on the empathic listening portion of the microskills framework, the activating influencing skills receive only secondary attention. Influencing skills such as empathic confrontation, feedback, self-disclosure, interpretation, psychoeducation, and therapeutic confrontation were added to the framework over the years. All these specifically affect the sympathetic nervous system, leading first to new thoughts and behaviors and later to activities that will enable Nelida to be more proud, culturally aware, and self-confident. Throughout the activating, influencing change process, which involves risk for the client, there is a constant need for safety and relationship. Thus, the newly rewired brain learns to balance activation and calming.

We have seen how Allen used attending and listening skills early in the session to develop feelings of safety and trust, thus enabling him to draw out Nelida's story of the microaggression and its impact on her.

Figure 5.2 presents the microskills hierarchy, outlining the systematic step-by-step communication skill units. Note that multicultural understanding, neuroscience, ethics, and positive psychology form the foundation, in recognition that communication style varies with individual cultural background and history. Professionally, it is essential that interpersonal communication be bounded by ethical practice. Finally, microskills practice is based on what we have called

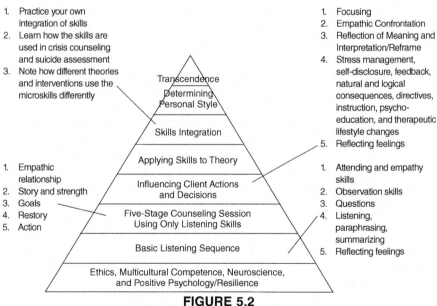

FIGURE 5.2

The Microskills Hierarchy:
A Pyramid for Building Cultural Intentionality

Consider that listening is obviously central in providing a safe relationship.

How would you personally define listening?

How might different theories listen differently—cognitive behavior, humanistic, narrative, multicultural, feminist, and so forth?

Research has shown that the listener inevitably influences the way in which clients construct and think about their issues ("There is no immaculate listening"). What type of listener are you?

the *positive asset search,* and the positive psychology–resilience foundation speaks to the issue that counseling and psychotherapy have too often focused on problems rather than on positive ways to build health and resilience.

Rewiring of Memories Into Positive Resilient Action

Counseling and therapy are typically thought of as changing the meaning of issues and thus moving toward action. This action is typically thought of as oriented externally in terms of new behavior, thoughts, and feelings. However, these changes also affect the body through blood flow, heart rate, neurotransmitters, hormones, and onward to the gut, cell, and DNA. These are powerful agents of change, and a strictly traditional cognitive behavior or humanistic orientation is limiting. Counseling and therapy are deeply intertwined with biological processes; being aware of this will enhance counselors' effectiveness.

Let us look at a counselor and client from a brain-based skills approach. What are some specifics that lead to the changes described in the preceding paragraph? The client, Nelida, shares her story; Allen listens, reflects, and seeks to help re-story the memory and its meaning. Two brains are active in the session, and each person's brain, including short- and long-term memory, may change during the interaction. Two sets of memories in the hippocampus meet in the here and now of conscious conversation. Working memory brings life and the possibility of change to the session. Ultimately, counseling change is an interactive process of influencing clients' working memory in positive ways. Counselors use working memory as an access to long-term memory, and significant change in long-term memory leads to changes in thoughts, feelings and emotions, and behaviors. Counseling is not a one-way process, and counselors also learn and change as they work with clients.

Working memory is the integrated centerpiece of action in counseling conversation. Working memory can be defined as the area in which people store high-speed data from here-and-now consciousness, as well as information from short- and long-term memory. Nelida and Allen can each likely store, at most, 18 items in working memory. However, the amount of information in working memory can change at any moment. For example, a highly emotional experience may leave the client with as few as one or two items in working memory. Similarly, counselors can become fixated on one slightly distorted view of what the client is saying, thus disrupting the therapeutic process.

In considering the change process that occurs through the interaction of client and counselor, counselors are also dealing with the relationship of the "executive CEO" prefrontal cortex with the amygdala and the limbic HPA hormonal axis. Attending behavior (attentional processes are heavily controlled by the thalamus and the prefrontal areas) remains foundational in determining whether declarative long-term memories are solidified in the hippocampus. However, emotional involvement through the energizing amygdala is necessary for working memory to function.

The listening process is ultimately aimed at understanding and calming, thus bringing in the importance of the vagus nerve and of developing new memories and stories that help promote a habit of clients' calming under stress. With an understanding of client issues and concerns, counselors can move toward influencing skills and activating change processes.

One can think of counseling and therapy from a time-based information processing approach in which consciousness represents the psychological present (close to alertness), which ranges in length from 100 to 750 ms and has access to short- and long-term memory (somewhat close to orienting). A person who meditates; someone experiencing a real runner's high; or a ballerina, tennis star, or serious painter—all are very close to living in the here and now of consciousness. Of course, few reach these goals without practice, which involves executive functions, limbic HPA hormones, the amygdala's stimulation, and memory in the hippocampus, and they all operate in the holistic brain. With practice, long-term memory becomes automated in procedural memory, thus allowing the person to be fully in the here and now. This is also a goal of counseling and therapy—to help clients learn new ways of being that eventually become so much a part of them that they seldom have to think about their actions.

Our Brain-Based Approach to the Case of Nelida

The Nelida and Allen interview starts with long-term, embedded memories. Microaggressions can rest deeply in the soul, and their emotional effects can be long lasting. Changing long-term memories is one challenging task that counselors and therapists face. They start this process, of course, by listening to client stories in a safe space.

As Nelida reexamined her memories of the microaggression, Allen encouraged her to externalize her perceptions and view the challenging situation as it might be seen by others, particularly Latina/Latino friends. In this case, Nelida had solid training in past courses in multicultural counseling and therapy and soon came to realize that she was not at fault for her accent and should not have blamed herself. Then Allen brought out positive stories and memories of her parents and grandparents, who were forced to leave Cuba immediately after the Castro regime took over. Her grandfather moved from being a store owner in Havana to cleaning floors in New York. Eventually, he moved to Miami and provided a good life for his family. Nelida saw him as a hero, and she began to take pride in her cultural heritage.

With support from Allen's alternate use of influencing and listening skills, and the strength of her grandfather, she renamed and reframed the classroom experience as oppression and racism while simultaneously expressing anger toward her ignorant classmates—a dramatic change in language and worldview in a relatively short time. Nelida moved from passive acceptance of the microaggression to active awareness and the need for her to change her behavior, her cognitions, and her emotions. A new form of executive functioning and emotional regulation occurred. In addition, she also spoke of sadness that she had not spoken up earlier and had internalized her oppression.

Here, you see the specific development of new neural connections and a rewiring that has led to a change in memory and resulted in immediate changes in behavior. These changes are lasting even today as Nelida moves into professional life. Her thoughts and feelings of cultural inferiority have been replaced by cultural pride. Nelida is now equipped for a more active stance toward the world. Executive functioning has changed, and emotions are regulated in new ways. In an atmosphere of safety and trust, Nelida became able to reframe the difficult classroom experience in a new way. To address the issue of living differently with new memories, the interview continued, and an action plan for interview follow-up was generated.

Reflective Questions

Consider that you have seen the microaggression reframed as oppression and that Nelida has externalized her cognitive and emotional issues. Before this, Nelida's microaggressions were internalized, lowering her self-confidence and leading to her feeling unsafe in the classroom. At the conclusion, you see that her brain has been rewired to take active resilient action when she encounters the next microaggression (as she indeed will; they do not go away).

Please review the case. What were the specific steps and microskills toward safety? What skills relate to reframing and action?

What can you take away from this session?

Conclusion

One key task of counseling is to help the client re-story past experiences and develop new memories and connections (behaviors, thoughts, feelings, meanings). Successful counseling and psychotherapy change the client and long-term memory in significant ways and even build new neural networks in the brain (neuroplasticity). The attending microskills presented earlier provide the cognitive and emotional "charge" to promote understanding and change. The influencing skills both start and solidify the change process.

Quiz

1. Which of the following is *not* one of the considerations that, as Porges (2011) suggested, is helpful to consider in establishing safety?
    a. Prosodic vocal tone (quality of intonation).
    b. Gestures and body language.
    c. Style of eye contact.
    d. Open-ended questions.
2. Which of the following is *not* a form of empathy?
    a. Cognitive.
    b. Situational.
    c. Affective.
    d. Mentalization.
3. In helping a client deal with microaggressions, the central goal is to:
    a. Listen carefully and fully.
    b. Provide a safe environment so that the client can talk easily.
    c. Use neuroscientific concepts to understand what is going on inside the client.
    d. Build resilience by strengthening the client so that the client can work with future insults and challenges more effectively and not internalize what others say about him or her.

References

Beauchamp, M. (2015). The social mysteries of the superior temporal sulcus. *Trends in Cognitive Science, 19,* 489–490.

Berglund, C. (2013). The neuroscience of empathy: Neuroscientists identify specific brain areas related to empathy. *Psychology Today.* Retrieved from https://www.psychologytoday.com/blog/the-athletes-way/201310/the-neuroscience-empathy

Council for Accreditation of Counseling and Related Educational Programs. (2015). *2016 CACREP standards.* Retrieved from http://www.cacrep.org/wp-content/uploads/2012/10/2016-CACREP-Standards.pdf

Engen, H. G., & Singer, T. (2013). Empathy circuits. *Current Opinion in Neurobiology, 23,* 275–282. http://dx.doi.org/10.1016/j.conb.2012.11.003

Eres, R., Decety, J., & Molenberghs, P. (2015). Individual differences in local gray matter density are associated with differences in affective and cognitive empathy. *NeuroImage, 117,* 305–310.

Fan, Y., Duncan, N., de Greck, M., & Northoff, G. (2011). Is there a core neural network in empathy? An fMRI based quantitative meta-analysis. *Neuroscience and Biobehavioral Reviews, 35,* 903–911.

Gendlin, E.T. (1970). A short summary and some long predictions. In J. T. Hart & T. M. Tomlinson (Eds.), *New directions in client-centered therapy* (pp. 544–562). Boston, MA: Houghton Mifflin.

Ghahremani, A., Rastogi, A., & Lam, S. (2015). The role of right anterior insula and salience processing in inhibitory control. *Journal of Neuroscience, 35,* 3291–3292.

Ivey, A., & Daniels, T. (2016). Systematic interviewing microskills: Developing bridges between the fields of communication and counseling psychology. *International Journal of Communication, 10,* 1–21.

Ivey, A., Ivey, M., & Zalaquett, C. (2015). *Essentials of intentional interviewing: Counseling in a multicultural world* (3rd ed.). San Francisco, CA: Brooks/Cole.

Ivey, A., Ivey, M., & Zalaquett, C. (2016). The neuroscience of listening, empathy, and microskills. *Counseling Today, 30*(8), 18–21.

Ivey, A., Ivey, M., & Zalaquett, C. (2017). *Intentional interviewing and counseling: Facilitating client development in a multicultural society* (9th ed.). San Francisco, CA: Brooks/Cole.

Ivey, A., Normington, C., Miller, D., Morrill, W., & Haase, R. (1968). Microcounseling and attending behavior: An approach to pre-practicum training. *Journal of Counseling Psychology, 15*(5, Pt. 2), 1–12.

Kawamichi, H., Yoshihara, K., Sasaki, A. T., Sugawara, S. K., Tanabe, H. C., Shinohara, R, . . . Sadato, N. (2015). Perceiving active listening activates the reward system and improves the impression of relevant experiences. *Social Neuroscience, 10,* 16–26. http://dx.doi.org/10.1080/17470919.2014.954732.

Lamm, C., Decety, J., & Singer, T. (2011). Meta-analytic evidence for common and distinct neural networks associated with directly experienced pain and empathy for pain. *NeuroImage, 54,* 2492–2502.

Mahy, C., Moses, L., & Pfeifer, J. (2014). How and where: Theory-of-mind in the brain. *Developmental Cognitive Neuroscience, 9,* 68–81.

Maslow, A. H. (1943). A theory of human motivation. *Psychological Review, 50,* 370–396. http://dx.doi.org/10.1037/h0054346

Petersen, S. E., & Posner, M. I. (2012).The attention system of the human brain: 20 years after. *Annual Review of Neuroscience, 35,* 73–89. http://dx.doi.org/10.1146/annurev-neuro-062111-150525

Porges, S. (2011). *The polyvagal theory: Neurophysiological foundations of emotions, attachment, communication, and self-regulation.* New York, NY: W. W. Norton.

Spunt, R. (2013). Mirroring, mentalizing, and the social neuroscience of listening. *International Journal of Listening, 27,* 61–72. http://dx.doi.org/10.1080/10904018.2012.756331

This chapter is also drawn from three publications with permission of the publishers: (a) "Systematic Interviewing Microskills: Developing Bridges Between the Fields of Communication and Counseling Psychology," by A. Ivey and T. Daniels, 2016, *International Journal of Communication, 10,* 1–21 (permission granted by Taylor & Francis); (b) "The Neuroscience of Listening, Empathy, and Microskills," by A. Ivey, M. Ivey, and C. Zalaquett, 2016, *Counseling Today, 30*(8), 18–21 (permission granted by the American Counseling Association); and (c) *Intentional Interviewing and Counseling: Facilitating Client Development in a Multicultural Society* (9th ed.), by A. Ivey, M. Ivey, and C. Zalaquett, 2017, San Francisco, CA: Brooks/Cole (permission granted by Brooks/Cole).

Chapter 6

Neuroscience-Informed Counseling Theory

SeriaShia Chatters, Carlos P. Zalaquett,
and Allen E. Ivey

This chapter provides an overview of the intersection between counseling theories and neuroscientific research. The interaction between neuroscience and counseling offers strong evidence of the effects of different therapies on the brain. Neuroscience informs theoretical orientation by providing the biological basis for how client issues are developed and resolved. An understanding of neuroscience and neurobiology can deepen understanding of how the brain responds to treatment. This chapter reviews a few select theories to demonstrate how they may benefit from the integration of neuroscience. The case of Natasha is presented to explore an integrative approach to neuroscience-informed counseling theory and neurocounseling intervention.

 ## 2016 CACREP Standards

This chapter addresses a section of the 2016 Council for Accreditation of Counseling and Related Educational Programs (CACREP) Standards pertinent to the common core area of Counseling and Helping Relationships (Standard II.F.5.):

- Theories and models of counseling (Standard II.F.5.a.)

This chapter also addresses the following Specialization Standard:

- Integration of theories relevant to counseling (Counselor Education and Supervision, Standard VI.B.1.b.)

■ ■ ■

Clinical Case Study: Natasha

Natasha is a 24-year-old Puerto Rican American woman who attended a counseling center at a mid-sized southwestern university because of stress and academic concerns. She previously served for 5 years in the U.S. Army. During that time, she was deployed on three occasions and saw action in both Gulf Wars, including Operation Iraqi Freedom and Operation Enduring Freedom. Natasha was recently divorced after a 3-year marriage that was emotionally and physically abusive. She was afraid of being physically attacked by her ex-husband, who had made a number of threats during the divorce. She also reported bouts of excruciating abdominal pain but attributed this pain to the stressful situation with her ex-husband. Natasha had originally been attending a college on the East Coast. One day, she abruptly stopped attending all of her classes at this college and moved to the opposite side of the continental United States to avoid the stress and fear triggered by the abusive relationship. Because she moved and neglected to drop her classes at the West Coast college, Natasha failed all of her courses for the spring semester. During the initial interview, Natasha reports, "I am a failure," and feels hopeless.

Neuroscience-Informed Theoretical Orientation

Research discoveries have spurred many questions among therapists regarding theoretical orientation, interventions, and treatment approach. For example, which theoretical orientation or intervention is the most effective at managing problematic neural pathways? With the brain's tendency toward negative affective bias (Hanson & Mendius, 2009), which theoretical orientation or intervention may assist clients to reduce bias, increase positive experiences, and encourage the thickening of preferred neural pathways? Although these questions have yet to be answered, research findings have had a significant impact on the understanding of the neurobiological underpinnings of cognition and how therapists may be able to affect the brain's structure. In this section, we briefly review how neuroscience informs three theoretical orientations: a cognitive approach, cognitive behavior therapy (CBT); a psychodynamic approach, interpersonal psychotherapy; and a postmodern approach, narrative therapy.

Reflective Question

What would you focus on first with Natasha—her cognitive distortions related to her academic failure, her current physical symptoms, her lack of social supports, or her narrative of the divorce?

CBT

CBT is a broad category encompassing several therapeutic approaches including rational emotive behavior therapy, cognitive therapy, cognitive behavior modification, and dialectic behavior therapy, among others. In general, CBT is a therapeutic approach that emphasizes the role of thinking in inducing and perpetuating client distress. CBT treatment strategies involve therapists' assisting clients to intentionally direct their thought patterns from dysfunctional to functional processes (David & Szentagotai, 2006; Paquette et al., 2003; Ressler & Mayberg, 2007). The use of CBT has considerable empirical support as an intervention for various disorders. We briefly review the neuroscience associated with CBT in the treatment of phobias, trauma, and depression.

CBT and Phobias

The impact of psychotherapy on brain activation has, over the past decade, primarily been studied in the context of phobias. Phobias, or extreme or irrational fear of or aversion to something or a specific situation, cause the client to elicit a specific or a conditioned fear response to a stimulus. Empirical studies have indicated that exposure therapy, a behavioral intervention rooted in systematic desensitization (Wolpe, 1958), is successful in relieving phobia symptoms. Paquette et al. (2003) studied brain activation and the use of CBT in the treatment of spider phobia. During pretest, study participants experienced a fear response to the photographic stimuli that was correlated with activation of the right dorsolateral prefrontal cortex (PFC) and parahippocampal gyrus. During postintervention, a significant reduction in activation was noted in those same areas. The authors believed that initial parahippocampal activation had led to the development of avoidance toward spiders, reinforcing the phobia. Paquette et al. hypothesized that reduced activation of the right dorsolateral PFC may be related to study participants' use of metacognitive strategies aimed at self-regulating the fear triggered by the spider film excerpts. In addition to parahippocampal activity, researchers have found activation in the right and left amygdalas, periamygdaloid, and medial PFC in the process of extinction (e.g., the reduction of the fear of spiders after repeated exposure to the stimulus). Similarly, a study of male and female Vietnam veterans found decreased activation in the medial PFC and increased activation in the left and right amygdalas and the periamygdaloid after veterans therapeutically processed traumatic experiences (Shin et al., 2002). This landmark study was followed by several studies that subsequently confirmed that CBT produced changes in the brain activation during the treatment of anxiety disorders (see Beauregard, 2007; Frewen, Dozois, & Lanius, 2008; Makinson & Young, 2012; Straube, Glauer, Dilger, Mentzel, & Miltner, 2006).

CBT and Trauma

As described in Chapter 4, a traumatic event can have a significant impact on the brain that may permanently stimulate atypical structural plastic changes within the amygdala, PFC, and other structures. Once symptoms of posttraumatic stress disorder (PTSD) are present, neurons in the amygdala may have formed neural networks associated with abnormal flashbacks, easily triggered by stimuli (Sapolsky, 2003). Although CBT may not be able to deconstruct these permanent changes, counseling may stimulate the formation of new or alternate neural pathways that may offset maladaptive circuitry associated with PTSD symptoms (Maguschak & Ressler, 2008; Quirk & Mueller, 2007). CBT may induce neuroplastic changes in structural interconnectedness in brain regions and neurons by promoting a reduced expression of learned fear and moderating the underlying neuronal pathways (De Raedt, 2006; K. C. Martin & Kandel, 1996; Ressler & Mayberg, 2007).

CBT and Depression

The psychological and somatic symptoms of depression have been correlated with several biological dysfunctions. The neurological impact of depression increases the volume of the amygdala (Roozendaal, McEwen, & Chatterji, 2009), decreases the volume of the hippocampus (MacQueen, Yucel, Taylor, Macdonald, & Joffe, 2008) and PFC (Joëls & Baram, 2009), and changes the connectivity between the amygdala and PFC (de Almeida et al., 2009) and the amygdala and hippocampus (Fu et al., 2008). Symptoms of mood dysregulation may be associated with decreased metabolism of the PFC (Galynker et al., 1998). Symptoms of apathy may be associated with elevated levels of cortisol in the bloodstream that affect reward circuits in the limbic system (Arnsten, 2009; Lieberman, 2006). Symptoms of excessive guilt and hopelessness are correlated with dysfunction of the hypothalamic–pituitary–adrenal axis, which is related to arousal of the sympathetic branch of the autonomic nervous system (Du et al., 2009; Fiocco, Wan, Weeks, Pim, & Lupien, 2006; Gillespie & Nemeroff, 2005; Segerstrom & Miller, 2004).

In addition to the aforementioned impact on the brain, Fu et al. (2008) found that amygdala–hippocampal activity was associated with depression and that dorsal anterior cingulate activity was a predictor of a positive treatment response to CBT. This is an important finding because of its potential translational implications. Dorsal anterior cingulate activity may be used to identify those individuals who are most and least likely to benefit from CBT, leading to more effective selection of treatment and utilization of resources.

Biofeedback can be added as a component of CBT and has been used in counseling for many years. One of the pioneers of biofeedback was Dr. Edmund Jacobson, who wrote some of the very first books on biofeedback and progressive muscle relaxation (Jacobson, 1934). Biofeedback is exactly what it sounds like: feedback to the client about certain aspects of his or her biology and body, such as information about breathing patterns, skin temperature control, galvanic skin responses, and muscle tension, to name a few. Each type of biofeedback is selected on the basis of the client's needs and concerns.

Studies investigating the efficacy of using biofeedback or adding it to traditional therapeutic interventions to treat anxiety (Karavidas et al., 2007; Siepmann, Aykac, Unterdörfer, Petrowski, & Mueck-Weymann, 2008) and depression (Karavidas et al., 2007) have found mixed results. Various forms of biofeedback appear to be effective in the treatment of panic disorder and PTSD, including respiratory sinus arrhythmia, electromyographic feedback, and heart rate variability training (Gevirtz & Dalenberg, 2008; Meuret et al., 2004). Neurofeedback is a form of biofeedback that has indications for use with children, adolescents, and adults experiencing a variety of issues including anxiety, brain injury, depression, trauma, substance use, and attention-deficit/hyperactivity disorder (Simkin, Thatcher, & Lubar, 2014).

Learning Theory in Neurofeedback

Neurofeedback is a treatment method designed to alter brain functioning through the use of signals provided to the client via various illustrations (e.g., thermometer, a flying plane, dimming or brightening the screen) that reflect changes in the client's real-time electroencephalogram (EEG). Neurofeedback is grounded in the behavioral learning theory of operant conditioning. During neurofeedback, clients receive positive reinforcement for reaching a state of optimal EEG activity in targeted brain regions. When a person displays desired brain activity in targeted regions, a video game, music, or a movie may play to reinforce optimal activity in that brain state. When the client is outside the limits of optimal arousal, the reinforcer is withdrawn, and the video game, music, or movie stops playing. This real-time positive feedback assists clients to train their brains to recognize optimal arousal and alter their approach in response. Neurofeedback has particular indications for attention-deficit/hyperactivity disorder and may be equally as effective as stimulant medication (Fuchs, Birbaumer, Lutzenberger, Gruzelier, & Kaiser, 2003). In a functional magnetic resonance imaging (fMRI) study, neurofeedback normalized functioning in the anterior cingulate cortex, which is associated with selective attention (Lévesque, Beauregard, & Mensour, 2006).

Psychodynamic Therapy

Psychodynamic therapy has been found to be an effective treatment for numerous mental disorders, most notably depression (Leichsenring, Rabung, & Leibing,

Reflective Question

How might you use CBT to address Natasha's cognitive distortions?

2004). Counseling in general seems to be helpful for depression by altering the density of serotonin (5-HT) receptors (Bhagwagar, Rabiner, Sargent, Grasby, & Cowen, 2004; Drevets et al., 1999; Sargent et al., 2000). Karlsson et al. (2010) conducted a study comparing the effects of psychotherapy and fluoxetine (Prozac) on the density of serotonin 5-HT1A receptors. Using binding potential values, a crucial measure in positron emission tomography (PET) studies to establish the density of available receptors (Laruelle, Slifstein, & Huang, 2002), they estimated the ratio of specific and nondisplaceable binding in the white matter of participants' brains. Pre- and posttreatment symptom improvement in both groups was similar, but only those receiving psychotherapy showed an increase in serotonin 5-HT1A binding in the dorsolateral PFC, ventrolateral PFC, ventral anterior cingulate cortex, inferior temporal gyrus, insular cortex, and angular gyrus.

Interpersonal Therapy and Depression

A specific form of psychodynamic therapy known as interpersonal psychotherapy (IPT) was developed specifically to treat depression (Weissman, Markowitz, & Klerman, 2000). IPT is a short-term, time-limited method based on Harry Stack Sullivan's interpersonal theory (Weissman & Markowitz, 1994). In IPT, clients appraise their current relationships and seek to improve interpersonal connectedness and social supports while coping with stress. Evidence for IPT's alteration of neurological functioning in the treatment of depression is emerging. In a study comparing the effects of IPT and paroxetine (Paxil; an antidepressant), a PET scanner was used to analyze clients' metabolic glucose levels (Brody et al., 2001). Posttreatment, glucose metabolism was reduced in the bilateral PFC for clients treated with the antidepressant and in the right PFC for clients treated with IPT. PET scans of clients in both groups showed an increased metabolism in the left temporal cortex. These results demonstrate that the depressed brain may exhibit increased glucose metabolism in the PFC and decreased metabolic activity in the left temporal cortex. Such findings may indicate that treatment for depression may require some normalization of metabolic activity in these areas.

Narrative Therapy

Narrative therapy is a postmodern approach that was developed in the 1980s by Michael White and David Epston and gained popularity in the 1990s (Beaudoin & Zimmerman, 2011; White, 2007; White & Epston, 1990). The primary impetus of narrative therapy is to assist clients in making meaning out of their experiences. In narrative therapy, clients explore

Reflective Question

How might you enhance Natasha's social support using an IPT framework?

opportunities to access preferred experiences or reauthor their narrative, and they learn how to separate their identities from their experiences or issues, better known as deconstruction or externalization (Beaudoin & Zimmerman, 2011; White, 2007). A client's narrative is a story the client tells the therapist about his or her issues. The therapist, working from a narrative approach, will apply various narrative techniques in the session, such as collaboratively reauthoring the client's narrative through a process called *coconstruction*. From a neurobiological perspective, the client's current perspective of his or her narrative could have neural networks associated with these problem-related experiences. These neural networks are significantly more developed than those associated with preferred experiences because of the brain's tendency toward conservatism (Beaudoin & Zimmerman, 2011). Problem-saturated stories are the result of the PFC attempting to create meaning from repetitive generation of negative affect. As mentioned earlier, the infrequency of positive experiences results in neural networks that are mainly associated with emotionally laden problematic experiences. As these networks become more sophisticated, they have a higher likelihood of being activated.

Reauthoring is a process by which clients reexamine problematic situations they handled in undesirable ways to rewrite them (White & Epston, 1990). The narrative achieved during the process of reauthoring more closely represents clients' preferred ways of being and is more congruent with their values (White, 2007). In narrative therapy, these new narratives are called *problem-free narratives, problem-minimized events*, or *unique outcomes*. Through the process of reauthoring the narrative, more adaptive neural pathways are strengthened.

During reauthoring, therapists encourage conversations that may shift the client's affective experiences and preconceived narratives by revisiting the experience. Each revisited conversation can encourage alterations to memories that may be infused with new meaning and emotions or moods (Sousa, 2011). These memories can be altered in a negative or positive way, so therapists must be careful during the reauthoring process. LeDoux (2003) indicated that once an experience is retrieved in therapy, it may return to storage in an altered form.

Future Directions in Neuroscience-Informed Theory

Counselors are using knowledge of neuroscience to inform conventional theory. For example, Ivey, Ivey, and Zalaquett (2015) advanced the application of neuroscience in counseling and social justice intervention using concepts such as neuroplasticity, attention and focus, wellness, and stress management. They have used their neuroscience-based model of neuroscience to guide the application of counseling mi-

Reflective Question

What parts of Natasha's narrative could you help her to reauthor?

croskills to increase empathy, clarify emotions, and advance individual wellness and strengths in counseling and social justice interventions (Ivey & Zalaquett, 2011). Another example from the counseling field is the development of neuroscience-informed CBT (n-CBT; Field, Beeson, & Jones, 2015). This approach modifies Ellis's (1962) ABC model that a person's belief in response to an antecedent is primarily responsible for emotional and behavioral consequences. The goal of n-CBT is to use conventional CBT techniques such as cognitive restructuring or behavioral activation (identified as Wave2 in n-CBT) while training the client to become aware of his or her physiological responses by using mindfulness, neurofeedback, biofeedback, and healthy coping techniques (identified as Wave1 in n-CBT; Field et al., 2015). We hope that further neuroscience-informed theories will emerge from within the counseling profession.

Our Brain-Based Approach to the Case of Natasha

Natasha came to the southwestern college's counseling center because of concern about her academic performance and growing stress. During Natasha's initial visit, she completed an intake and several assessments to determine an initial diagnosis. Clients who met the criteria for anxiety- or stress-related disorders were offered psychotherapy, biofeedback, or both. During this first session, she was provided with assistance regarding her academic situation. This brought great relief to her because she was able to continue her studies at her new university. Being far away from her abusive ex-husband greatly reduced the anxiety she had felt for the past 3 years.

By the end of the first session, we agreed to use a combination of CBT, IPT, and narrative therapy along with biofeedback training. Natasha received weekly counseling appointments and weekly biofeedback appointments to reduce stress and physical tension. Some of Natasha's session goals were to increase her relaxation response using biofeedback-guided training. Natasha's skin response (through electromyography) and finger temperature were measured. Natasha worked to reduce all of the indicated feedback values. Feedback regarding her progress was communicated to her through use of a light (with red indicating a high level of response and green indicating a low level), a numerical display (with high numbers indicating a high level of response), and sound (with a loud sound indicating a high level of response). Using all three forms of feedback allowed for individualized preferences because changes in each measure of feedback were correlated. Natasha responded very well to the biofeedback training. During the next 6 weeks, she made great progress in reducing her tension and stress.

During counseling, CBT and IPT were first used to stabilize Natasha. CBT addressed core cognitive distortions such as her current

If you were working with Natasha as a client, what neuroscience-informed therapeutic direction would you have chosen, and why?

identity as a failure and feelings of hopelessness. IPT addressed the need to increase Natasha's social support system. Natasha was connected to local resources as a means of helping her become more socially connected. Natasha also decided to reach out to a family member to whom she felt close. Narrative therapy was introduced later to help Natasha reauthor her relationship narrative with her ex-husband. This work was more challenging for Natasha because she came to realize that relationship had been informed by problematic attachment patterns in early childhood. Through reauthoring, Natasha overcame her reticence about deserving a healthy, nonabusive relationship that was marked by nonpossessive caring. At the conclusion of Natasha's sessions, she reported increased engagement in her academic activities and more connectedness in social activities.

Conclusion

A counselor's theoretical orientation is the lens through which they view their client and conceptualize the case. Case conceptualization ultimately informs treatment planning and the selection of interventions throughout the therapeutic process. A counselor's theoretical orientation can often be a part of their identity as a counselor and may determine how they believe client issues develop and how they believe issues are resolved. In the case of Natasha, her therapist decided to use narrative and cognitive behavior–based biofeedback training in the form of electromyography and finger temperature training. The use of these therapeutic interventions has empirical support as an adjunct to conventional therapeutic interventions. As you reflect on our approach to Natasha's case, consider the following question.

Quiz

1. Researchers began studying the neurobiological outcomes of the use of therapeutic interventions by investigating:
   a. Depression.
   b. Anxiety.
   c. Phobias.
   d. Obsessions and compulsions.

2. The primary brain structure affected during the application of therapeutic interventions such as CBT and IPT is:
   a. The brain stem.
   b. The PFC.
   c. The limbic system.
   d. b and c.

References

Arnsten, A. F. T. (2009). Stress signaling pathways that impair prefrontal cortex structure and function. *Nature Reviews Neuroscience, 10,* 410–422.

Beaudoin, M. N., & Zimmerman, J. (2011). Narrative therapy and interpersonal neurobiology: Revisiting classic practices, developing new emphases. *Journal of Systemic Therapies, 30,* 1–13. http://dx.doi.org/10.1521/jsyt.2011.30.1.1

Beauregard, M. (2007). Mind does really matter: Evidence from neuroimaging studies of emotional self-regulation, psychotherapy, and placebo effect. *Progress in Neurobiology, 81,* 218–236.

Bhagwagar, Z., Rabiner, E. A., Sargent, P. A., Grasby, P. M., & Cowen, P. J. (2004). Persistent reduction in brain serotonin: A receptor binding in recovered depressed men measured by positron emission tomography. *Molecular Psychiatry, 9,* 386–392.

Brody, A. L., Saxena, S., Stoessel, P., Gillies, L. A., Fairbanks, L. A., Alborzian, S., . . . Ho, M. K. (2001). Regional brain metabolic changes in patients with major depression treated with either paroxetine or interpersonal therapy: Preliminary findings. *Archives of General Psychiatry, 58,* 631–640.

Council for the Accreditation of Counseling and Related Educational Programs. (2015). *2016 CACREP standards.* Retrieved from http://www.cacrep.org/wp-content/uploads/2012/10/2016-CACREP-Standards.pdf

David, D., & Szentagotai, A. (2006). Cognitions in cognitive behavioral psychotherapy: Toward an integrative model. *Clinical Psychology Review, 26,* 284–298.

de Almeida, J. R. C., Versace, A., Mechelli, A., Hassel, S., Quevedo, K., Kupfer, D. J., & Phillips, M. L. (2009). Abnormal amygdala-prefrontal effective connectivity to happy faces differentiates bipolar from major depression. *Biological Psychiatry, 66,* 451–459.

De Raedt, R. (2006). Does neuroscience hold promise for the further development of behavior therapy? The case of emotional change after exposure in anxiety and depression. *Scandinavian Journal of Psychology, 47,* 225–236.

Drevets, W. C., Frank, E., Price, J. C., Kupfer, D. J., Holt, D., Greer, P. J., . . . Mathis, C. (1999). PET imaging of serotonin 1A receptor binding in depression. *Biological Psychiatry, 46,* 1375–1387.

Du, J., Wang, Y., Hunter, R., Wei, Y., Blumenthal, R., Falke, C., . . . Manji, H. K. (2009). Dynamic regulation of mitochondrial function by glucocorticoids. *Proceedings of the National Academy of Sciences of the United States of America, 106,* 3543–3548.

Ellis, A. (1962). *Reason and emotion in psychotherapy.* New York, NY: Stuart.

Field, T. A., Beeson, E. T., & Jones, L. K. (2015). The new ABCs: A counselor's guide to neuroscience-informed cognitive-behavior therapy. *Journal of Mental Health Counseling, 37,* 206–220.

Fiocco, A. J., Wan, N., Weekes, N., Pim, H., & Lupien, S. J. (2006). Diurnal cycle of salivary cortisol in older adult men and women with subjective complaints of memory deficits and/or depressive symptoms: Relation to cognitive functioning. *Stress, 9,* 143–152.

Frewen, P. A., Dozois, D. J., & Lanius, R. A. (2008). Neuroimaging studies of psychological interventions for mood and anxiety disorders: Empirical and methodological review. *Clinical Psychology Review, 28,* 228–246.

Fu, C. H. Y., Williams, S. C. R., Cleare, A. C., Scott, J., Mitterschiffthaler, M. T., Walsh, N. D., . . . Murray, R. M. (2008). Neural responses to sad facial expressions in major depression following cognitive behavioral therapy. *Biological Psychiatry, 64,* 505–512.

Fuchs, T., Birbaumer, N., Lutzenberger, W., Gruzelier, J. H., & Kaiser, J. (2003). Neurofeedback treatment for attention-deficit/hyperactivity disorder in children: A comparison with methylphenidate. *Applied Psychophysiology and Biofeedback, 28,* 1–12.

Galynker, I. I., Cai, J., Ongseng, F., Finestone, H., Dutta, E., & Serseni, D. (1998). Hypofrontality and negative symptoms in major depressive disorder. *Journal of Nuclear Medicine, 39,* 608–612.

Gevirtz, R., & Dalenberg, C. (2008). Heart rate variability biofeedback in the treatment of trauma symptoms. *Biofeedback, 36*(1), 22–23.

Gillespie, C. F., & Nemeroff, C. B. (2005). Hypercortisolemia and depression. *Psychosomatic Medicine, 67*(Suppl. 1), S26–S28.

Hanson, R., & Mendius, R. (2009). *Buddha's brain.* Oakland, CA: New Harbinger.

Jacobson, E. (1934). *You must relax: Practical methods for reducing tensions of modern living.* New York, NY: McGraw-Hill.

Ivey, A., Ivey, M. B., & Zalaquett, C. (2015). *Essentials of intentional interviewing: Counseling in a multicultural world* (3rd ed.). Belmont, CA: Brooks/Cole.

Ivey, A. E. & Zalaquett, C. (2011). Neuroscience and counseling. *Journal for Social Action in Counseling and Psychology, 3,* 103–116. Retrieved from http://www.psysr.org/jsacp/ivey-v3n1-11_103-116.pdf

Joëls, M., & Baram, T. Z. (2009). The neuro-symphony of stress. *Nature Reviews Neuroscience, 10,* 459–466. doi: 10.1038/nrn2632

Karavidas, M. K., Lehrer, P. M., Vaschillo, E., Vaschillo, B., Marin, H., Buyske, S., . . . & Hassett A. (2007). Preliminary results of an open label study of heart rate variability biofeedback for the treatment of major depression. *Applied Psychophysiology and Biofeedback, 32*(1), 19–30. https://dx.doi.org/10.1007/s10484-006-9029-z

Karlsson, H., Hirvonen, J., Kajander, J., Markkula, J., Rasi-Hakala, H., Salminen, J. K., . . . Hietala, J. (2010). Research letter: Psychotherapy increases brain serotonin 5-HT 1A receptors in patients with major depressive disorder. *Psychological Medicine, 40,* 523–528.

Laruelle, M., Slifstein, M., & Huang, Y. (2002). Positron emission tomography: Imaging and quantification of neurotransporter availability. *Methods, 27,* 287–299.

LeDoux, J. (2003). The emotional brain, fear, and the amygdala. *Cellular and Molecular Neurobiology, 23,* 727–738.

Leichsenring, F., Rabung, S., & Leibing, E. (2004). The efficacy of short-term psychodynamic psychotherapy in specific psychiatric disorders: A meta-analysis. *Archives of General Psychiatry, 61,* 1208–1216.

Lévesque, J., Beauregard, M., & Mensour, B. (2006). Effect of neurofeedback training on the neural substrates of selective attention in children with attention-deficit/hyperactivity disorder: A functional magnetic resonance imaging study. *Neuroscience Letters, 394,* 216–221.

Lieberman, A. (2006). Depression in Parkinson's disease—A review. *Acta Neurologica Scandinavica, 113,* 1–8.

MacQueen, G. M., Yucel, K., Taylor, V. H., Macdonald, K., & Joffe, R. (2008). Posterior hippocampal volumes are associated with remission rates in patients with major depressive disorder. *Biological Psychiatry, 64,* 880–883.

Maguschak, K. A., & Ressler, K. J. (2008). J3-catenin is required for memory consolidation. *Nature Neuroscience, 11,* 1319–1326. http://dx.doi.org/l0.1038/nn.2198

Makinson, R. A., & Young, J. S. (2012). Cognitive behavioral therapy and the treatment of posttraumatic stress disorder: Where counseling and neuroscience meet. *Journal of Counseling & Development, 90,* 131–140.

Martin, K. C, & Kandel, E. R. (1996). Cell adhesion molecules, CREB, and the formation of new synaptic connections. *Neuron, 17,* 567–570.

Meuret, A. E., Wilhelm, F. H., & Roth, W. T. (2004). Respiratory feedback for treating panic disorder. *Journal of Clinical Psychology, 60*(2), 197–207.

Paquette, V., Levesque, J., Mensour, B., Leroux, J.-M., Beaudoin, G., & Bourgouin, P. (2003). "Change the mind and you change the brain": Effects of cognitive-behavioral therapy on the neural correlates of spider phobia. *NeuroImage, 18,* 401–409.

Quirk, G. J., & Mueller, D. (2007). Neural mechanisms of extinction learning and retrieval. *Neuropsychopharmacology, 33,* 56–72.

Ressler, K. J., & Mayberg, H. S. (2007). Targeting abnormal neural circuits in mood and anxiety disorders: From the laboratory to the clinic. *Nature Neuroscience, 10,* 1116–1124.

Roozendaal, B., McEwan, B. S., & Chattarji, S. (2009). Stress, memory and the amygdala. *Nature Reviews Neuroscience, 10,* 423–433.

Sapolsky, R. M. (2003). Stress and plasticity in the limbic system. *Neurochemical Research, 28,* 1735–1742.

Sargent, P. A., Kjaer, K. H., Bench, C. J., Rabiner, E. A., Messa, C., Meyer, J., . . . Cowen, P. J. (2000). Brain serotonin 1A receptor binding measured by positron emission tomography with [11C] WAY-100635: Effects of depression and antidepressant treatment. *Archives of General Psychiatry, 57,* 174–180.

Segerstrom, S. C., & Miller, G. E. (2004). Psychological stress and the human immune system: A meta-analytic study of 30 years enquiry. *Psychological Bulletin, 130,* 601–630.

Shin, L. M., Orr, S. P., Carson, M. A., Rauch, S. L., Macklin, M. L., Lasko, N. B., . . . Pitman R. K. (2004). Regional cerebral blood flow in the amygdala and medial prefrontal cortex during traumatic imagery in male and female Vietnam veterans with PTSD. *Archives of General Psychiatry, 61,* 168–176. doi:10.1001/archpsyc.61.2.168

Siepmann, M., Aykac, V., Unterdörfer, J., Petrowski, K., & Mueck-Weymann, M. (2008). A pilot study on the effects of heart rate variability biofeedback in patients with depression and in healthy subjects. *Applied Psychophysiology and Biofeedback, 33,* 195–201. doi: 10.1007/s10484-008-9064-z

Simkin, D. R., Thatcher, R. W., & Lubar, J. (2014). Quantitative EEG and neurofeedback in children and adolescents: Anxiety disorders, depressive disorders, comorbid addiction and attention-deficit/ hyperactivity disorder, and brain injury. *Child and Adolescent Psychiatric Clinics of North America, 23,* 427–464.

Sousa, D. A. (2011). *How the brain learns* (4th ed.). Thousand Oaks, CA: Corwin.

Straube, T., Glauer, M., Dilger, S., Mentzel, H. J., & Miltner, W. H. (2006). Effects of cognitive-behavioral therapy on brain activation in specific phobia. *NeuroImage, 29,* 125–135.

Weissman, M. M., & Markowitz, J. C. (1994). *Interpersonal psychotherapy of depression.* New York, NY: Jason Aronson.

Weissman, M. M., Markowitz, J. W., & Klerman, G. L. (2000). *Comprehensive guide to interpersonal psychotherapy.* New York, NY: Basic Books.

White, M. (2007). *Maps of narrative practice.* New York, NY: Norton.

White, M., & Epston, D. (1990). *Narrative means to therapeutic ends.* New York, NY: Norton.

Wolpe, J. (1958). *Psychotherapy by reciprocal inhibition.* Stanford, CA: Stanford University Press.

Chapter 7

Neurocounseling Assessment

Lori A. Russell-Chapin

This chapter presents a comprehensive assessment model that is needed for an efficacious treatment outcome. It addresses the importance of including a comprehensive assessment for every new counseling client. In neurocounseling, the main goal of treatment is achieving emotional, behavioral, and physiological self-regulation. The clinical evaluation becomes even more in-depth because medical history, head injuries, pregnancy, and birth complications are always essential to understanding the complexity and perhaps even origins of presenting symptoms and brain dysregulation. Both qualitative and quantitative evaluations need to be used. The battery of tests must include a thorough psychosocial and medical history and self-report checklists and inventories that follow a wellness profile for conceptualization of a successful treatment plan. If warranted, quantitative electroencephalograms (EEGs) and continuous performance tests add another dimension to the neurocounseling assessment. This chapter includes suggestions and examples of possible tests to be included in the overall assessment. On the basis of those baseline scores and interviews, an effective conceptualization and treatment plan can be developed. The ensuing plan will then include goals evolving from both the assessment and the partnership between the client and counselor.

2016 CACREP Standards

This chapter addresses sections of the 2016 Council for Accreditation of Counseling and Related Educational Programs (CACREP) Standards pertinent to the common core area of Assessment and Testing (Standard II.F.7.):

- Methods of effectively preparing for and conducting initial assessment meetings (Standard II.F.7.b.)

- Procedures for identifying trauma and abuse and for reporting abuse (Standard II.F.7.d.)
- Use of assessments for diagnostic and intervention planning purposes (Standard II.F.7.e.)
- Use of assessment results to diagnose developmental, behavioral, and mental disorders (Standard II.F.7.l.)
- Ethical and culturally relevant strategies for selecting, administering, and interpreting assessment and test results (Standard II.F.7.m.)

This chapter also addresses the following Specialization Standards:

- Characteristics, risk factors, and warning signs of individuals at risk for mental health and behavioral disorders (College Counseling and Student Affairs, Standard IV.E.2.d.)
- Characteristics, risk factors, and warning signs of students at risk for mental health and behavioral disorders (School Counseling, Standard V.G.2.g.)

■ ■ ■

Clinical Case Study: Carrie

A family member referred Carrie because she believed Carrie was slowly killing herself with anorexia. Carrie is a 30-year-old Caucasian woman who had completed two different residential treatment programs for her eating disorder. Carrie also believed she was in trouble and was feeling hopeless and desperate. Her very low weight of 75 pounds was causing multiple emotional and physiological high-risk problems.

The initial interview consisted of a thorough psychosocial and medical history. The neurocounseling interview required additional questions such as information about her birth and delivery, head traumas, surgeries, and use of technology, including laptops, smartphones, and tablets.

During our initial interview, Carrie appeared extremely bright. However, despite entering graduate school and continuing to hold down a part-time job in the helping professions, her overall demeanor was timid. Carrie's voice was almost inaudible, and eye contact was minimal. Her physical appearance was startling and scary to me. I knew that Carrie was very sick and that we had a very long neurocounseling journey ahead of us.

She was compliant and completed the battery of tests that were required. Carrie's baseline pretreatment scores along with her posttreatment assessment scores are discussed throughout this chapter, in the order in which each assessment was presented. The inventories or types of inventories included in Carrie's assessment battery were as follows:

- Psychosocial–medical history interview
- Neurological Risk Assessment
- Neurocounseling observational notes
- Insomnia checklist
- Depression checklist
- Anxiety checklist
- Body Perception Questionnaire–Short Form
- Trauma checklist
- Millon Clinical Multiaxial Inventory–III (MCMI-III)
- Learning difficulties assessment
- Test of Variable Attention (TOVA)
- Five-channel EEG
- Full 19-channel EEG

My first task with Carrie was to let her know that I knew she had a great deal of expertise and knowledge about her body and even food. She shyly smiled. This treatment had to be different because Carrie was beginning to give up on life. In my mind, building rapport and a therapeutic alliance were essential. Although we were going to conduct neurofeedback (NFB), biofeedback, and traditional talk counseling, my first session focused on building trust and rapport. Carrie shared that she was consuming approximately 700 calories a day and running more than 8 miles daily. I asked her if she thought that was the amount of exercise that a healthy person needs daily. She said yes. It was then that I learned that Carrie had never had a menstrual cycle. She had struggled with and eating disorder since she was 12 years old. After our first session, I realized that Carrie knew very little about healthy living. Thus, our counseling goals targeted improvements in healthy living and wellness in all aspects of daily life.

Assessment

Assessment has many meanings, and numerous different types of assessments are available. The *Cambridge Free English Dictionary* (2016) defines *assessment* as the act of judging or deciding the amount,

Reflective Questions

What are your major concerns in working with Carrie?

How might she be at high risk?

value, quality, or importance of something. In neurocounseling, that definition makes sense, because the counselor must gather information on enough data points to make an efficacious decision about counseling treatment, goals, and outcomes.

A clinical assessment needs to include all major aspects of the client's life, and it also needs to include possible generational history as well. The epigenetics involved in a client's history could hold an essential key to the puzzle and presenting concern. If a client does not have that generational history and relatives are still living, this part of the assessment may even be fun for the client to seek. Recounting that history back to the counselor is often therapeutic in itself.

The clinical neurocounseling assessment must contain both qualitative and quantitative portions from many different sources. The qualitative and subjective portions often build necessary rapport and therapeutic alliance. The client needs to believe that the counselor truly understands the problems involved. The quantitative and objective measures often offer the counselor and client a unique perspective from a normative and comparison point of view. Assisting a client in observing how a particular score deviates from an average provides one more data point for looking at the client's problem from a different vantage point. The major advantages of having multiple sources of qualitative and quantitative information are developing patterns from these assessments. If results from all tests and interviews are similar, then it is often easier and provides a stronger case for diagnosis, conclusions, and treatment strategies (Chapin & Russell-Chapin, 2014). If the results show a wide range of discrepancies, then additional specific assessments may be required.

Psychosocial–Medical History Interview

Many counselors allow the psychosocial history to be a part of the initial intake by using a checklist or standardized form. The client can fill out the intake form ahead of time and bring it to the first session. This process does possibly save time, but the beginning stages of rapport building are lost. According to Demos (2005), a basic psychosocial medical history must include questions about personal family history, school history and performance, psychological history, and medical history. Information about lifestyle from a wellness perspective is important too. Inquiries about nutrition, sleep hygiene, exercise, work satisfaction and work environment, spirituality and religion, drug uses, and any other possible resources and liabilities are musts to include in the psychosocial and medical history.

Reflective Question

What are the advantages of using both qualitative and quantitative measurements in Carrie's situation?

During the psychosocial–medical history interview, many details of Carrie's life unfolded. A large family of origin may have allowed Carrie to get lost in the family dynamics. A fire in the family home resulted in the loss of many of her treasured family heirlooms. Two head injuries may have affected Carrie's situation. Early traumas, such as bowel infections as a preschooler, influenced Carrie's overall development. Carrie had a bowel resection, and her physician completed an ileostomy surgery to facilitate weight gain. As part of her medical care, Carrie attends regular appointments with her physician to review the success of the ileostomy intervention.

Neurological Risk Assessment

If clients are not good historians, having them complete the Neurological Risk Assessment is a useful beginning because it gently nudges the client into remembering certain potential sources of dysregulation. The Neurological Risk Assessment (see Figure 7.1) is a paper-and-pencil checklist that offers 11 different categories of possible neurological risks ranging from genetic predispositions to environmental toxins. If the client does not remember or know, then bringing in another family member may be wise. Congruent information is the key, and the main goal for the counselor is to focus on any aspects of the interview that may explain possible sources of brain dysregulation, such as head injuries, birthing complications, emotional or physical trauma, substance abuse and prenatal exposure to toxins, and high fevers. The total number of items checked off show potential neurological risks and brain dysregulation. Even one checked area may suggest brain dysregulation (Chapin & Russell-Chapin, 2014, pp. 8–10). This assessment also assists in developing treatment goals and priorities. Carrie listed seven of the 11 sources of neurological risks, suggesting many possible reasons for her dysregulation ranging from surgical anesthesia to psychosocial stressors.

Neurocounseling Observational Notes

The counselor needs to use knowledge of neurocounseling and keen observational and listening skills and take notes on many direct and often indirect behaviors of and anecdotes from the client. For example, if the client is often late or gets lost coming to the office, jot that down in the case notes. If the client states she or he has difficulty with relationships and cannot seem to finish tasks, write that down. These observations and statements are clues to the client's brain dysregulation. Every detail can lead the counselor to additional information about the functioning of the client's brain. Carrie spoke very quietly and was often difficult to hear. She rarely looked directly at people, especially me as her counselor. She said she hoarded food in her room. Carrie's handshake was limp but warm. Her breathing

		Neurological Dysregulation Risk Assessment
		Name:_____ Age:_____ Date:_____
		Current Problem, Symptom, or Complaint: _____
		Please read each potential source of neurological dysregulation and indicate whether or not it may be a risk factor for you or your child.
❏ Yes	❏ No	**Genetic Influences:** Grandparents, parents, or siblings with mental health or learning disorders (including attention-deficit/hyperactivity disorder), posttraumatic stress disorder, depression, generalized anxiety disorder, substance abuse, personality or other severe psychological disorders (bipolar or schizophrenia).
❏ Yes	❏ No	**Prenatal Exposure:** Maternal distress, psychotropic medication use, alcohol or substance abuse, nicotine use, or possible exposure to environmental toxins including genetically modified foods, pesticides, petrochemicals, xenestrogens in plastics, heavy metals (lead/mercury), and fluoride, bromine, and chlorine in water.
❏ Yes	❏ No	**Birth Complications:** Forceps or vacuum delivery, oxygen loss, head injury, premature birth, difficult or prolonged labor, obstructed umbilical cord, or fetal distress.
❏ Yes	❏ No	**Disease and High Fever:** Sustained fever above 104 degrees due to bacterial infection, influenza, strep, meningitis, encephalitis, Reye's Syndrome, PANDAS, or other infections or disease processes.
❏ Yes	❏ No	**Current Diagnosis:** Of mental health, physical health, alcohol abuse, or learning disorder.
❏ Yes	❏ No	**Poor Diet and Inadequate Exercise:** Diet high in processed food; preservatives; simple carbohydrates (sugar and flour); genetically modified foods; foods treated with herbicides; pesticides, and hormones; low daily water intake, high caffeine intake; and lack of adequate physical exercise (20 minutes, 7 times a week).
❏ Yes	❏ No	**Emotionally Suppressive Psychosocial Environment:** Being raised or currently living in poverty; domestic violence; physical, emotional, or sexual abuse; alcoholic or mentally unstable family environment; emotional trauma; neglect; institutionalization; and inadequate maternal emotional availability or attachment.
❏ Yes	❏ No	**Mild to Severe Brain Injury:** Experienced one or more blows to the head from a sports injury, fall, or auto accident (with or without loss of consciousness), or episodes of open head injury, coma, or stroke.
❏ Yes	❏ No	**Prolonged Life Distress:** Most commonly due to worry about money, work, economy, family responsibilities, relationships, personal safety, and/or health causing sustained periods of anxiety, irritability, anger, fatigue, lack of interest, low motivation or energy, nervousness, and/or physical aches and pains.
❏ Yes	❏ No	**Stress-Related Disease:** Includes heart disease, kidney disease, hypertension, obesity, diabetes, stroke, hormonal, and/or immunological disorders.
❏ Yes	❏ No	**Prolonged Medication Use, Substance Use, or Other Addictions:** Including legal or illegal drug use, substance abuse, or addiction (alcohol, drugs, nicotine, caffeine, medication, gambling, sex, spending, etc.) and overuse of screen technologies (cell phones, video games, television, computers, Internet, etc.).
❏ Yes	❏ No	**Seizure Disorders:** Caused by birth complications, stroke, head trauma, infection, high fever, oxygen deprivation, and/or genetic disorders and includes epilepsy, pseudoseizures, or epileptiform seizures.
❏ Yes	❏ No	**Chronic Pain:** Related to accidents, injury, or a disease process. Including back pain, headache and migraine pain, neck pain, facial pain, and fibromyalgia.

FIGURE 7.1

Assessment Checklist

was shallow. Her clothes were clean and baggy. She never smiled during the first interview.

Screening Inventories

The results of the intake history inform what objective test to give the client. Even though the client's history may not suggest a background of depression or anxiety, having the client fill out those self-reports often elicits additional information. When dealing with symptoms of learning difficulties and attention, tests of continuous performance provide good objective information, as do paper-and-pencil checklists. When selecting a checklist, ensure that it is both reliable (measures the same information every time and is scored consistently over multiple administrations) and valid (correlates with the presenting problem being assessed). The following assessments are typical in a neurocounseling evaluation.

Insomnia

Many counseling clients experience sleep concerns. Gaining a clear picture of how troubling their sleep disruptions are is important to the client's overall health. Several inventories exist to assess sleep problems. The Insomnia Severity Index (Morin, Belleville, Belanger, & Ives, 2011) is a very short and concise inventory consisting of seven items that take approximately 5 minutes to complete. Clients indicate the severity of their sleep disruption during the past 2 weeks. Clients rate the severity of insomnia symptoms that include difficulties falling asleep, nighttime awakening, and early morning awakening. Carrie's self-report score indicated that she was struggling with clinical insomnia of moderate severity. She indicated feeling worried and distressed about her sleep problems, which were causing interference in her daily life.

Depression

Many depression screening tools are available. A commonly used assessment is the Beck Depression Inventory, Second Edition (BDI-II; Beck, Steer, & Brown, 1996). The BDI-II is a relatively short test that takes around 15 minutes to complete. Clients self-report the degree to which they are experiencing depressive symptoms for the past 2 weeks on a 4-point scale. Total scores indicate the severity of depressive symptoms as low to none, mild, moderate, or severe. Carrie's overall score indicated that she reported experiencing depressive symptoms to a severe degree.

Anxiety

As with depression, many anxiety inventories are on the market. A commonly used anxiety screening is the Burns Anxiety Inventory (Burns, 1993). This tool can usually be completed in 15 minutes because it has only 33 items. The client is asked to rate each statement according to how much a particular feeling has bothered him or her in the past several days. The inventory surveys mostly physiological manifestations of anxiety, such as heart racing, sweaty palms, and detachment from one's bodily sensations. As with the BDI-II, clients self-report the degree to which they have experiences anxiety on a 4-point scale. Total scores indicate low to absent, mild, moderate, or severe levels of anxiety. Carrie's overall score was very high, indicating that she was experiencing not only severe but also extreme levels of anxiety. Some of Carrie's responses on question items guided treatment planning, such as her acknowledgment of feeling tense and stressed, with racing thoughts and fear of criticism by others and of being alone

Body Perception

The Body Perception Questionnaire–Short Form is a 45-item Likert-type scale questionnaire and is divided into two categories: Body Awareness and Autonomic Nervous System Reactivity (Porges, 1993). Although they are self-reported by the client, the ratings offer essential biofeedback information about perceptions and awareness of the body and its natural responses and a possible picture of the state of the client's fight, flight, or freeze reactions. Carrie rated only six items at the second highest rating of "usually." The rest of her ratings were in the "occasionally" category. These scores suggest that Carrie is not very aware of her body and its needs. This may offer some insight into her ability to detach mind from body.

Trauma

The counselor again has plenty of options when selecting a trauma checklist that fits the client's needs. Many inventories are available for children and adults. One such trauma checklist that is freely available is the PTSD Checklist for DSM-5 (PCL–5; Weathers, Litz, Keane, Palmieri, Marx, & Schnurr, 2013). This self-report has 17 test items and takes only approximately 15 minutes to complete. The client is asked to rate how bothered an experience makes him or her feel on a scale ranging from 1 (*not at all*) to 5 (*extremely*). An example of a statement is "feeling jumpy or easily startled." The counselor adds up the total score, with higher scores indicating greater severity of trauma symptoms. Carrie's high score on the PCL–5 suggested that posttraumatic stress disorder is a possibility.

Other Screening Inventories and Assessments

Another test that may be used is the Bender Visual-Motor Gestalt Test, Second Edition (Brannigan & Decker, 2003). This test assists in determining the impact of traumatic brain injuries. The main emphasis of the Bender Visual-Motor Gestalt is a psychological assessment of the client's visual–motor functioning, visual perception, neurological impairments, and emotional disturbances. Carrie was not administered this test.

Personality Inventories

Many standardized, valid, and reliable personality inventories are available. The MCMI-III, developed by Theodore Millon, is often used in neurocounseling assessments (Dumont, Willis, Viezel, & Zibulsky, 2014). This test gives information about personality disorders and presenting symptoms. The information gained from the MCMI-III once again assists in treatment and goal setting for the client.

The MCMI-III is a 175-item paper-and-pencil or computerized test that takes approximately 30 to 40 minutes to complete. The client rates the items as true or false and is instructed about the importance of responding truthfully to each item. The test analysis includes three validity components of disclosure, desirability, and debasement. These validity scales offer vital information to the counselor about the client's response style. Self-report inventories are prone to response bias, and validity scales help the counselor to understand whether the client is overdisclosing or underdisclosing. Clients can underdisclose to minimize problems in an attempt to appear desirable ("faking good"). Clients can overdisclose to exaggerate symptoms as part of a cry for help ("faking bad"). Understanding a client's response style helps the counselor understand the validity and accuracy of the client's self-reported symptoms.

After the test results were customized to Carrie, four scores were in the personality disorder range: schizoid, avoidant, depressive, and dependent. Carrie's severe presenting symptoms were high anxiety and dysthymia. Under severe clinical syndromes, a very high score on major depression also appeared. Her validity scales showed a profile of a person who was overly trusting and would self-disclose too much and too fast. Her profile indicated that she had very little positive regard for herself and was extremely self-critical.

Learning Difficulties Assessments

Numerous clients have learning and developmental difficulties. A multitude of self-report paper-and-pencil inventories and checklists address attentional problems. Note that some client problems can be related to overall aptitude, intelligence, or both. This type of testing was not needed for Carrie because she was actively holding down a part-time job with positive results and entering graduate school.

Attention Deficit

One example of a learning difficulties assessment is the Amen Clinic ADD Type Questionnaire (Amen, 2001). This instrument takes approximately 20 minutes to complete and has 71 items that assess six subtypes of attention-deficit/hyperactivity disorder (ADHD): inattention, hyperactive, overfocused, temporal lobe, limbic, and ring of

123

fire. This inventory has two columns. The client completes the first column, and the client's significant other completes the second column. Both parties rate the degree to which they believe the client is experiencing certain symptoms. This allows the counselor to compare and analyze responses. The severity of symptoms such as distractibility is measured on a 5-point scale. The test provides interpretation of both overall scores and self-reported scores on subscales.

Carrie did not ask any other member of her family to fill out this inventory. Her self-report scores were calculated, and she had significant problems in the overfocused and limbic categories of the questionnaire. These results might suggest that Carrie has great difficulty with obsessive–compulsive traits.

Continuous Performance Tests

Computerized continuous performance tests offer quantitative information about a person's attention. The TOVA is an auditory and visual nonlanguage test in which the person uses a microswitch to indicate his or her response (Greenburg & Waldman, 1993). Clinicians are looking for both visual and auditory errors of omission and commission. In other words, the visual test scores might indicate whether the client clicked the microswitch too often when the X was presented, making errors of commission, or did not click when the X was presented, making errors of omission. In the auditory version, the client might click too often or too little when the stimulus sound is presented.

Carrie's TOVA auditory test did not fall within normal limits. Her scores suggested possible attention problems as well as ADHD. Her self-report did not suggest ADHD. To rule out further concerns, a hearing test from an audiologist might be recommended. Her visual scores on the TOVA were at the low end of normal.

Quantitative EEG

Still another type of assessment for trauma is the administration of a quantitative electroencephalogram (qEEG). Either a five-channel or a full 19-channel qEEG can be administered, depending on the client's need. EEG technology captures electrical energy at different frequencies, known as brain waves. Brain waves are often labeled by categories that correlate to possible behaviors. There are more categories than the typical five of delta, theta, alpha, beta, and gamma, but these five are the basics. Delta waves are often viewed at 0 to 3 Hz, or 0 to 3 cycles per second. These waves are slow, low waves and are associated with sleep and sometime with trauma-related problems. Theta waves are typically 4 to 7 Hz and are associated with drowsiness and meditation. They are also slower waves. Alpha waves are categorized as 8 to 12 Hz and are needed for idling and transitioning from one brain wave state to another. Beta waves range from 13 to 30 Hz. They are considered busy waves. Low beta waves from 12 to 15 Hz assist in focused attention and problem solving. When a person is too high in beta waves, there may be anxiety. Gamma waves are 30 Hz or more and are often found in bursts of insight.

Five-Channel qEEG

Because of Carrie's severe and chronic condition, she was given a five-channel qEEG. This shorter and quicker version of the EEG measured brain waves at the five brain locations of Cz at the top of the head; F/3 and F/4 at the left and right front of the head, respectively; Fz at the middle front of the scalp; and O1 at the back of the left side of the head (see Figure 7.2 for locations). The five-channel EEG often provides enough valuable data to proceed with treatment. It also saves time and financial expenditures. This type of EEG is often called the Quick Q (Swingle, 2008) and often only takes 20 minutes to administer. The five-channel qEEG provides the overall representative state of the client's brain, and trauma may also be seen at the back of the head in the occipital lobes.

Carrie's EEG showed many healthy and normal responses, which was surprising and confusing because of the severe conditions and symptoms that were presented. Sleep disturbances were illuminated at O1 with low theta and beta ratios. Dysregulations were found in the prefrontal lobes at F3 and F4, probing for depression and lethargy. The Fz site found low gamma and beta ratios, suggesting excessive passivity. Because of the severity of Carrie's symptoms and relatively healthy five-channel qEEG, the 19-channel qEEG was recommended.

Nineteen-Channel qEEG

When clients come to the counselor with chronic issues and perhaps head injuries such as concussion, additional examination with a 19-channel qEEG may be required. The 19-channel qEEG records at 19 locations instead of five. Instead of attaching the electrodes with individual sensors, the client wears a cap with 19 different sensors inside it that will measure the entire brain. The technician will analyze the report after artifacting out muscle movements. The report will provide data on brain wave amplitudes, ratios between brain wave bandwidths, possible topological brain maps, and comparisons from normative databases. Both the five-channel and 19-channel qEEGs may offer information about possible NFB treatments. The 19-channel qEEG offers a more comprehensive assessment of neurological dysregulation.

The results of the 19-channel qEEG were more comprehensive, showing overall trauma and dysregulation throughout the other brain sensor

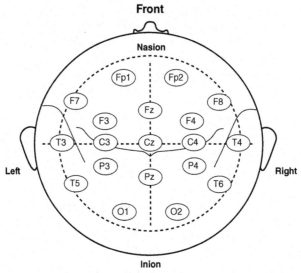

FIGURE 7.2

Head Map Functions

FIGURE 7.2 KEY

Nasion = The intersection of the frontal bone and two nasal bones of the human skull.

Inion = The most prominent projection of the occipital bone at the posterioinferior (lower rear) part of the human skull.

Fp1 ≈ Attention, concentration, planning, verbal episodic retrieval, visual working memory, orchestrates network planning, decision making, and task completion. Increased or excess theta causes attention deficit/hyperactivity disorder. Increased or excess beta causes rigidity of focus.

Fp2 ≈ Emotional attention, judgment, sense of self, self/impulse control, face/object processing, emotional inhibition, verbal episodic memory. Increased or excess theta causes impulsivity, poor social awareness, and anxiety. Increased or excess beta causes emotional overcontrol, decreased nuance.

Fz = Motor planning of both lower extremities (BLEs) and mid-line, running, walking, kicking, response and emotional inhibition, grooming. Increased or excess theta causes attention deficit/hyperactivity disorder. Increased or excess beta causes attention and motivational problems, obsessive-compulsive disorder.

F7 = Verbal expression, speech fluency, cognitive mood regulation, visual and auditory working memory, attentional gate, Broca's area. Increased or excess theta causes speech and work finding problems. Increased or excess beta causes increased input control.

F3 = Motor planning, right upper extremities (RUE), right fine motor coordination, visual episodic retrieval, mood elevation, object processing, emotional interpretation, positive mood. Increased or excess theta causes depression and decreased executive function. Increased or excess beta causes obsessive-compulsive disorder.

F4 = Motor planning, left upper extremities (LUE), left fine motor coordination, verbal episodic and semantic retrieval, regulation of attention or impulse. Increased or excess theta causes lack of tact, disorganized dialogue, poor use of analogy and irony. Increased or excess beta causes hypervigilance.

F8 = Emotional expression, drawing, endogenous mood regulation, face recognition, emotional processing, visual/spatial working memory, sustained attention. Increased or excess theta causes lack of prosody. Increased or excess beta causes oversensitivity to speech intonation in others.

(Continued)

FIGURE 7.2 KEY *(Continued)*

T3 = Logical, verbal memory formation and storage, phonologic processing, hearing. Increased or excess theta causes memory and language problems. Increased or excess beta causes irritability. C3 = Sensorimotor integration RUE, alerting response, right hand writing, short-term momory. Increased or excess theta causes poor handwriting. Increased or excess beta causes motor hyperactivity.

Cz = Sensorimotor integration of BLE, ambulation, basal ganglia, thalamic efferents, substantia nigra. Increased or excess theta causes attention deficit/hyperactivity disorder. Increased or excess beta causes attention and motivational problems.

C4 = Sensorimotor integration LUE, calming response, left hand writing, short-term momory. Increased or excess beta causes hypervigilance.

T4 = Emotional and autobiographical memory formation and storage, hearing, personality, musical ability, organization. Increased or excess theta causes anger, sadness, aggression, tone of voice interpretation problems.

T5 = Logical, verbal understanding, word recognition, auditory processing, short-term memory, inner voice, meaning construction. Increased or excess theta causes anger, sadness, aggression, tone of voice interpretation problems.

P3 = Right side perception and cognitive processing, spatial relations, multimodal sensations, calculations, praxis, verbal reasoning. Increased or excess theta causes problems with memory, organization, digit span, calculations. Increased or excess beta causes increased thinking or worrying.

Pz = Perception midline, spatial relation, praxis, route finding, attention shifting/integration. Increased or excess beta causes problems with perseveration, sensory vigilance.

P4 = Left side perception and cognitive processing, spatial relations, multimodal interactions, praxis, nonverbal reasoning, visual-spatial sketchpad, vigilance, victim mentality. Increased or excess theta causes increased self concern and rationalization. Increased or excess beta causes emotional rumination.

T6 = Emotional understanding, facial and symbol recognition, auditory processing, long-term memory. Increased or excess theta causes poor memory for faces and melodies.

O1 = Right visual processing, pattern recognition, color, movement, black and white and edge perception.

O2 = Left visual processing, pattern recognition, color, movement, black and white and edge perception.

---

sites. Cognitive inefficiency and memory problems were discovered, with low amplitudes of alpha brain waves. A decrease in the brain's slow wave activity has been found with posttraumatic stress disorder. This suppresses traumatic experiences, resulting in emotional, behavioral, and physiological consequences (Chapin & Russell-Chapin, 2014). Low alpha waves at the midline and occipital lobes are often seen in EEGs and are related to emotional trauma (Swingle, 2008). The two EEG test results assisted in the development of a thorough treatment plan.

Assessment-Based Treatments

Several treatment approaches exist that use assessment data as part of the treatment process. In Carrie's case, potentially useful approaches included biofeedback, diaphragmatic breathing, skin temperature control, heart rate variability training, and NFB.

Diaphragmatic Breathing

Carrie was trained in diaphragmatic breathing. As an assessment tool, diaphragmatic breathing provides the counselor with beginning data on the client's possible problems. Taking a baseline of a client's breathing patterns offers clues about anxiety and other lifestyle issues in general, such as body tension and muscle rigidity.

The average normal adult breathing rate is between 12 and 15 breaths per minute (Schwartz & Andrasik, 2003). Young children from ages 2 to 5 years breathe faster, around 25 to 30 breaths per minute, and children ages 5 to 12 take 20 to 25 breaths per minute. Adolescents typically breathe 15 to 20 times per minute. Getting a baseline breathing measurement for a client helps establish a goal for treatment that is often targeted at a relaxed, peak performance state of six breaths per minute. Relaxed breathing not only alleviates anxiety but assists the brain in better absorption of glucose and oxygen (Schwartz & Andrasik, 2003).

Biofeedback

Because Carrie had already been through several residential treatment programs, biofeedback was recommended as the first treatment strategy. Her biofeedback interventions were skin temperature control and heart rate variability (HRV) training.

A skin temperature control assessment is important to include as part of evaluation and treatment. Obtaining a baseline–pretreatment value is simple to achieve. Ask the client to gently hold a thermometer for approximately 1 minute. Record the temperature.

HRV is a biofeedback technique that teaches heart rhythm feedback or beat-to-beat changes in heart rate to enhance self-regulation (Chapin & Russell-Chapin, 2014; McCraty, Atkinson, Tomasino, & Bradley, 2009). HRV is a measure of the variation in time between heartbeats that can be used to determine the amount of stress the body is under. A lower HRV signifies a predominant activation of the sympathetic nervous system. There are many HRV software and hardware packages on the market. emWave is produced by the Institute of HeartMath (Boulder Creek, CA). It uses a plethysmograph that slides into a small cuff on the big finger of the nondominant hand or an ear sensor clip to measure heart rate variability. Another instrument is RESPeRATE (RESPeRATE Inc., Minden, NV), Food and Drug Administration–approved for blood pressure control, that allows clients to practice breathing by watching visual corrective feedback.

NFB

NFB is a noninvasive brain-based treatment for a variety of mental health concerns, including symptom reduction of ADHD, depression, anxiety, and other clinical issues. NFB can also be used to enhance peak performance. NFB uses EEG technology to collect brain wave data about treatment response at the sites identified in Figure 7.2. The head map of functions in Figure 7.2 illustrates the diverse and specific functions of the differing brain site locations and functions, assisting the counselor in correlating possible brain sites and functions with actual treatment activity and goals.

Clients receive feedback about their brain activity and can adjust their performance accordingly. If NFB is warranted on the basis of client evaluation, then the counselor obtains brain wave data at pre- and posttest measurements. NFB software calculates numerous statistical compilations for brain wave amplitude, illustrating objective data from the differences in a single session or over multiple sessions.

Carrie's Treatment Response

Carrie was seen twice per week, with careful monitoring of symptoms and measurable biweekly goals. Her progress was gradual but optimistic. Carrie was taught HRV using the emWave software. She became proficient at the low levels, and she was able to practice this heart rate coherence during her everyday living activities. Because of her low body weight, Carrie was usually cold. Teaching Carrie skin temperature activities helped to bring her skin temperature to at least 86 degrees. The goal is 90 degrees for a relaxed state of peak performance. As her trust began to grow, Carrie agreed to slowly increase her calorie consumption to 1,200 calories and decrease her running to 5 miles per day. Her weight increased by 10 pounds. By our 10th neurofeedback session, Carrie began to look me directly in the eyes. Carrie stated that she felt safe in my office. I asked her to look in the mirror and describe what she saw. Carrie turned to me and exclaimed, "There is life in my eyes!" Truly, there was vibrancy in Carrie for the first time.

My Brain-Based Approach to the Case of Carrie

Using the case of Carrie, I have demonstrated my brain-based approach to assessment and neurocounseling throughout the chapter. Each assessment offered additional information that assisted in developing a carefully crafted treatment plan based on all the data and patterns. In this case, the client's symptoms were very severe. Ethically responsible principles and judgments must be considered at every step of the treatment process.

Reflective Question

Why might it be helpful to combine several assessment-based treatment tools to help Carrie, rather than selecting only one?

Conclusion

The case of Carrie demonstrates how useful a thorough and comprehensive assessment battery can be. Each assessment was a unique yet interdependent aspect of the treatment. Many of the evaluations discussed in this chapter are consistently used in regular counseling. However, when the goal is neurocounseling, or bridging brain and behavior, assessments that address body perception, EEG, baseline skin temperature and HRV, and insomnia are routinely used as part of the overall assessment battery. These neurocounseling tests offer additional information about the client's physiology and provide baseline measures to begin goal development. Although every counselor does not need to be an expert in all of these neurocounseling measurements, it is recommended that counselors be neurowise and nimble rather than neuronaïve about the importance of neurocounseling information to the overall assessment, treatment, and health of the client.

Reflective Question

If only a few assessments could be used with Carrie, what essential evaluations would you choose?

Quiz

1. Which statement about validity and reliability is most true?
   a. The test needs to be valid and reliable.
   b. The test only needs to be valid.
   c. The test only needs to be reliable.
   d. It is more important to be reliable than valid.

2. The main goal of a neurocounseling assessment is:
   a. A comprehensive evaluation.
   b. Physiological, emotional, and behavioral self-regulation.
   c. An evaluation for conceptualization and treatment.
   d. None of the above.

3. Which of the following are possible sources of brain dysregulation?
   a. Genetic predisposition.
   b. Substance abuse.
   c. High fever.
   d. All of the above.

Reflective Question

For the Case Study

How might the use of neurocounseling assessments in the case of Carrie result in more effective treatment?

References

Amen, D. (2001). *Healing ADD: The breakthrough program that allows you to see and heal the six types of ADD.* New York, NY: Putnam.

Beck, A. T., Steer, R. A., & Brown, G. K. (1996). *Manual for the Beck Depression Inventory-II.* San Antonio, TX: Psychological Corporation.

Brannigan, G. G., & Decker, S. L. (2003). *Bender visual-motor gestalt test, second edition.* Itasca, IL: Riverside.

Burns, D. D. (1993). *Ten days to self esteem.* New York, NY: Quill.

Cambridge Free English Dictionary. (2016). Retrieved from http://dictionary.cambridge.org/dictionary/english/assessment

Chapin, T., & Russell-Chapin, L. (2014). *Neurotherapy and neurofeedback: Brain-based treatment for psychological and behavioral problems.* New York, NY: Routledge.

Council for the Accreditation of Counseling and Related Educational Programs. (2015). *2016 CACREP standards.* Retrieved from http://www.cacrep.org/wp-content/uploads/2012/10/2016-CACREP-Standards.pdf

Demos, J. N. (2005). *Getting started with neurofeedback.* New York, NY: Norton.

Dumont, R., Willis, J. O., Viezel, K., & Zibulsky, J. (2014). Millon Clinical Multiaxial Inventory—III. In C. R. Reynolds, K. J. Vannest, & E. Fletcher-Janzen (Eds.), *Encyclopedia of special education.* New York, NY: Wiley. http://dx.doi.org/10.1002/9781118660584.ese1564

Greenberg, L. M., & Waldman, I. D. (1993). Developmental normative data on the Test of Variables of Attention (T.O.V.A.). *Journal of Child Psychology and Psychiatry, 34,* 1019–1030.

McCraty, R., Atkinson, M., Tomasino, D., & Bradley, R. T. (2009). The coherent heart: Heart–brain interactions, psychophysiological coherence, and the emergence of system-wide order. *Integral Review, 5*(2), 10–115.

Morin, C. M., Belleville, G., Belanger, L., & Ives, H. (2011). The Insomnia Severity Index: Psychometric indicators to detect insomnia cases and evaluate treatment response. *Sleep, 34,* 601–608.

Porges, S. (1993). *Body perception questionnaire short form.* Retrieved from http://www.stephenporges.com

Schwartz, M., & Andrasik, F. (2003). *Biofeedback: A practitioner's guide* (3rd ed.). New York, NY: Guilford Press.

Swingle, P. (2008). *Brain neurotherapy; The clinician's guide.* Vancouver, British Columbia, Canada: Author.

Weathers, F. W., Litz, B. T., Keane, T. M., Palmieri, P. A., Marx, B. P., & Schnurr, P. P. (2013). *The PTSD checklist for DSM-5 (PCL-5).* Retrieved from http://www.ptsd.va.gov/professional/assessment/documents/PCL-5_Standard.pdf

Chapter 8

Wellness and Optimal Performance

Theodore J. Chapin

The battle for the hearts, minds, and souls of those seeking health is ever present in modern society. On one side stand those who favor a disease and illness model that often reflects a cost-conscious, depersonalized, and medication-based approach to diagnosis and treatment. On the other side are those who favor a holistic, mind–body–spirit model that is individualized and wellness focused and seeks optimal functioning. It is against this backdrop that this chapter explores the concept of wellness and extends this discussion to focus on the foundational role of several neurocounseling-based strategies for optimal performance. These concepts are illustrated and applied through the case study of William, a man who struggles with excess weight, anxiety, compulsiveness, trauma, and depressed mood.

 2016 CACREP Standards

This chapter addresses a section of the 2016 Council for Accreditation of Counseling and Related Educational Programs (CACREP) Standards pertinent to the common core area of Human Growth and Development (Standard II.F.3.):

- Ethical and culturally relevant strategies for promoting resilience and optimum development and wellness across the life span (Standard II.F.3.i.)

■ ■ ■

Clinical Case Study: William

William is a 51-year-old man. He was the oldest of three boys. William was an above-average student and was active in scouting, sports, and a conservative Christian church. His mother was a devoted though compulsive homemaker, and his father was an emotionally constricted disciplinarian who used excessive corporal punishment. William experienced his first bout of depression during his freshman year of college. He was reportedly overwhelmed by the academic and social demands of independent college life. He was later married and divorced, which seemed to increase his anxiety and compulsiveness. He then remarried and had two children. He pursued a successful career, though he was once asked to resign after repeated criticism from his superiors. This triggered a second episode of depression. Over the past decade, William's body has gone from muscular and athletic to moderately obese. Recently, William suffered severe physical and emotional trauma after an elective surgery. William sought help to better manage his emotions and regain his physical fitness.

Wellness

For decades, counseling has been at the forefront in considering the importance of physical and spiritual health when providing mental health services. The wellness movement was spurred when Halbert Dunn (1961), a physician and consultant to the World Health Organization, challenged the then-prevailing belief that health was solely the absence of disease. Dunn instead suggested that health was a state of physical, mental, and social well-being. Dunn described wellness as integrated functioning of maximized individual potential.

Hettler (1984) was among the first to propose a wellness model, followed by a wellness model that emerged from the counseling profession in 1988 called the *wheel of wellness* (Myers, Sweeney, & Witmer, 2000) and later the *indivisible self* (Myers & Sweeney, 2005). In recent years, a brain-based wellness model has emerged called the *healthy mind platter* (Rock, Siegel, Poelmans, & Payne, 2012). Rock et al. (2012) developed the model depicted in Figure 8.1 to explain how optimal brain functioning can be maintained through daily healthy mental habits.

The three models described here all propose similar lifestyle areas deemed important to a person's well-being. These lifestyle areas were called *wellness dimensions* by Hettler (1984), *wellness factors* by Myers and Sweeney (2005), and *mental activities* by Rock et al. (2012). The following section uses Hettler's six wellness dimensions as an

FIGURE 8.1

The Healthy Mind Platter for Optimal Brain Matter™

Note. Healthy Mind Platter for Optimal Brain Matter © 2011 by David Rock and Daniel J. Siegel, MD. Used with permission. All rights reserved.

organizing framework for the healthy mind platter's mental activities to advance an integrative brain-based approach to wellness assessment and psychoeducation. Together, these wellness dimensions and mental activities provide a template and guide for the development of a healthy lifestyle. The following section also includes a wellness assessment for the case of William to elucidate the importance of screening for lifestyle habits during intake. It is important to mention that lifestyle habits are an often unrecognized yet debilitating influence on a person's overall health.

Occupational and Intellectual Wellness: Focus Time, Playtime, Downtime

Occupational wellness involves personal satisfaction and enrichment in one's life work. Intellectual wellness recognizes the value of learning and cognitive stimulation. These wellness domains are consistent with the healthy mind platter's mental activities of focus time, playtime, and downtime. *Focus time* pertains to goal-directed brain states in the completion of tasks. Persons may experience what Csikszentmihalyi (1990) called the *flow state*, defined as full immersion in the task at hand with energized focus and enjoyable involvement. His initial observations of the flow state were with artists, particularly painters, who became so deeply involved in their work that they would often go significant periods of time without food, water, and sleep. In describing their experiences, they used the metaphor of being carried away in a current of water (Csikszentmihalyi, 1975). Today, many sports psychologists describe a similar phenomenon when they talk about being "in the zone" (Strack, Linden, & Wilson, 2011). Flow can occur across many types of human endeavors, including education, music, sports, gaming, spiritual and religious practice, and work. Along with physical exercise, focused attention may help to prevent the development of Alzheimer's disease (Baumgart et al., 2015).

Playtime refers to engagement in creative and spontaneous activity that results in new neural connections in the brain and reduces the potential for aggressive and emotionally dysregulated behavior (van den Berg et al., 1999). *Downtime* refers to relaxation that lacks a specific goal or focus rather than active leisure activities. Downtime helps the brain to recharge by activating different regions, namely the default mode network for task-negative states (Rock et al., 2012). Put simply, downtime is about being in the moment rather than doing tasks (Rock et al., 2012, p. 8). Downtime provides space for preconscious processing in the right hemisphere of the brain, leading to the development of new insights (Segal, 2004).

William reported that intellectual wellness was a strength area. He felt actively engaged in work-related activities (focus time). He was also an avid reader. William noted that he frequently reverted to passive activities when returning home from work, such as watching television for long periods. He rarely engaged in defocused downtime and wanted to engage in more meaningful leisure activities (playtime).

Physical Wellness: Physical Time, Sleep Time

Physical wellness includes engaging in healthy behavior through sleep, exercise, diet, and self-care. This wellness domain is consistent with two mental activities in the healthy mind platter: physical time and sleep time. *Physical time* is defined as physical activity, preferably aerobic, that strengthens the brain, such as by stimulating neuronal growth (known as neurogenesis). Ratey (2008) found that 40 minutes of aerobic exercise three times a week stimulates neurological production of brain-derived neurotrophic factor. He described this as "Miracle-Gro" for the brain and said that it is important for both energy metabolism and synaptic plasticity because it activates glutamate, increases antioxidant production, and grows new brain cells. Although exercise has been more widely known to be as effective as antidepressant medication in reducing symptoms of major depression (Blumenthal et al., 1999), it is less known that exercise can also increase the size of the hippocampus and improve memory in older adults (Erickson et al., 2011). In this study, 40 minutes of brisk walking resulted in a 2% increase in hippocampal volume in the intervention group, compared with a 1.4% decrease in the control group, which had engaged in nonaerobic yoga and resistance-band training.

Sleep time is the mental activity that facilitates the brain's consolidation of learning and memory, and the brain's resting state helps people recover from activities. Sleep has a restorative function; during sleep, glial cells clean the brain of toxins and debris (Xi et al., 2013). Sleep appears to be related to neuroplasticity via synaptic potentiation and cellular gene and protein translation, as well as efficient memory processing from initial learning (encoding) to long-term memory (consolidation) across whole brain networks (Abel, Havekes, Saletin, & Walker, 2013). Thus, people who lack quality sleep are unable to recover fully from the day, and their consolidation of learning and memories is impaired. Inadequate sleep has also been linked to the development of depression (Nakata, 2011).

William reported receiving inconsistent quality sleep. On some nights, he was able to fall asleep quickly with no nighttime or early morning awakening. On other nights, he stayed up late to watch television or drank alcohol during the evening, both of which had an impact on the quality of his sleep. Most of all, William wanted to regain his athletic figure and seemed highly motivated to restart an active workout regimen.

Social Wellness: Connecting Time

Social wellness reflects the quality of interpersonal relationships and community interaction. This wellness domain is comparable to the mental activity of connecting time in the healthy mind platter. *Connecting time* refers to engagement in face-to-face relationships and with the natural world, activating circuitry in the brain. In an older landmark study, social relationships predicted mortality over a 9-year period even when physical health, health behaviors, and socioeconomic status were controlled for (Berkman & Syme, 1979). In their review of 81 studies, Uchino, Holt-Lunstad, Uno, Betancourt, and Garvey (1999) found that social support had positive effects on blood pressure in addition to the cardiovascular, endocrine, and immune systems.

William reported having lifelong friends and a strong marriage, although he admitted to neglecting parts of these relationships. For example, he often lacked energy to go out and socialize on the weekends. He felt connected to his children.

Emotion and Spiritual Wellness: Time-In

Emotional wellness values awareness and acceptance of feelings, as well as an optimistic approach to life. Spiritual wellness involves one's spiritual practice, search for meaning and purpose, and tolerance of others' beliefs and traditions. Engagement in spiritual practice and acceptance of experience are comparable to the healthy mind platter's mental activity of time-in. *Time-in* involves quiet internal reflection and meditation. Many spiritual meditation techniques exist, all of which involve a quiet environment, a comfortable posture, a focus of attention, and an open reflective attitude. Meditation has been linked to several neurological benefits, including increased cortical thickness (gyrification) of gray matter that promotes improved information processing (Luders et al., 2012), increased gray matter of the hippocampus involved in the formation of new memories (Holze et al., 2011), the slowing of age-related neurological decline (Luders, 2013), and increased activation of the default mode network, associated with attention, mind wandering, retrieval of episodic memory, and emotional processing (Xu et al., 2014). A meta-analysis of 47 mindfulness trials with 3,515 participants found moderate evidence for improved anxiety, depression, and pain; some evidence for reduced stress and improved quality of life; and low or insufficient evidence for improved mood, attention, eating habits, sleep, and weight and reduced substance use (Goyal et al., 2014). Meditation appears to have comparable outcomes to other active treatments such as medication, exercise, and behavioral therapies. Clearly, time-in and meditation should be part of a comprehensive wellness plan and not a stand-alone strategy.

William was dissatisfied with his current religious and spiritual involvement. He felt that his current religious experience was fairly dogmatic and did not leave space for exploration. William engaged in little time-in activity beyond attending church. He had little interest in engaging in a more traditional, quiet, and still meditative process. William was open to meditating while being physically active, such as walking, gardening, or biking or being immersed in a creative project.

Neurocounseling Strategies to Enhance Wellness

Neurocounseling strategies involve the use of brain-based interventions to facilitate client change (Montes, 2013). They use both traditional talk therapy methods and a variety of specialized neurologically based techniques. Several neurocounseling strategies were applied to the case of William, including Therapeutic Lifestyle Changes, biofeedback, and neurofeedback.

Therapeutic Lifestyle Changes

The daily habits people form and the lifestyle choices they make play an important role in their overall health and functioning. Ivey, Ivey, and Zalaquett (2014) identified 17 stress management strategies that enhance wellness called *Therapeutic Lifestyle Changes*. Three of the five most important lifestyle changes were identified as nutrition and weight management, sleep, and exercise. Along with screen time, these factors are known to facilitate or hinder healthy self-regulation (Chapin & Russell-Chapin, 2014). When the brain and body are in a constant state of distress (sympathetic fight, flight, or freeze) as a result of bad habits and poor

Reflective Question

How might William's level of engagement in different mental activities be related to his primary emotional and behavioral problems?

lifestyle choices, wellness and optimal performance are not possible. Problematic habits must first be ameliorated before healing recovery (parasympathetic response) can occur.

Nutrition and Weight Management

Excessive consumption of simple carbohydrates such as sugar, pasta, and other white foods such as potatoes, flour, and white rice has been found to have an adverse impact on the brain's neurological functioning, affecting memory and neuronal plasticity (Molteni, Barnard, Ying, Roberts, & Gomez-Pinilla, 2002). In addition, it has been identified as a significant factor in the development of metabolic disease, cardiovascular disease, obesity, and Type 2 diabetes (Stanhope, Schwarz, & Havel, 2013). According to Amen (2001), the best diet for neurological regulation and optimal production of neurotransmitters consists of protein (e.g., lean meat, fish, organic dairy, and nuts), complex carbohydrates (e.g., fresh vegetables and fruit), and both saturated fats (e.g., dairy, coconut oil) and monounsaturated fats (e.g., omega-3 fatty acids, olive oil).

Although nothing substitutes for the nutritional value of a healthy diet, careful use of selective dietary supplements can improve neurological and immunological functioning (Balch, 2010). A few of the more important supplements found to reduce and manage the neurological inflammation that interferes with optimal brain functioning include omega-3s found in fish oil, curcumin from the spice turmeric, vitamin D, and N-acetylcysteine. The fatty acids in omega-3s are converted into oxylipins that initiate and terminate the immune response and promote neuronal repair (Zivkovic, Telis, German, & Hammock, 2011). Curcumin also serves an anti-inflammatory function that reduces oxidative stress caused by various diseases including diabetes, cancer, arthritis, cardiovascular disease, and Alzheimer's disease (Ghosh, Banerjee, & Sil, 2015). Vitamin D, usually acquired with exposure to sunlight, has been found to promote immune functioning and general physical and mental health (Aranow, 2011). Finally, N-acetylcysteine acts to support the production of glutathione, essential for synaptic plasticity (Dean, Giorlando, & Berk, 2011). It has been found to be helpful in the treatment of addictions, bipolar disorder, obsessive–compulsive disorder, trichotillomania, and schizophrenia. Counselors should acquire specialized training if they want to suggest dietary supplements to clients or consider referring their client to a nutritionist or a functional medicine professional.

Sleep

The National Sleep Foundation recently released its updated recommendations for healthy sleep (Hirshkowitz et al., 2015). It recommended 9 to 11 hours of sleep for school-age children (6–13 years old), 8 to 10 hours for teenagers (14–17 years old), 7 to 9 hours for adults (18–64 years old), and 7 to 8 hours for older adults (65 years and older). Sleep duration does not always equate to sleep quality. Education in sleep hygiene can help

139

ensure ready sleep onset, deep quality rest and recovery, and refreshed awakening (Chen, Kuo, & Chueh, 2010). General suggestions for healthy sleep hygiene include limiting the use of alcohol, caffeine, and nicotine; avoiding eating, drinking, or exercising before bedtime; creating a cool, quiet, and dark sleep environment; keeping a regular sleep routine; using the bedroom only for sleep or intimacy; using natural light when one wakes and during the day to replenish natural melatonin; and limiting naps. If a person experiences ongoing problems with sleep, further treatment options include melatonin supplementation and neurofeedback.

Screen Time

Screen time on cell phones, computers, video games, and television continues to increase as it becomes more deeply integrated into schools, the workplace, and leisure activity. Its use has become so pervasive that average screen time use has surpassed sleep and other vital life activities. Screen time use has rocketed to 6 hours a day for tweens, 9 hours a day for teens, and 7 hours a day for adults (Swingle, 2015). Currently, 12% of all U.S. users would meet the criteria for addiction with significant neurological impact (Swingle, 2015). Wellness and optimal performance are best achieved through a lifestyle that takes advantage of the benefits of technology without its supplanting other healthy interests. To maintain optimal health and performance, Swingle (2015) recommended limiting screen time to 1 to 2 hours a day beyond use involved in school and work, stopping screen time 1 to 2 hours before bed (including television), avoiding toddler use of screen time before age 2 years, restricting child use of screen time between ages 2 and 6 years, and maintaining engagement in other activities including face-to-face social interaction and outdoor recreation.

Exercise

One relatively inexpensive and effective way to maintain wellness and optimal performance is daily aerobic exercise (Chapin & Russell-Chapin, 2014). Not only does exercise provide obvious physical and long-term health benefits, but it also promotes neurological, cognitive, and mental health.

Biofeedback and Neurofeedback

In a compilation of work on the application of biofeedback and neurofeedback in sports psychology, optimal self-regulation is described as involving both bottom-up and top-down strategies (Strack et al., 2011). Two bottom-up strategies include the biofeedback training techniques of peripheral skin temperature and heart rate variability. Elevated peripheral skin temperature (warm hands and feet) indicates relaxed muscles

Reflective Question

Which Therapeutic Lifestyle Changes could be helpful to enhance William's performance, based on the results of his wellness assessment?

and a slowed, steady heart rate. Healthy heart rate variability, accomplished through slow, diaphragmatic breathing, indicates the achievement of a parasympathetic response or physiological state of calm recovery. The zone for optimal performance can be achieved by rhythmically paced, smooth breathing; attention focused on the heart; and thoughts directed toward a positive outcome. Com-

Reflective Question

You have now provided William with psychoeducation on Therapeutic Lifestyle Changes and collaboratively formed a wellness plan. As a next step in the treatment process, how might you use biofeedback and neurofeedback with William?

bined, these promote calm focus and smooth recovery. For example, consider a golfer who hits an errant shot and becomes overly upset and anxious, resulting in loss of composure and several more shanked shots. By relaxing one's muscles, maintaining even blood flow throughout the body, breathing evenly, and steadying one's overall level of arousal, recovery and focus can be more readily restored and optimal performance better realized.

Top-down strategies for optimal performance involve neurofeedback training in optimal brain wave functioning. Neurofeedback is a form of biofeedback applied to the brain's electrical activity. It uses the EEG, computer technology, and principles of reinforcement to identify, target, increase, or decrease certain helpful or unhelpful brain wave patterns that affect performance (Chapin & Russell-Chapin, 2014). Most often, the first step in neurofeedback treatment is to evaluate current brain wave functioning and any abnormal brain wave patterns related to attention-deficit/hyperactivity disorder, anxiety, trauma, and obsessive–compulsive disorder with the initial goal of modifying these brain waves toward more normal functioning. Next, optimal brain wave patterns for a given behavior are strengthened. In sports, this may involve strengthening alpha brain waves for improved calm focus. In the arts, it may involve strengthening theta–alpha waves for improved creativity. In business and public speaking, it may involve training alpha waves for calm focus and low beta waves for improved cognitive efficiency (Chapin & Russell-Chapin, 2014). Even the process of aging that is characterized by a steady decline in alpha waves has seen the application of neurofeedback to help forestall cognitive decline. This technique is called "brain brightening" and involves alpha wave training four times a year to maintain cognitive efficiency (Budzynski, 1996).

My Brain-Based Approach to the Case of William

Overall assessment of William's current level of wellness found his primary strength area to be his intellectual wellness and the most prominent areas of concern to be physical, emotional, and spiritual wellness. The problem areas detected in William's wellness assessment led to intervention through Therapeutic Lifestyle Changes. William began to consume a diet of protein, fruit, and vegetables. He limited his intake of sugar and simple carbohydrates. He also began taking several dietary supplements, including fish oil and curcumin, vitamin D, and N-acetylcysteine. William began working out an hour a day. His exercise routine consisted of performing a variety of exercises, stretching, lifting light weights, and biking. He maintained a steady sleep routine of 7 to 8 hours in a dark, cool room. Over time, William lost 80 pounds and gained more energy to attend to neglected aspects of his work relationships, friendships, and marriage.

Psychotherapy, biofeedback, and neurofeedback were integrated into William's treatment. Through psychotherapy, William searched for meaning in life events and began to change the way he perceived them. William converted his outrage about receiving corporal punishment into motivation to learn about parenting. William realized that his previous marriage and divorce had spurred him to become fully responsible and not be stuck in the life that he and others thought he should live. Although his forced resignation had felt very demoralizing at the time, it had motivated him to start his own business. In his trauma after elective surgery, William had learned about the fragility of life and the fallibility of others.

William developed improved self-regulation through biofeedback and neurofeedback training. His biofeedback consisted of heart rate variability and peripheral skin temperature training to increase his ability to generate a calming, parasympathetic response. His neurofeedback consisted of four protocols, one intended to reduce his tendency toward overactivation, another to process his traumatic experiences, a third to reduce his obsessive–compulsive tendencies, and a fourth to reduce negative self-talk and associated depressed mood.

William's improved performance led to several significant life achievements. Over time, William built a strong professional reputation, owned his own business, became a professional author, and provided trainings locally, nationally, and occasionally in other countries.

Conclusion

A healthy, meaningful, and high-performing life cannot be achieved solely through amelioration of illness, disease, or pathology. By harnessing the mind–body connection implicit in neurocounseling interventions such as Therapeutic

Reflective Questions

After reading through this chapter, which threat to optimal performance might continue to be William's weakest?

What else needs to be done to help William?

142

Lifestyle Changes, biofeedback, neurofeedback, and meditation, clients can more fully hope to overcome dysfunctional physical, emotional, or behavioral states and realize the promise of wellness and optimal performance.

Reflective Question

What might have been missed had the wellness assessment not been conducted?

Quiz

1. Which of the following is not one of the six dimensions of Hettler's model of wellness?
   a. Physical.
   b. Emotional.
   c. Spiritual.
   d. Health.

2. Which of the following is not a healthy lifestyle strategy?
   a. Moderate use of alcohol.
   b. Dietary supplements.
   c. Exercise.
   d. Screen time.

3. Which of the following mental activities does not help clients to regulate their emotions?
   a. Time-in.
   b. Focus time.
   c. Playtime.
   d. Sleep time.

References

Abel, T., Havekes, R., Saletin, J., & Walker, M. (2013). Sleep, plasticity, and memory from molecules to whole-brain networks. *Current Biology, 23,* 774–788.

Amen, D. (2001). *Healing ADD: The breakthrough program that allows you to see and heal the six types of ADD.* New York, NY: Putnam.

Aranow, C. (2011). Vitamin D and the immune system. *Journal of Investigative Medicine, 59,* 881–886.

Balch, P. A. (2010). *Prescription for nutritional healing: A practical A-Z reference to drug-free remedies using vitamins, minerals, herbs & food supplements* (5th ed.). New York, NY: Avery.

Baumgart, M., Snyder, H. M., Carrillo, M. C., Fazio, S., Kim, H., & Johns, H. (2015). Summary of the evidence on modifiable risk factors for cognitive decline and dementia: A population-based perspective. *Alzheimer's & Dementia, 11,* 718–726.

Berkman, L. F., & Syme, L. S. (1979). Social networks, host, resistance, and mortality: A nine-year follow-up study of Alameda County residents. *American Journal of Epidemiology, 109,* 186–204.

Blumenthal, J., Babyak, M., Moore, K., Craighead, W., Herman, S., Khatri, P., & Ranga Krishnan, K. (1999). Effects of exercise training on older adults with major depression. *Archives of Internal Medicine, 19,* 2349–2356.

Budzynski, T. (1996). Brain brightening: Can neurofeedback improve cognitive process? *Biofeedback, 24*(2), 14–17.

Chapin, T., & Russell-Chapin, L. (2014). *Neurotherapy and neurofeedback: Brain-based treatment for psychological and behavioral problems.* New York, NY: Routledge.

Chen, P., Kuo, H., & Chueh, K. (2010). Sleep hygiene education: Efficacy on sleep quality in working women. *Journal of Nursing Research, 18,* 282–289.

Council for Accreditation of Counseling and Related Educational Programs. (2015). *2016 CACREP standards.* Retrieved from http://www.cacrep.org/wp-content/uploads/2012/10/2016-CACREP-Standards.pdf

Csikszentmihalyi, M. (1975). *Beyond boredom and anxiety.* San Francisco, CA: Jossey-Bass.

Csikszentmihalyi, M. (1990). *Flow: The psychology of optimal experience.* New York, NY: Harper & Row.

Dean, O., Giorlando, F., Berk, M. (2011). N-acetylcysteine in psychiatry: Current therapeutic evidence and mechanisms of action. *Journal of Psychiatry & Neuroscience, 36,* 78–86. doi: 10.1503/jpn.100057

Dunn, H. (1961). *High level wellness.* Arlington, VA: Beatty.

Erickson, K., Voss, M., Prakash, R., Basak, C., Szabo, A., Chaddock, L., . . . Kramer, A. (2011). Exercise training increases size of hippocampus and improves memory. *Proceedings of the National Academy of Sciences of the United States of America, 108,* 3017–3022.

Ghosh, S., Banerjee, S., & Sil, P. (2015). The beneficial role of curcumin on inflammation, diabetes and neurogenerative disease: A recent update. *Food Chemical Toxicology, 83,* 111–124.

Goyal, M., Singh, S., Sibings, E., Gould, N., Rowland-Seymour, A., Sharma, R., . . . Haythornthwaite, J. (2014). Meditation programs for psychological stress and well-being: A systematic review and meta-analysis. *JAMA, 174,* 357–368.

Hettler, B. (1984). Wellness: Encouraging a lifetime of pursuit of excellence. *Health Values, 8*(4), 13–17.

Hirschkowitz, M., Whiton, K., Albert, S. M., Alessi, C., Bruni, O., DonCarlos, L., . . . & Ware, J. C. (2015). National Sleep Foundation's updated sleep duration recommendations: Final report. *Sleep Health, 1*(4), 233–243. http://dx.doi.org/10.1016/j.sleh.2015.10.004

Holze, B., Carmody, J., Vangel, M., Congleton, C., Yerramsetti, S., Gard, T., & Lazar, S. (2011). Mindfulness practice leads to increases in regional brain gray matter density. *Psychiatry Research, 191,* 36–43.

Ivey, A. E., Ivey, M. B., & Zalaquett, C. (2014). *Intentional interviewing and counseling* (8th ed). Belmont, CA: Brooks/Cole.

Luders, E. (2013). Exploring age-related brain degeneration in meditation practitioners. *Annuls of the New York Academy of Science, 1307,* 62–72.

Luders, E., Kurth, F., Mayer, E., Toga, A., Narr, K., & Gaser, C. (2012). The unique brain anatomy of meditation practitioners: Alteration in cortical gyrification. *Frontiers in Human Neuroscience, 6,* 1–9.

Molteni, R., Barnard, R., Ying, Z., Roberts, C., & Gomez-Pinilla, F. (2002). A high-fat, refined sugar diet reduces hippocampal brain-derived neurotrophic factor, neuronal plasticity, and learning. *Neuroscience, 112,* 803–814.

Montes, S. (2013). The birth of the neurocounselor. *Counseling Today, 56*(7), 32–40.

Myers, J. E., & Sweeney, T. J. (2005). The indivisible self: An evidence-based model of wellness. *Journal of Individual Psychology, 61,* 234–245.

Myers, J. E., Sweeney, T. J., & Witmer, J. M. (2000). The wheel of wellness counseling for wellness: A holistic model for treatment planning. *Journal of Counseling & Development, 78,* 251–266.

Nakata, A. (2011). Work hours, sleep sufficiency, and prevalence of depression among full-time employees: A community-based cross-sectional study. *Journal of Clinical Psychiatry, 72,* 605–614.

Ratey, J. (2008). *Spark: The revolutionary new science of exercise and the brain.* New York, NY: Little, Brown.

Rock, D., Siegel, D. J., Poelmans, S. A. Y., & Payne, J. (2012). The healthy mind platter. *NeuroLeadership Journal, 4,* 1–23.

Segal, E. (2004). Incubation in insight problem-solving. *Creativity Research Journal, 16,* 141–148.

Stanhope, K., Schwarz, J., & Havel, P. (2013). Adverse metabolic effects of dietary fructose: Results from the recent epidemiological, clinical, and mechanistic studies. *Current Opinions in Lipidology, 24,* 198–206.

Strack, B., Linden, M., & Wilson, V. (2011). *Biofeedback and neurofeedback applications in sport psychology.* Wheat Ridge, CO: Association for Applied Psychophysiology and Biofeedback.

Swingle, M. (2015). *I-mind: How cell phones, computers, gaming and social media are changing our brains, our behavior and the evolution of the species.* Portland, OR: Inkwater.

Uchino, B. N., Holt-Lunstad, J., Uno, D., Betancourt, R., & Garvey, T. S. (1999). Social support and age-related differences in cardiovascular function: An examination of potential mediators. *Annual Behavioral Medicine, 21,* 135–142.

van den Berg, C. L., Hol, T., Van Ree, J. M., Spruijt, B. M., Everts, H., & Koolhaas, J. M. (1999). Play is indispensable for an adequate development of coping with social challenges in the rat. *Developmental Psychobiolology, 34,* 129–138.

Xi, L., Kang, H., Xu, Q., Chen, M. J., Liao, Y., Thiyagarajan, M., . . . Nedergaard, M. (2013). Sleep drives metabolic clearance from the adult brain. *Science, 342,* 373–377.

Xu, J., Vik, A., Groote, I., Lapopoulos, J., Holen, A., Ellingsen, O., . . . Davanger, S. (2014). Nondirective meditation activates default mode network and areas associated with memory retrieval and emotional processing. *Frontiers in Human Neuroscience, 8,* 86.

Zivkovic, A., Telis, N., German, J., & Hammock, B. (2011). Dietary omega-3 fatty acids aid in the modulation of inflammation and metabolic health. *California Agriculture, 65,* 106–111.

Part III
NEUROADAPTATION
AND ADDICTION

The third section of the text explores special issues in neurocounseling pertaining to neuroadaptation, including substance use, the process of addiction, and psychopharmacology. These topics require an understanding of previous chapter information about neurotransmission, epigenetics, and neuroadaptation.

■ ■ ■

Chapter 9

Clinical Neuroscience of Substance Use Disorders

Sean B. Hall and Kiera D. Walker

The purpose of this chapter is to summarize emerging findings on the basic neuroscience of addiction in an effort to help counselors enhance their case conceptualization and to link evidence-based interventions to empirically derived targets. Throughout the chapter, the term *drug* is used to refer to an external (exogenous) chemical substance that has addictive properties and includes alcohol in addition to other drugs.

 2016 CACREP Standards

This chapter addresses a section of the 2016 Council for Accreditation of Counseling and Related Educational Programs (CACREP) Standards pertinent to the common core area of Human Growth and Development (Standard II.F.3.):

- Theories and etiology of addictions and addictive behaviors (Standard II.F.3.d.)

This chapter also addresses the following Specialization Standards:

- Theories and models of addiction related to substance use as well as behavioral and process addictions (Addictions Counseling, Standard V.A.1.b.)

- Neurological, behavioral, psychological, physical, and social effects of psychoactive substances and addictive disorders on the user and significant others (Addictions Counseling, Standard V.A.1.e.)
- Techniques and interventions related to substance abuse and other addictions (Addictions Counseling, Standard V.A.3.d.)
- Neurological and medical foundation and etiology of addiction and co-occurring disorders (Clinical Mental Health Counseling, Standard V.C.1.d.)
- Neurobiological and medical foundation and etiology of addiction and co-occurring disorders (Clinical Rehabilitation Counseling, Standard V.D.1.e.)

■ ■ ■

 ## Clinical Case Example: Crystal

To many in her community, Crystal was known for her magnetic personality and carefree approach to life. She had a reputation for being spirited, fearless, and willing to circumvent the rules for any new adventure that came her way. Nevertheless, beyond her closest friends, few knew about the anguish and turmoil Crystal endured at home. Without parental supervision, Crystal began sneaking away to attend local parties on the weekends. One evening, Crystal tried intravenous heroin for the first time. This warm and blissful sensation was in stark contrast to her typical, albeit hidden, melancholy. Over the next 4 years, Crystal began using heroin more frequently until it became part of her daily routine. As Crystal's use became more frequent, her tolerance began to increase and the pleasurable feelings she once experienced began to disappear. Aside from frequent job loss and intermittent incarcerations, Crystal was also experiencing negative health consequences related to sharing needles. One day, Crystal realized that her desire to use had been replaced by a need to avoid the anxiety, malaise, and physical discomfort associated with withdrawal.

Neuroadaptation in Addiction

Drug addiction is conceptualized as a chronic and progressive illness characterized by the compulsion to consume a desired drug at the expense of other reinforcers and one's physical safety (Koob, Arends, & Le Moal, 2014). Addiction researchers often study how the brain adapts to chronic drug use—more precisely, (a) how might drugs of abuse induce psychopathology in motivation and executive function and (b) how might these deficits contribute to chronic or compulsive drug use? One possible answer includes the finding that the pharmacological properties of drugs have the capacity to trigger changes in neuroplasticity. For instance, cocaine may alter gene expression, which translates into structural changes to the neuron's dendrites. Such modifications have the capacity to sensitize neurons to both drug reward and associated stimuli. This, in turn, can alter behavior by modulating the liking and wanting properties of the drug (De Roo, Klauser, Garcia, Poglia, & Muller, 2008).

Conceptual Frameworks

Under the incentive–sensitization hypothesis of addiction, reward is composed of three separable elements: wanting (appetitive process), liking (consummatory process), and learning (predictive associations or cognitive representations). The term *liking* may be subdivided into the subjective experience of pleasure and the objective neural or behavioral reactions to rewarding stimuli (Berridge, Robinson, & Aldridge, 2009). *Wanting* refers to the subjective need or desire to consume the drug and is driven by the attribution of incentive salience to a stimulus. Formally, incentive salience is regarded as a type of motivation that mobilizes one to approach and consume rewards in the presence of conditioned cues. Last, *predictive learning* refers to the associations formed between drug cues and expected rewards. Taken together, the incentive–sensitization hypothesis (Berridge & Robinson, 1998) suggests that drugs of abuse remodel the brain systems responsible for the attribution of incentive salience, which sensitizes one to drug stimulation or drug-related cues.

Solomon's (1980) opponent-process theory of acquired motivation provides another useful lens for interpreting the transition from voluntary to chronic use. This model refers to the vacillation between two opposing psychological processes. Accordingly, after repeated exposure to a stimulus, the intensity of the primary process decreases and the secondary process increases. In other words, during chronic drug use, the individual becomes less sensitive to the hedonic properties of the drug (tolerance) and more sensitive to unpleasant interoceptive (the sense of internal body states) and emotional states associated with cessation (Koob et al., 2014).

Conceptually, it is thought that the allostatic dysregulation of brain reward systems may underlie these opponent processes. The term *allostasis* refers to the body's capacity to adjust its set points (ideal calibration for optimal functioning) in an effort to maintain homeostasis (McEwen, 2000). It is thought that chronic drug use may redefine a new and enduring set point, at which more of the drug is needed to achieve the desired effect. In other words, neuroadaptations in response to more frequent drug exposure continuously increase the negative hedonic set point (secondary process) while reducing the intensity and duration of the positive hedonic reaction (primary process; Koob et al., 2014).

Epigenetic Factors in Addiction

The human genome is a complex system capable of synthesizing 2 million proteins (Clamp et al., 2007) designed to carry out functional tasks essential for sustaining life. Whereas deoxyribonucleic acid (DNA) contains genetic instructions, ribonucleic acid (RNA) molecules are involved in the transmission of genetic information and expression of genes. This process (known as transcription) occurs in the cell's nucleus through gene expression, whereby RNA polymerase and associated proteins called *transcription factors* use the DNA sequence as a template for synthesizing messenger RNA (mRNA). Generally, the transcription of mRNA can be influenced by direct modification of the DNA sequence or through epigenetic factors. The term *epigenetic* characterizes modifications to gene expression that can be maintained from one generation to the next but are not caused by alterations to the DNA sequence. Epigenetic factors activate or silence gene expression by modifying the chromatin structure (Masterpasqua, 2009). Chemical processes such as methylation (addition of a methyl group) and deacetylation (removal of an acetyl group) help to regulate this process through the modification of DNA and histone proteins (proteins that help package and arrange DNA in anatomical units known as nucleosomes; Feil & Fraga, 2012). For example, when specific enzymes (histone methyl-transferases or DNA methyl-transferases) methylate (add a methyl group to) either DNA or histone proteins, the structure of chromatin is compressed. Once compressed, sections of the chromatin will be inaccessible to transcription factors. Without access to DNA, the expression of genes in this region will be silenced (Nestler, Hyman, & Malenka, 2009). Notably, accumulating evidence has appeared to suggest that drugs of abuse exploit this mechanism to induce persistent behavioral and cognitive modifications (Robison & Nestler, 2012).

Neurotransmission can be thought of as communication between the genome of a presynaptic neuron and the genome of its postsynaptic counterpart (Stahl, 2013). Although signal transduction (see Chapter 2) begins minutes after activation by an extracellular stimulus (e.g., neurotransmission), persistent effects on gene expression and protein synthesis may take considerable time to materialize (days to several weeks). In contrast, immediate early genes, considered to be the gateway to genomic response (Saha & Dudek, 2013), are activated shortly after neurotransmission with translation from mRNA beginning in about 15 minutes. However, because they have a short half-life (between 1 and 2 hours), their effect on gene expression is temporary (Robison & Nestler, 2012). Once transcribed from mRNA, the immediate early genes, *cJun* and *cFos,* are transcribed into mRNA; they are, in turn, translated into their protein product, Jun and Fos (Stahl, 2013). The Jun family of proteins consists of c-Jun, JunB, and JunD, whereas the Fos family of proteins consists of c-Fos, FRA1, FRA2, FosB, and ΔFosB.

Notably, ΔFosB has received increasing attention in the addiction literature. As a transcription factor, it is thought to influence behavior change via alterations in the expression of other genes. Unlike other immediate early

Reflective Question

What might have increased the likelihood of Crystal's becoming addicted to heroin?

genes, ΔFosB is uniquely stable, which may indicate that its effects are more enduring (Nestler, Barrot, & Self, 2001). Recent evidence has also appeared to demonstrate that chronic drug use induces an accumulation of ΔFosB in the nucleus accumbens, the dorsal striatum, and (to a lesser extent) the prefrontal cortex. According to Nestler et al. (2001), ΔFosB may function as a molecular switch, capable of exerting long-term effects on synaptic plasticity (Chen, Kelz, Hope, Nakabeppu, & Nestler, 1997).

Remarkably, many drugs of abuse remodel (e.g., through enlargements, protrusions, and modifications to the convexity or concavity of dendritic spines) the brain's reward pathway (van Huijstee & Mansvelder, 2015). These structural changes are thought to affect key processes involved in neurotransmission, which in turn fuel the cognitive and behavioral phenotypes (e.g., liking, wanting, craving) associated with substance abuse (Robison & Nestler, 2011). Accumulating evidence has suggested that ΔFosB may be linked to increased drug sensitivity, incentive salience, and compulsive behavior (Robison & Nestler, 2011). It should be noted that these changes are not permanent (ΔFosB is no longer detectable 1–2 months after withdrawal). The precise mechanisms that mediate the relationship between synaptic remodeling and long-term behavioral phenotypes remain an active area of research (van Huijstee & Manvelder, 2015).

Addiction Cycle

Binge and Intoxication (Positive Reinforcement)

For addiction researchers, dopamine (DA) has been an active line of inquiry in increasing knowledge of reward and motivation. Broadly, DA is thought to play a role in movement, goal-directed behavior, cognition, attention, and reward (Schultz, 2002). The primary reward circuit, known as the mesocorticolimbic DA system, is divided into the mesolimbic and mesocortical pathways (see Figure 9.1). Dopaminergic (DAergic) projections in the mesolimbic pathway have been implicated in reward prediction (Nieh, Kim, Namburi, & Tye, 2013), whereas neurons in the mesocortical pathway have been linked to executive functions such as working memory, behavioral flexibility, and decision making (Floresco & Magyar, 2006).

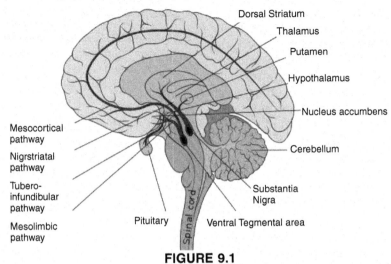

FIGURE 9.1

Major Dopamine Pathways

The pleasurable sensations that follow acute drug use have also been linked to increased levels of DA in the mesolimbic pathway (projections from the ventral tegmental area to the nucleus accumbens; Volkow & Morales, 2015). Generally, DA binds with at least five subtypes of G protein–coupled receptors (D1-type through D5-type receptors) distributed throughout various regions of the brain. However, DA cells in the ventral tegmental area are made up of GABAergic medium spiny neurons (MSNs), which express either D1-type (D1R) or D2-type (D2R) receptors (Robison & Nestler, 2011). In addition, these MSNs may operate in either a tonic or phasic firing state. During tonic firing, DAergic cells release short (single-spike, 1–8 Hz), spontaneous bursts of DA into the extracellular space. In contrast, phasic firing refers to a series of high-frequency bursts (15 Hz; induced by glutamatergic stimulation), which flood the synaptic cleft with DA. According to Schultz (2002), phasic firing in DA neurons is induced by a stimulus that holds motivational value. Relatedly, given that peak reward occurs when DA rapidly floods each pathway (which activates D2R and inhibits D1R), it should be noted that routes of administration more commonly associated with rapid uptake (e.g. inhalation, intravenous) are more rewarding and therefore more addictive (Volkow & Morales, 2015).

DAergic neurons in the mesolimbic pathway (ventral tegmental area projections toward the nucleus accumbens) are also separable into a direct pathway and an indirect pathway. Notably, medium spiny neurons (MSNs) in the direct pathway modulate persistent reward, and

MSNs in the indirect pathway regulate transient punishment (Volkow & Morales, 2015). To enhance reward prediction, glutamatergic tracts from the amygdala, the hippocampus, and the ventral prefrontal cortex also innervate the aforementioned projections. Recall that the amygdala generates an emotional response to environmental stimuli, the hippocampus aids in both memory formation and consolidation, and the prefrontal cortex is involved in executive function and limbic regulation (Calabrese et al., 2014). When stimulated by enough DA to trigger phasic firing, these mechanisms help the individual form associations between reward cues and the drug of abuse (Volkow & Morales, 2015). Once an association is formed, exposure to reward cues can activate a conditioned response, whereby phasic firing is triggered in expectation of reward.

Withdrawal and Negative Affect (Negative Reinforcement)

During chronic drug use, temporary cessation has been linked to a withdrawal syndrome characterized by physical (specific to the drug of choice) and psychological (motivational deficits) symptoms, such as irritability, dysphoric mood (dissatisfaction, agitation, or both), alexithymia (difficulty expressing or experiencing emotion), and anhedonia (inability to experience pleasure; Koob et al., 2014). Remember from the opponent-process model that pleasant (positive hedonic) and unpleasant (negative hedonic) responses are inversely related. Consequently, as excessive drug use stimulates the brain's natural reward system (primary process), the central division of the extended amygdala initiates an antireward response (secondary process). More simply, as people become less sensitive to the rewarding effects of the drug, they become more sensitive to unpleasant symptoms associated with cessation (Koob et al., 2014).

As drug dependence progresses, the brain's reward system is weakened, and the motivational deficits associated with withdrawal begin to emerge. These processes are governed by within- and between-system changes. Within-system changes affect reward circuitry and are mediated by neuroplastic alterations among MSNs in the nucleus accumbens. Ultimately, within-system changes are associated with decreased sensitivity in the mesocorticolimbic system to DA stimulation, thereby reducing both the liking and the wanting properties of the drug (Koob et al., 2014). Alternatively, between-system changes in the extended amygdala affect the way the body responds to stress. Consider that corticotropin-releasing hormones from neurons in the hypothalamus trigger the release of adrenocorticotropic hormone and glucocorticoids (cortisol) from the hypothalamic–pituitary–adrenal axis (Bamberger, Shulte, & Chrousos, 1996). Withdrawal from chronic drug use has been linked to dysregulation in this axis, including elevated levels of adrenocorticotropic hormone, cortisol, and corticotropin-releasing hormones in the extended amygdala (Koob et al., 2014).

Together, withdrawal and between-system adaptations may underlie compulsive drug use in an effort to stave off the dysphoric mood states present during withdrawal. For example, as the liking and wanting properties of a drug abate (within-system changes), compulsive use becomes increasingly motivated by the desire to reestablish a baseline qualia and reduce the negative hedonic states associated with withdrawal syndrome (Redish, Jensen, & Johnson, 2008).

Preoccupation and Anticipation (Craving)

The preoccupation–anticipation stage outlines the neurobiological systems thought to underlie both craving and reinstatement (relapse). It is well known that the appetitive urge to relapse (craving) can be activated when clients are exposed to a drug-, cue-, or stress-induced trigger (Carter & Tiffany, 1999), but why do people have such a difficult time suppressing this urge? Notably, evidence has suggested that chronic drug abuse alters more than just motivation; it also impairs critical brain regions for exerting top-down control over behavior. According to Redish, Jensen, and Johnson (2008), people are more vulnerable to developing an addiction when pathways that contribute to a person's habit supersede the person's inhibitory pathways that affect planning. Consequently, an important body of literature has emerged examining how executive dysfunction may mediate the loss of inhibitory control and reward-related processing among addicts (Berridge & Robinson, 1998).

In one study, Hayashi, Ko, Strafella, and Dagher (2013) were able to reduce cravings by inactivating the dorsolateral prefrontal cortex (area at the top and side of the prefrontal cortex) during exposure to drug-related cues. By deactivating the dorsolateral prefrontal cortex, they were able to disrupt signaling between the medial orbitofrontal cortex (which marks the subjective value of a reward), the anterior cingulate cortex (ACC; responsible for response selection, planning, and self-monitoring), and the ventral striatum (which converts motivation to action). Hayashi et al. reasoned that the medial orbitofrontal cortex monitored the subjective value of the drug and that the dorsolateral prefrontal cortex was used to determine temporal availability (whether the drug is available now or in the future). According to Koob et al. (2014), these findings may indicate the presence of an inhibitory ("stop") signal, primarily mediated by the ventrolateral prefrontal cortex and the orbitofrontal cortex, and a reward-seeking ("go") signal, primarily mediated by the ACC and dorsolateral prefrontal cortex.

Researchers are also beginning to unpack the insula's role in attention and decision making and how such mechanisms influence the decision to use drugs despite negative consequences. The insula has the capacity to integrate external stimuli, interoceptive (awareness of internal body states) signals, and motivational states while also tapping into other key networks, including the executive function and motor systems (DeVito et al., 2013). It is thought that the insula may rely on interoceptive signals to "mark" the reward potential of certain outcomes, allowing individuals

to discriminate between outcomes with more or less hedonic value. For addicts, interoceptive signals may be used to erroneously predict the benefits of drug-seeking behavior (Naqvi, Gaznick, Tranel, & Bechara, 2014). Consequently, accumulating evidence has lent support to these hypotheses because increased activity in the insula has been associated with the tendency to choose smaller–sooner rewards (regarded as a marker of impulsivity; Claus, Kiehl, & Hutchison, 2011), failure to adjust one's behavior after making an error (Paulus, Lovero, Wittmann, & Leland, 2008), and greater incentive to act on uncertainty ("action pressure"; Leland, Arce, Feistein, & Paulus, 2006). In summary, these findings suggest that abnormal functioning in the insula during addiction may increase both impulsivity and difficulty in identifying risky situations (Naqvi et al., 2014).

On a related note, the somatic marker model of addiction suggests that chronic users may also be biased toward immediate drug rewards and have difficulty accessing the unpleasant emotional consequences associated with relapse or long-term use (Verdejo-García & Bechara, 2009). For instance, hyperactivity in the amygdala system heightens the emotional impact of immediate drug rewards while reducing the hedonic value of natural reinforcers. At the same time, impairments in the ventromedial prefrontal cortex suppress the availability of unpleasant emotions (e.g., shame, guilt, regret) associated with the long-term consequences of drug use. Consequently, choosing a long-term outcome requires an emotional signal with the strength to overcome the incentive salience attached to immediate drug rewards. In other words, bottom-up (mediated by hyperactivity in the amygdala) signals bias addicts toward immediate rewards by interrupting the top-down (mediated by the ventromedial prefrontal cortex) signals for triggering emotional states associated with unpleasant, long-term consequences. The aforementioned research may have important implications for counselors, because these mechanisms may be ideal targets for cognitive interventions.

Clinical Implications

A large literature has emerged that explores the therapeutic efficacy of counseling for addictive behaviors. These results appear to suggest that various interventions are indeed capable of stimulating clinically significant change among individuals diagnosed with substance use disorders. For instance, recent meta-analyses have appeared to support the efficacy of cognitive behavior therapy (Magill & Ray, 2009), motivational interviewing (Jensen et al., 2011), acceptance and commitment therapy (Lee, Woolee, Levin, & Twohig, 2015), 12-step treatments (Project MATCH Research Group, 1997), and contingency management (Benishek et al., 2014). However, on average, the magnitude of treatment effects ranges from small to medium, suggesting that these interventions may be, at most, moderately effective (Feldstein Ewing, Filbey, Sabbineni, Chandler, & Hutchison, 2011). In addition, well-designed comparative effectiveness trials have failed to detect significant differences across modalities, suggesting that the active ingredients assumed to underlie therapeutic action either are tapping a common pathway or have not been fully articulated (Crits-Christoph et al., 1999; Project MATCH Research Group, 1997; UK Alcohol Treatment Trial Research Team, 2005). Such findings underscore the difficulty in detecting the salutary components of psychotherapy for addiction and, therefore, may undermine the ability to use this knowledge to optimize treatment effects (Morgenstern & McKay, 2007).

Given these challenges, researchers are starting to use sophisticated research designs and advanced neuroimaging technology to further unpack the basic neurobiological mechanisms of behavior change. For example, functional magnetic resonance imaging (fMRI) relays information about activity in specific brain regions. These images are derived from changes in the magnetic susceptibility of blood as oxygenation levels vary over time. More specifically, the brightness of a voxel (three-dimensional pixel used in computer imaging) varies on the basis of the concentration levels of oxygenated blood (increased oxygenated blood flow corresponds to a brighter image). By adjoining thousands of voxels together in a three-dimensional space, a real-time representation of the brain emerges. Using these images, researchers and clinicians can observe alterations in neuronal activity across a region of interest at different points in time (de Charms, 2008). These methods are allowing researchers to observe how changes in fMRI signaling can be used to infer that neurocognitive adaptations have occurred. For instance, Vollstädt-Klein et al. (2011) found evidence to support that cue-exposure treatment for alcohol use disorder may contribute to reductions in the incentive salience of alcohol cues and suppress the recruitment of attentional resources for processing alcohol-related stimuli, extinction of addiction memory, and increased executive control. These interpretations of the data were based on reduced activity in the mesocorticolimbic pathway, the ACC, insula, and the precentral gyrus.

Similarly, Feldstein Ewing et al. (2011) found that change talk ("It is time to stop drinking") in motivational interviewing may inhibit activity in the mesocorticolimbic pathway, resulting in reduced

> Describe the evidence-based treatment plan you would use if you were Crystal's counselor.

craving and incentive salience during high-risk situations. Moreover, DeVito et al. (2012) observed reduced activity in the ACC, right inferior frontal gyrus, dorsolateral prefrontal cortex, and midbrain among subjects who completed a computerized cognitive behavior therapy intervention. These findings suggest that computerized cognitive behavior therapy may be effective at increasing executive control, reducing impulsivity, and reducing the motivational salience of drug-related cues.

Last, an emerging line of research has begun to explore the utility of real-time fMRI feedback for enhancing the therapeutic benefit of behavioral interventions for substance use disorders. Although still in the early phases of development, researchers have demonstrated decreased ACC (craving) activation in response to visual cues among smokers (Hartwell et al., 2016) and patients diagnosed with alcohol use disorder (Karch et al., 2015). These data appear to demonstrate that clients may be able to leverage fMRI data to alter the neurophysiology of brain regions associated with addictive behaviors

It is clear from these findings that advancements in neuroscience have provided researchers with new tools to better understand how counseling interventions may affect key neural pathways implicated in the pathophysiology of substance use disorders. As social and behavioral scientists, counselors must translate these findings and modify their interventions to accommodate emerging developments. This understanding will allow counselors to create reasonably accurate frameworks to guide their provision of safe, effective, and efficient therapy. Without accounting for these developments, interventions may be driven by imprecise therapeutic targets, which may translate into prolonged distress, slow therapeutic progress, or submaximal outcomes.

Quiz

1. DAergic neurons in the mesolimbic pathway are largely associated with:
   a. Reward prediction.
   b. Executive function.
   c. Movement disorders.
   d. Decision making.

2. Which of the following is *not* an evidence-based counseling intervention for addiction?
   a. Motivational interviewing.
   b. Cognitive behavior therapy.
   c. Contingency management.
   d. Interpersonal and social rhythm therapy.
3. Which of the following elements make up the addiction cycle?
   a. Detoxification, initial recovery, and relapse prevention.
   b. Liking, needing, and opponent processes.
   c. Binge–intoxication, withdrawal and negative affect, and preoccupation–anticipation.
   d. Positive reinforcement, negative reinforcement, and decision making.

References

Bamberger, C. M., Schulte, H. M., & Chrousos, G. P. (1996). Molecular determinants of glucocorticoid receptor function and tissue sensitivity to glucocorticoids. *Endocrine Reviews, 17,* 245–261. doi:10.1210/edrv-17-3-245

Benishek, L. A., Dugosh, K. L., Kirby, K. C., Matejkowski, J., Clements, N. T., Seymour, B. L., & Festinger, D. S. (2014). Prize-based contingency management for the treatment of substance abusers: A meta-analysis. *Addiction, 109,* 1426–1436. http://dx.doi.org/10.1111/add.12589

Berridge, K. C., & Robinson, T. E. (1998). What is the role of dopamine reward: Hedonic impact, reward learning, or incentive salience? *Brain Research Reviews, 28,* 309–369.

Berridge, K. C., Robinson, T. E., & Aldridge, J. W. (2009). Dissecting components of reward: "Liking," "wanting," and learning. *Current Opinion in Pharmacology, 9,* 65–73. http://dx.doi.org/10.1016/j.coph.2008.12.014

Calabrese, F., Rossetti, A. C., Racagni, G., Gass, P., Riva, M. A., & Molteni, R. (2014). Brain-derived neurotrophic factor: A bridge between inflammation and neuroplasticity. *Frontiers in Cellular Neuroscience, 8,* 430. http://dx.doi.org/10.3389/fncel.2014.00430

Carter, B. L., & Tiffany, S. T. (1999). Meta-analysis of cue-reactivity in addiction research. *Addiction, 94,* 327–340. doi:10.1046/j.1360-0443.1999.9433273.x

Chen, J., Kelz, M. B., Hope, B. T., Nakabeppu, Y., & Nestler, E. J. (1997). Chronic Fos-related antigens: Stable variants of ΔFosB induced in brain by chronic treatments. *Journal of Neuroscience, 17,* 4933–4941.

Clamp, M., Fry, B., Kamal, M., Xie, X., Cuff, J., Lin, M. F., . . . Lander, E. S. (2007). Distinguishing protein-coding and noncoding genes in the human genome. *Proceedings of the National Academy of Sciences of the United States of America, 104,* 19428–19433. http://dx.doi.org/10.1073/pnas.0709013104

Claus, E. D., Kiehl, K. A., & Hutchison, K. E. (2011). Neural and behavioral mechanisms of impulsive choice in alcohol use disorder. *Alcoholism: Clinical and Experimental Research, 35,* 1209–1219. http://dx.doi.org/10.1111/j.1530-0277.2011.01455.x

Crits-Christoph, P., Siqueland, L., Blaine, J., Frank, A., Luborsky, L., Onken L. S., . . . Beck, A. T. (1999). Psychosocial treatments for cocaine dependence: National Institute on Drug Abuse Collaborative Cocaine Treatment Study. *Archives of General Psychiatry, 56,* 493–502.

de Charms, R. C. (2008). Applications of real-time fMRI. *Nature Reviews Neuroscience, 9,* 720–729.

De Roo, M., Klauser, P., Garcia, P. M., Poglia, L., & Muller, D. (2008). Spine dynamics and synapse remodeling during LTP and memory processes. *Progress in Brain Research, 169,* 199–207

DeVito, E. E., Meda, S. A., Jiantonio, R., Potenza, M. N., Krystal, J. H., & Pearlson, G. D. (2013). Neural correlates of impulsivity in healthy males and females with family histories of alcoholism. *Neuropsychopharmacology, 38,* 1854–1863. http://dx.doi.org/10.1038/npp.2013.92

DeVito, E. E., Worhunsky, P. D., Carroll, K. M., Rounsaville, B. J., Kober, H., & Potenza, M. N. (2012). A preliminary study of the neural effects of behavioral therapy for substance use disorders. *Drug and Alcohol Dependence, 122,* 228–235. http://dx.doi.org/10.1016/j.drugalcdep.2011.10.002

Feil, R., & Fraga, M. F. (2012). Epigenetics and the environment: Emerging patterns and implications. *Nature Reviews Genetics, 13,* 97–109. http://dx.doi.org/10.1038/nrg3142.

Feldstein Ewing, S. W., Filbey, F. M., Sabbineni, A., Chandler, L. D., & Hutchison, K. E. (2011). How psychosocial alcohol interventions work: A preliminary look at what fMRI can tell us. *Alcoholism: Clinical and Experimental Research, 35,* 643–651. http://dx.doi.org/10.1111/j.1530-0277.2010.01382.x

Floresco, S. B., & Magyar, O. (2006). Mesocortical dopamine modulation of executive functions: Beyond working memory. *Psychopharmacology, 188,* 567–585. doi:10.1007/s00213-006-0404-5

Hartwell, K. J., Hanlon, C. A., Li, X., Borckardt, J. J., Canterberry, M., Prisciandaro, J. J., . . . Brady, K. T. (2016). Individualized real-time fMRI neurofeedback to attenuate craving in nicotine-dependent smokers. *Journal of Psychiatry & Neuroscience, 41,* 48–55. http://dx.doi.org/10.1503/jpn.140200

Hayashi, T., Ko, J. H., Strafella, A. P., & Dagher, A. (2013). Dorsolateral prefrontal and orbitofrontal cortex interactions during self-control of cigarette craving. *Proceedings of the National Academy of Sciences of the United States of America, 110,* 4422–4427. http://dx.doi.org/10.1073/pnas.1212185110

Jensen, C. D., Cushing, C. C., Aylward, B. S., Craig, J. T., Sorell, D. M., & Steele, R. G. (2011). Effectiveness of motivational interviewing interventions for adolescent substance use behavior change: A meta-analytic review. *Journal of Consulting and Clinical Psychology, 79,* 433–440. http://dx.doi.org/10.1037/a0023992

Karch, S., Keeser, D., Hümmer, S., Paolini, M., Kirsch, V., Karali, T., . . . Pogarell, O. (2015). Modulation of craving related brain responses using real-time fMRI in patients with alcohol use disorder. *PLoS ONE, 10,* e0133034. http://dx.doi.org/10.1371/journal.pone.0133034

Koob, G. F., Arends, M. A., & Le Moal, M. (2014). *Drugs, addiction, and the brain.* Waltham, MA: Elsevier.

Lee, E. B., Woolee, A., Levin, M. E., & Twohig, M. P. (2015). An initial meta-analysis of acceptance and commitment therapy for treating substance use disorders. *Drug and Alcohol Dependence, 155,* 1–7. http://dx.doi.org/10.1016/j.drugalcdep.2015.08.004

Leland, D. S., Arce, E., Feistein, J. S., & Paulus, M. P. (2006). Young adult stimulant users' increased striatal activation during uncertainty is related to impulsivity. *NeuroImage, 33,* 735–731. http://dx.doi.org/10.1016/j.neuroimage.2006.07.011

Lynch, P. J. (Ill.). (2015). *Dopaminergic pathways* [Digital image]. Retrieved from https://commons.wikimedia.org/wiki/File:Dopaminergic_pathways.svg

Magill, M., & Ray, L. A. (2009). Cognitive-behavioral treatment with adult alcohol and illicit drug users: A meta-analysis of randomized controlled trials. *Journal of Studies on Alcohol and Drugs, 70,* 516–527.

Masterpasqua, F. (2009). Psychology and epigenetics. *Review of General Psychology, 13,* 194–201. http://dx.doi.org/10.1037/a0016301

McEwen, B. S. (2000). Allostasis and allostatic load: Implications for neuropsychopharmacology. *Neuropsychopharmacology, 22,* 108–124. http://dx.doi.org/10.1016/S0893-133X(99)00129-3

Morgenstern, J., & McKay, J. R. (2007). Rethinking the paradigms that inform behavioral treatment research for substance use disorders. *Addiction, 102,* 1377–1389. doi:10.1111/j.1360-0443.2007.01882.x

Naqvi, N. H., Gaznick, N., Tranel, D., & Bechara, A. (2014). The insula: A critical neural substrate for craving and drug seeking under conflict and risk. *Annals of the New York Academy of Sciences, 1316,* 53–70. http://dx.doi.org/10.1111/nyas.12415

Nestler, E. J., Barrot, M., & Self, D. W. (2001). ΔFosB: A sustained molecular switch for addiction. *Proceedings of the National Academy of Sciences of the United States of America, 98,* 11042–11046. http://dx.doi.org/10.1073/pnas.191352698

Nestler, E. J., Hyman, S. E., & Malenka, R. C. (2009). *Molecular neuropharmacology: A foundation for clinical neuroscience* (2nd ed.). New York, NY: McGraw-Hill.

Nieh, E. H., Kim, S.-Y., Namburi, P., & Tye, K. M. (2013). Opto-genetic dissection of neural circuits underlying emotional valence and motivated behaviors. *Brain Research, 1511,* 73–92. http://doi.org/10.1016/j.brainres.2012.11.001

Paulus, M. O., Lovero, K. L., Wittmann, M., & Leland, D. S. (2008). Reduced behavioral and neural activation in stimulant users to different error rates during decision-making. *Biological Psychiatry, 63,* 1054– 060. http://dx.doi.org/10.1016/j.biopsych.2007.09.007

Project MATCH Research Group. (1997). Matching alcoholism treatments to client heterogeneity: Project MATCH posttreatment drinking outcomes. *Journal of Studies on Alcohol, 58,* 7–29.

Redish, A. D., Jensen, S., & Johnson, A. (2008). A unified framework for addiction: Vulnerabilities in the decision process. *Behavioral and Brain Sciences, 31,* 415–487. http://doi.org/10.1017/S0140525X0800472X

Robison, A. J., & Nestler, E. J. (2011). Transcriptional and epigenetic mechanisms of addiction. *Nature Reviews Neuroscience, 12,* 623–637. http://dx.doi.org/10.1038/nrn3111

Saha, R. N., & Dudek, S. M. (2013). Splitting hares and tortoises: A classification of neuronal immediate early gene transcription based on poised RNA polymerase II. *Neuroscience, 247,* 175–181. doi: 10.1016/j.neuroscience.2013.04.064

Schultz, W. (2002). Getting formal with dopamine and reward. *Neuron, 36,* 241–263.

Solomon, R. L. (1980). The opponent-process theory of acquired motivation: The costs of pleasure and the benefits of pain. *American Psychologist, 35,* 691–712. http://psycnet.apa.org/index.cfm?fa=fulltext.journal&jcode=amp&vol=35&issue=8&page=691&format=PDF

Stahl, S. (2013). *Stahl's essential pharmacology: Neuroscientific basis and practical application* (4th ed.). New York: NY: Cambridge University Press.

UK Alcohol Treatment Trial (UKATT) Research Team. (2005). Effectiveness of treatment for alcohol problems: Findings of the randomized UK Alcohol Treatment Trial (UKATT). *BMJ, 331,* 541–547. http://dx.doi.org/10.1136/bmj.331.7516.541

van Huijstee, A. N., & Mansvelder, H. D. (2015). Glutamatergic synaptic plasticity in the mesocorticolimbic system in addiction. *Frontiers in Cellular Neuroscience, 8,* 466. http://dx.doi.org/10.3389/fncel.2014.00466

Verdejo-García, A., & Bechara, A. (2009). A somatic marker theory of addiction. *Neuropharmacology, 56,* 48–62. http://dx.doi.org/10.1016/j.neuropharm.2008.07.035

Volkow, N. D., & Morales, M. (2015). The brain on drugs: From reward to addiction. *Cell, 162,* 712–725

Vollstädt-Klein, S., Loeber, S., Kirsch, M., Bach, P., Richter, A., Bühler, M., von der Goltz, C., . . . Kiefer, F. (2011). Effects of cue-exposure treatment on enural cue reactivity in alcohol dependence: A randomized trial. *Biological Psychiatry, 69,* 1060–1066. http://dx.doi.org/10.1016/j.biopsych.2010.12.016

Chapter 10

Psychopharmacology Basics

Nancy Sherman and Thomas A. Field

Psychopharmacological medications can play an important role in wellness and recovery for some individuals and conditions, and they have become a staple of mental health treatment for many. It is currently estimated that one in five people in the United States takes a psychotropic medication (Medco Health Solutions, 2010). Although these medications cannot cure mental disorders, they may play an important role in alleviating symptoms. To best care for clients, counselors should have a working knowledge of how psychotropic medications work in the brain, common side effects, when to refer for a medication evaluation, and which mental disorders may benefit from an additional or alternative approach to medication. Counselors must also be aware of medical conditions and nonpsychotropic medications that may be the cause of psychological symptoms. Basic pharmacological information is presented, although not everything you will need to know about psychotropic medication is within the scope of this chapter.

Counselors may well be the primary source of information for clients about their medication because primary care providers prescribe more psychotropic drugs than psychiatrists. Furthermore, counselors typically see clients on a weekly schedule, whereas prescribers of psychotropic medications may only see their clients once every 4 to 6 weeks at most. It is therefore critical for counselors to have some basic knowledge of psychotropic drug classification, pharmacokinetics, and neurobiological action. Counselors should also possess knowledge of psychiatric medication use with children and older adults. With this information, counselors can help clients better understand what they need to know about taking psychotropic medication.

The case of Charlie is presented to illustrate basic elements of psychopharmacology and the use of psychotropic (psychiatric) medication. Key terms such as *pharmacokinetics* and *neurotransmission* are defined and explained. Information on classification, contraindications, and abuse potential of psychotropic drugs is provided as well as information on how these drugs work in the brain and body. Special considerations for use of psychiatric medication with children and older adults are presented. A brain-based approach is proposed for medication referral, medication monitoring, and medication psychoeducation.

 ## 2016 CACREP Standards

This chapter addresses sections of the 2016 Council for Accreditation of Counseling and Related Educational Programs (CACREP) Standards pertinent to the following Specialization Standards:

- Classifications, indications, and contraindications of commonly prescribed psychopharmacological medications for appropriate medical referral and consultation (Addiction Counseling, Standard V.A.2.h.)
- Classifications, indications, and contraindications of commonly prescribed psychopharmacological medications for appropriate medical referral and consultation (Clinical Mental Health Counseling, Standard V.C.2.h.)
- Classifications, indications, and contraindications of commonly prescribed psychopharmacological medications for appropriate medical referral and consultation (Clinical Rehabilitation Counseling, Standard V.D.2.l.)
- Physical, mental health, and psychopharmacological factors affecting marriages, couples, and families (Marriage, Couple, and Family Counseling, Standard V.F.2.l.)
- Common medications that affect learning, behavior, and mood in children and adolescents (School Counseling, V.G.2.h.)

■ ■ ■

 ## Clinical Case Study: Charlie

Charlie is a 5-year-old boy who lives with his mother and stepfather. Charlie is one of four children, two of whom are step-siblings. His parents both work, and the children often stay with their maternal grandmother after school. Charlie's grandmother spoke to me about her concern that he had been prescribed risperidone (Risperdal) by his family physician. She had looked the drug up on the Internet and learned it was for people with schizophrenia (or "crazy people," as she described them). The doctor had told her that risperidone had been around for a long time and should work well for Charlie's problems. Although she was concerned about the drug, she also said that Charlie's behavior had markedly improved and that he slept through the night for the first time in years.

Charlie had been hyperactive since he was a baby. From age 4 years, Charlie had been treated for attention-deficit/hyperactivity disorder with a variety of medications, first with stimulant medication and later with others. Nothing seemed to help until the risperidone. In addition to the hyperactivity, Charlie had difficulty learning social skills and playing with other children. He was obsessed with dinosaurs and had some repetitive behavior. Charlie had only been treated by his pediatrician/family practice doctor and had received no counseling or psychiatric evaluation. Charlie's family had concerns about the long-term effects of the medication and believed the physician was not monitoring it.

Neurobiology of Psychotropic Drugs

As described in Chapter 1, brain communication takes place between neurons. Neurons communicate with each other through neurotransmitters. When a neuron is excited, an electrical current travels through an axon to a terminal button. The neuron (presynaptic neuron) must then release neurotransmitters across a space called a *synapse* to another neuron (postsynaptic neuron). Each particular type of neurotransmitter binds to a specific receptor. Receptors are named according to the type of neurotransmitter with which they prefer to bind. For example, serotonin binds to serotonin receptors.

Psychotropic drugs can act in several different ways. One way is by mimicking the effects of naturally occurring neurotransmitters. Drugs can also block neurotransmission, as well as alter the common storage, release, and removal of neurotransmitters. One important mechanism by which psychotropics act is to block the reuptake of a neurotransmitter released from the presynaptic terminal. Selective serotonin reuptake inhibitors work in this way by blocking the reuptake of serotonin and leaving more of the neurotransmitter in the synapse. Increasing the levels of serotonin in the synapse is believe to improve mood (Preston, O'Neal, & Talaga, 2013). Drugs that bind and enhance the function of receptors are known as *agonists* and medicines that bind and thereby block normal function are known as *antagonists*.

Reflective Question

What other possible interventions might be helpful to Charlie and his parents?

167

Pharmacokinetics

Pharmacokinetics can be defined as the study of what happens to a drug when it enters the body. The four pharmacokinetic processes that occur are absorption, distribution, metabolism, and excretion. Every drug has a unique kinetic profile composed of these four factors (Preston et al., 2013).

Absorption is how a drug enters the bloodstream. Most psychotropic drugs are administered by mouth, and so the majority of medications are absorbed through the stomach and small intestines. For this reason, the rate of absorption is affected by a full or empty stomach and drug solubility, in addition to the amount of blood flow. Some psychotropics are injected intravenously (directly into the bloodstream) or intramuscularly (into the muscle). The route of administration affects the absorption of the drug. For example, drugs administered intravenously are absorbed more quickly than those administered orally or intramuscularly. Other routes of administration for psychotropic medications include sublingual (under the tongue) and transdermal (through the skin, usually by adhesive patch).

Distribution refers to the circulation of medication throughout the body via the bloodstream after absorption. The amount of blood supply to an area determines the rate of distribution. For example, the heart and brain have an increased blood supply, so medication will act more quickly in these areas. The drug is also distributed to areas of metabolism and excretion. Factors influencing the distribution of medicine include the chemical consistency of the medication, the amount administered, other drugs taken, local blood flow, and membrane permeability.

Metabolism is the process of how the body changes drugs to eliminate them. As the drugs enter the body, they are treated as foreign substances and are chemically altered by metabolism, producing by-products called *metabolites*. Some metabolites produce the desired therapeutic effect and reduce the individual's symptoms. Other metabolites affect different body tissues and result in undesirable side effects. When liver function is impaired, there is a risk of having excessive levels of the drug. Toxicity or poisoning can occur. If the liver metabolizes the drug too quickly, the person may not get enough of the drug to experience a therapeutic level that reduces symptoms.

All drugs are eventually removed from the body during a process called *excretion*. Most drugs are excreted through urine that is processed by the kidneys. Without adequate kidney function, toxic levels of a drug can accumulate in the bloodstream. Drugs are metabolized and eliminated at varying rates. The half-life of a drug is the amount of time it takes for the plasma concentration of the blood to be reduced by one half. When a person takes medication on a regular basis, there is an ongoing process of drug absorption from each dose and, at the same time, an ongoing process of drug removal by metabolism and elimination. Steady state occurs when the amount of drug taken is equivalent to the amount of drug eliminated. Drugs usually take between five and six half-lives before reaching steady state. Drugs with shorter half-lives reach steady state quickly, and those with longer half-lives are slower to reach steady state (Kramer, 2003). Drug side effects can be less severe or even eliminated after a steady state is reached. For example, selective serotonin reuptake inhibitors have reduced gastrointestinal side effects after reaching steady state (Kramer, 2003).

As depicted in Figure 10.1, an individual's response to a drug is affected by many factors that have an impact on the psychokinetic

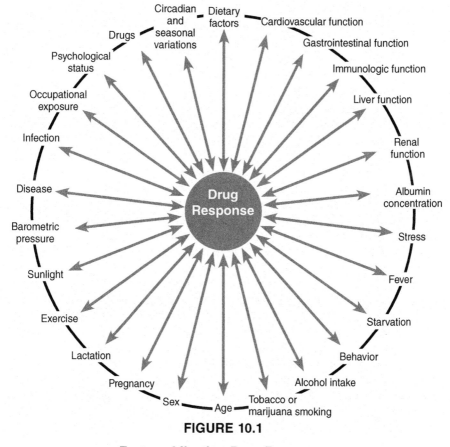

FIGURE 10.1

Factors Affecting Drug Response

Note. From *Merck Manual Consumer Version* (http://www.merckmanuals.com/consumer), edited by Robert Porter, 2015, Kenilworth, NJ: MerckSharp & Dohme Corporation, a subsidiary of Merck & Co., Inc. Copyright 2015 by MerckSharp & Dohme Corporation, a subsidiary of Merck & Co., Inc. Reprinted with permission. The *Merck Manual Consumer Version* is also known as the *Merck Manual* in the United States and Canada and the *MSD Manual* in the rest of the world.

processes. These factors include age, genetic factors, expectation of the drug's effect, interactions with other medicines, and others. Because of these factors, determining drug dosage and route of administration can be a complex issue. In complex client cases, it is important to consider referring clients for medication evaluation

to a specialized psychopharmacologist such as a psychiatrist or psychiatric nurse practitioner because of their extensive knowledge of psychotropic medications.

Use of Psychiatric Drugs With Children and Older Adults

Two groups of particular concern when prescribing psychiatric drugs are children and older adults. According to Preston et al. (2015), medical professionals have only recently recognized major differences in neurobiological development and metabolism for child and older adult populations. The pharmacokinetics of drugs in children is different from adults because of age, body composition, liver and kidney function, and maturation of enzymatic systems (Preston et al., 2015). Medication dosing for children must consider such factors, making prescribing a complex art for many psychopharmacologists. For example, a 12-year-old who weights 200 pounds would likely require a different therapeutic dose than a 12-year-old who weighs 100 pounds. The therapeutic dose may also differ between a 12-year-old and a 17-year-old who both weight 200 pounds.

In older adults, the pharmacokinetic action of psychotropic drugs differs from that in younger adults. Age-related changes cause drugs to stay active longer in the body, prolonging the effect and potentially increasing side effects. In older adults, water in the body decreases and the amount of fat increases. This combination can result in higher concentrations of water-soluble drugs because there is less water to dilute them and more fat in which to store medications (Ruscin & Linnebur, 2016). The liver does not metabolize drugs as efficiently in older adulthood, and the kidneys are less able to excrete drugs into urine resulting in less elimination.

Psychotropic Drug Classification

Psychotropic drugs are placed in different categories and classified according to their primary effect on the brain and central nervous system. Table 10.1 displays neurotransmitters targeted by psychopharmacological drugs. The main classifications for psychiatric medications

TABLE 10.1

Neurotransmitters Targeted by Psychopharmacological Drugs

Class	Drug	Dopamine	GABA	Norepinephrine	Serotonin
Anxiolytic (benzodiazepine)	Ativan, Klonopin, Valium, Xanax		Enhance		
Antidepressant (SSRI)	Celexa, Lexapro, Luvox, Paxil, Prozac, Zoloft				Enhance
Antidepressant (SNRI)	Cymbalta, Pristiq, Strattera			Enhance	Enhance
Antidepressant (NDRI)	Wellbutrin	Enhance		Enhance	
Antidepressant (SMS)	Trinellix			Enhance	
Antipsychotic (first generation)	Haldol, Thorazine	Reduce			
Antipsychotic (second generation)	Abilify, Clozaril, Geodon, Invega, Risperdal, Seroquel, Zyprexa	Reduce			
Stimulant	Adderall, Concerta, Focalin, Ritalin, Vyvanse	Enhance			

Note. Enhance = the axon releases more of the neurotransmitter or the dendrite receives more of the neurotransmitter by inhibiting reuptake to the axon. Reduce = the axon releases less of the neurotransmitter or the dendrite receives less of the neurotransmitter by blocking the receiving channels. Drugs are listed by their trade name rather than their generic name. Mood stabilizers are not included in this table. GABA = gamma-aminobutyric acid; SSRI = selective serotonin reuptake inhibitor; SNRI = selective norepinephrine reuptake inhibitor; NDRI = norepinephrine and dopamine reuptake Inhibitor; SMS = serotonin modulator and stimulator.

are antidepressants, anxiolytics, mood stabilizers, antipsychotics, and stimulants. For each classification, we explore contraindications for use and abuse potential. A drug has a contraindication when its use can have serious adverse effects, particularly if the drug interacts with other medications a person is taking. Abuse potential is the likelihood that a person might abuse a drug because of the hedonic effect the drug elicits. The only psychotropic drug classes that have abuse potential are the antianxiety and stimulant medications. It should be noted that psychotropic drugs reduce symptoms and improve quality of life but are not a cure for any mental disorder.

Antidepressants

Antidepressants are the most commonly prescribed psychotropic drug class, taken by 11% of Americans older than age 11 years (Centers for Disease Control and Prevention, 2011). Antidepressants are typically used to treat depression, along with anxiety and obsessive–compulsive disorder. Antidepressants are relatively safe medications, with low abuse potential. Currently, the most commonly prescribed types of antidepressants are selective serotonin reuptake inhibitors and selective norepinephrine reuptake inhibitors because they have less pronounced side effects compared with older agents such as monoamine oxidase inhibitors and tricyclics. All antidepressant medications seem to have equivalent effectiveness in relieving depression symptoms, although some antidepressants work better than others depending on the person. Antidepressants have relatively long half-lives, with agents such as fluoxetine (Prozac) taking 6 weeks to reach therapeutic level (steady state). When a client feels an antidepressant is not relieving symptoms after taking it as prescribed for at least 2 months, counselors should encourage and coach the client to talk to his or her psychopharmacologist. Because of the risk of a serious adverse reaction called *serotonin syndrome,* a person should take only one antidepressant at a time unless titrating from one medication to another.

Anxiolytics

Anxiety-related disorders are treated with anxiolytics, in addition to antidepressants. The most commonly used anxiolytics are benzodiazepines, used to reduce symptoms of acute anxiety such as panic attacks, extreme worry, and fear. Benzodiazepines increase the neurotransmission of gamma-aminobutyric acid, producing a sedating, sleep-inducing, muscle-relaxing, and anti-anxiety effect. Benzodiazepines work much faster than antidepressants, with effects observable in minutes. Their short half-life and hedonic properties mean that benzodiazepines such as Klonopin, Xanax, and Valium have a high abuse potential and should only be prescribed on a short-term or as-needed basis. Tolerance can occur, and sudden withdrawal can be severe (Sadock & Sadock, 2014). For this reason, benzodiazepines should be prescribed to persons with active substance use disorders with caution. Benzodiazepines are contraindicated during pregnancy because their use during the first trimester has been shown to cause birth defects and other infant problems (Sadock & Sadock, 2014). Benzodiazepines should be prescribed with caution to older adults, who may become more somnolent and confused when using them (Ruscin & Linnebur, 2016). This cognitive impairment can result in falls and fractures. Billioti de Gage et al. (2014) found that benzodiazepine use was also associated with increased risk of Alzheimer's disease in a large sample of older adults.

Beta-blockers may be also used to manage the physical effects of anxiety such as rapid heartbeat, trembling, and sweating by blocking the release of epinephrine and norepinephrine. Other anxiolytics include buspirone (Buspar), which is often used to augment (i.e., used concurrently with) antidepressant treatment. Barbiturates are an older group of antianxiety agents that are less commonly used today because of their side effect profile.

Mood Stabilizers

Mood stabilizers are used to treat mania in bipolar disorder and mood swings associated with other mental disorders. Lithium is the most popular mood stabilizer. Only recently has research understood how it works in the brain. A meta-analysis of brain imaging data from people with bipolar disorder obtained from 11 international research groups found that individuals with bipolar disorder not taking lithium had reduced cerebral and hippocampal volumes compared with a comparison group of people without bipolar disorder (Hallahan et al., 2011). People with bipolar disorder who were taking lithium had significantly increased hippocampal and amygdala volume, suggesting that use of lithium can make up for structural brain alterations in people with bipolar disorder (Hallahan et al., 2011). Anticonvulsant medication developed to treat seizure disorders has also been shown to have mood-stabilizing actions.

Mood stabilizer medications can have serious and severe side effects and must be monitored closely for development of problems. For example, failure to remain adequately hydrated when taking lithium can result in lithium toxicity. Thus, people taking lithium should avoid diuretics such as caffeine and alcohol and drink plenty of water. Most mood stabilizers are contraindicated during pregnancy (Sadock & Sadock, 2014), and pregnant women with bipolar disorder typically have to stop these medications, resulting in increased risk of manic episodes.

Antipsychotics

Antipsychotic medications are major tranquilizers that are effective in reducing symptoms of psychosis such as hallucinations and delusions that are associated with schizophrenia and acute mania. The abuse potential for antipsychotic drugs is small. Older agents are called first-generation antipsychotics and can have the problematic side effect of involuntary muscle movements known as extrapyramidal symptoms. If these persist, they can become a chronic condition known as tardive dyskinesia. Newer second-generation atypical antipsychotics are less likely to cause extrapyramidal side effects, although they are more likely to cause metabolic side effects resulting in weight gain, increased cholesterol, and increased blood sugar that can progress to Type 2 diabetes (Sadock & Sadock, 2014). Because of these problematic side effects, adherence to antipsychotic treatment can be a significant treatment barrier. Antipsychotics work by blocking the dopamine receptor (agonists). Newer second-generation atypical antipsychotics also block the serotonin receptor. Atypical antipsychotics are also indicated for use in extreme aggression found in autism, and aripiprazole (Abilify) is Food and Drug Administration–approved for adjunctive treatment in major depression and Tourette's disorder.

Stimulants

Stimulants are most commonly prescribed to treat symptoms of attention-deficit/hyperactivity disorder by increasing dopamine transmission in the synapse through either enhanced presynaptic release or reuptake inhibition. Stimulants increase alertness, attention, and energy as well as elevate blood pressure, respiration, and heart rate (Sadock & Sadock, 2014). Most stimulants are either amphetamine (e.g., Adderall) or methylphenidate (e.g., Ritalin) products. Stimulants are also used to treat narcolepsy and chronic depression that has not responded to other treatment. Stimulants have a high abuse potential because of several factors. First, they have hedonic properties when taken at a high dose. Second, stimulants improve performance for most people, and high school and college students may purchase or share stimulants to improve attention and concentration during academic study sessions or examinations. Third, persons with eating disorders can misuse stimulants for their side effect of appetite suppression. Although more empirical research is needed, a longitudinal study found no evidence of problematic long-term effects such as stunted growth (Harstad et al., 2014). As with all psychotropic medications, pregnant women should discuss the use of stimulants with their prescriber.

Medication Referrals and Consultation

Referral to a prescriber of psychotropic medication is indicated by several factors (Field, 2016). Clients who are experiencing an acute change in their functioning are in need of a general medical evaluation first and may need a subsequent medication referral. Referrals are also indicated for acute conditions such as delirium, seizures, and neurovegetative symptoms of depression (e.g., changes in sleep, appetite, concentration, anhedonia, hypoactivity, and loss of energy). When a client is experiencing symptoms of schizophrenia or mania, referral to a psychopharmacologist as part of the treatment plan is considered a best practice.

Counselors should immediately refer clients to their psychopharmacologist when they are experiencing serious and potentially life-threatening side effects, such as Stevens-Johnson syndrome with use of lamotrigine (Sadock & Sadock, 2014). Similarly, clients who are withdrawing from chemical addictions may require specialized medical treatment to avoid medical complications associated with withdrawal. Clients with medical

Reflective Questions

Risperidone is an atypical antipsychotic medication.

Why might Charlie be taking this medication?

What are the benefits and risks?

issues should be carefully monitored. If their condition progressively declines, such as with neurocognitive disorders, the psychopharmacologist should be notified.

Consultation With Psychopharmacologists

When providing counseling services, consultation with psychopharmacologists can be crucial to ensuring the client is receiving integrated services in a complementary fashion that enhances the overall effectiveness of treatment (Field, 2016). For example, clients who are taking stimulants for attention-deficit/hyperactivity disorder may be better able to attend during therapy sessions, and their adherence to medication may optimize counseling sessions. Clients who feel their antidepressant has stopped working effectively may have less energy to attend to the tasks of therapy (DeRubeis, Siegle, & Hollon, 2008). Consultation often requires that the client sign a release so that protected health information from one provider can be shared with another. In the case of Charlie, the counselor should reach out to the primary care physician to better understand the provider's diagnosis and medication management plan. Although Charlie does not appear to be experiencing schizophrenia or mania, he is currently taking an antipsychotic, considered to be a medication that is best prescribed by a specialist (i.e., psychopharmacologist). One might wonder whether Charlie needs to be seen by a psychopharmacologist to ensure that he is receiving the best possible care in a complex case. This discussion with the primary care physician could be crucial.

Counselors can prepare for consultation meetings by preparing a list of symptoms that the client is experiencing, using terminology from the mental status examination. Counselors should also know the medications taken by the client and any client-reported side effects. Counselors should also avoid making medication recommendations because this is outside their scope of practice and may cast doubt on other information the counselor has shared (Field, 2016).

Consultations With Clients

At times, the client may ask the counselor for information about his or her medication. The counselor's role in this situation is to reinforce the importance of the client's relationship with the psychopharmacologist and prepare the client to bring up concerns regarding the medication with his or her medical provider in their next appointment (Field, 2016). Clients may feel anxious

Reflective Question

Practice role-playing a consultation with the primary care physician about Charlie's case.

How might you bring up concerns about the need for more specialized care?

about this encounter and hesitate to bring up important information about medication-related concerns. Clients can feel more prepared by writing down questions and role-playing the conversation, and the counselor could even attend the next medication management appointment (Field, 2016). The counselor could also discuss his or her ancillary role

Reflective Question

Read through the case of Charlie again.

Practice role-playing how to prepare Charlie's family for their next appointment with the primary care physician.

in monitoring the client's symptoms and side effects. Although medication-related questions should be deferred to the client's psychopharmacologist, the counselor can provide information about how to adhere to a medication regimen. As with other neuroscientific information, counselors should present information to clients about medications in a clear, concise manner that "distills without diluting" information (Field, 2016, p. 4). For example, it is more important for a client to understand that an antidepressant needs to be taken once a day to reach steady state than to understand the half-life and pharmacokinetics of antidepressants.

Our Brain-Based Approach to the Case of Charlie

Charlie's parents were lacking information about their son's condition. After consulting with the primary care provider, I (Nancy Sherman) received information that Charlie had been comprehensively assessed and diagnosed with autism. He was taking risperidone for acute aggressive episodes at home. I used this information to discuss Charlie's diagnosis and all available treatment options with his mother and grandmother. After this conversation, they understood the importance of an integrative approach. With Charlie's assent, my neurocounseling approach was to incorporate applied behavior analysis with neurofeedback to provide positive reinforcement for developing frustration tolerance and functional communication through classical and operant conditioning. A referral was made to a practitioner specializing in applied behavior analysis treatment. The treatment plan included medication management for risperidone, with a goal for the family to eventually wean Charlie off the drug at the direction of the primary care provider. An important adjunctive intervention was to provide parent education and space for the family to process their adjustment to and feelings of loss at their son's autism diagnosis. By reviewing all treatment options, the client and family were able to make an informed choice about what approach worked best for them.

What might the counselor have missed had she not consulted with the primary care provider?

Conclusion

Although counselors are not medical professionals, they need to have a working knowledge of the uses and misuses of psychotropic drugs to provide the best treatment possible. Counselors develop the type of therapeutic relationship that is often not possible with a medical professional. In this relationship, clients can learn about how their medication works, the potential for side effects and problem use, and how to take their medication as prescribed. Counselors can provide proper monitoring and prepare clients to discuss their medication with their psychopharmacologist. When the client is a child, the counselor should include parents when asking questions about medication response.

Quiz

1. When the amount of the drug available to the body is the same as the amount being eliminated, then _____ has been achieved.
   a. Half-life.
   b. Pharmacokinetic balance.
   c. Steady state.
   d. Partial state.
2. Which of the following is not a pharmacokinetic process?
   a. Excretion.
   b. Metabolism.
   c. Absorption.
   d. Accumulation.
3. What type of receptor would a serotonin neurotransmitter bind to?
   a. Serotonin receptor.
   b. Dopamine receptor.
   c. Serotonin neurotransmitters do not bind to receptors.
   d. GABA receptor.

References

Billioti de Gage, S., Moride, Y., Ducruet, T., Kurth, T., Verdoux, H., Tournier, . . . Bégaud, B. (2014). Benzodiazepine use and risk of Alzheimer's disease: Case-control study. *BMJ, 349,* 349. http://dx.doi.org/10.1136/bmj.g5205

Centers for Disease Control and Prevention. (2011). Antidepressant use in persons aged 12 and older: United States, 2005-2008. *National Center for Human Statistics Data Brief, 2011*(76), 1–8.

Council for the Accreditation of Counseling and Related Educational Programs. (2015). *2016 CACREP standards.* Retrieved from http://www.cacrep.org/wp-content/uploads/2012/10/2016-CACREP-Standards.pdf

DeRubeis, R. J., Siegle, G. J., & Hollon, S. D. (2008). Cognitive therapy versus medication for depression: Treatment outcomes and neural mechanisms. *Nature Reviews Neuroscience, 9,* 788–796. http://dx.doi.org/10.1038/nrn2345

Field, T. A. (2016). *The clinical mental health counselor's role in medication management* (AMHCA Clinical Practice Brief). Alexandria, VA: American Mental Health Counselors Association. Retrieved from http://www.amhca.org

Hallahan, B., Newell, J., Soares, J. C., Brambilla, P., Strawkowski, S. M., Fleck, D. E., . . . McDonald, C. (2011). Structural magnetic resonance imaging in bipolar disorder: An international collaborative mega-analysis of individual adult patient data. *Biological Psychiatry, 69,* 326–335. https://www.ncbi.nlm.nih.gov/pubmed/21030008

Harstad, E. B., Weaver, A. L., Katusic, S. K., Colligan, R. C., Kumar, S., Chan, E., . . . Barberesi, W. J. (2014). ADHD, stimulant treatment, and growth: A longitudinal study. *Pediatrics, 134,* e935–e944. http://dx.doi.org/10.1542/peds.2014-0428

Kramer, T. A. M. (2003). Side effects and therapeutic effects. *Medscape General Medicine, 5*(1), 28.

Medco Health Solutions. (2010). *America's state of mind.* Franklin Lakes, NJ: Author. Retrieved from http://apps.who.int/medicinedocs/en/d/Js19032en/

Preston, J. D., O'Neal, J. H., & Talaga, M. C. (2013). *Handbook of clinical psychopharmacology for therapists* (7th ed.). Oakland, CA: New Harbinger.

Ruscin, J. M., & Linnebur, S. A. (2016). *Aging and drugs.* Retrieved from http://www.merckmanuals.com/professional/SearchResults?query=Aging+and+Drugs&icd9=MM138%3bMM139%3bMM140%3bMM141%3bMM142

Sadock, B. J., & Sadock, V. A. (2014). *Synopsis of psychiatry* (11th ed.). New York, NY: Lippincott, Williams & Wilkins.

Part IV
EMERGING NEUROSCIENCE-INFORMED MODALITIES

The fourth section of the book introduces you to emerging neuroscience-informed approaches to the specialized modalities of group work and career counseling. The chapters included in this section present novel approaches to integrating neuroscience into counseling practice.

■ ■ ■

Chapter 11

Neuro-Informed Group Work

Chad Luke and Joel F. Diambra

Neuroscience has the potential to explain, inform, and guide the group process. The integration of neuroscience with group counseling need not create a whole new paradigm of group counseling. Rather, neuroscience both explicates group processes and adds illustrative, metaphorical imagery. These benefits can help clients make effective use of their time in group. With that foundation in mind, we describe the group process from beginning to end from a neuroscience-informed perspective. This chapter describes a neuroscience-informed approach to group counseling that is organized by the stages of the group process, with special consideration to applying therapeutic factors of group work (Yalom, 1995; Yalom & Leszcz, 2005) through the lens of neuroscience. We consider the stages of planning, preparing participants, setting the stage by establishing group norms, and getting to the working stage so that members experience therapeutic factors of group work. This chapter describes the case of Susan to help you facilitate the group process by understanding the neuroscience of group interaction. Reflection questions are provided at the end of each section to assist you in taking a thoughtful approach to facilitating the group process.

2016 CACREP Standards

This chapter addresses sections of the 2016 Council for Accreditation of Counseling and Related Educational Programs (CACREP) Standards pertinent to the common core area of Group Counseling and Group Work (Standard II.F.6.):

- Therapeutic factors and how they contribute to group effectiveness (Standard II.F.6.c.)
- Characteristics and functions of effective group leaders (Standard II.F.6.d.)
- Types of groups and other considerations that affect conducting groups in varied settings (Standard II.F.6.f.H1.)

■ ■ ■

 ## Clinical Case Study: Susan

Susan is a 35-year-old woman referred to group by her individual counselor to address issues related to life transitions. She has been a willing participant in individual counseling for the past 6 weeks, but both she and her counselor feel as though they have reached the point at which she would make greater gains in group counseling. On entry into the group, Susan describes a number of transitions in her life, including a career change, family conflicts, and relationship challenges with her husband of 13 years. It is clear from the start that Susan is in pain, feels stuck at this point in her life, and has been primed to describe her struggles in great detail. It also becomes readily apparent in the group counseling environment that some members appear overwhelmed by the amount of speech Susan uses to describe her feelings. There is also a sense that these lengthy descriptions create more distance between Susan and other group members as opposed to drawing her closer to them. The counselor recognizes this because she closely observes the nonverbal responses of other members as Susan shares; in addition, she can sense the energy in the room—it appears to flatten as Susan speaks. The counselor attempts to solicit feedback from group members regarding Susan's participation, but the members seem unable or unwilling to articulate their experience.

The counselor does two things at this point: First, she pauses to observe and reflect on what is happening in the group during these times. The counselor asks Susan whether the reactions and responses of the group to what she is saying remind her of people in her life and how they may respond to her. Susan affirms that she rarely, if ever, feels heard and valued, and now that she thinks about it, this seems to be happening in the group as well. The counselor also asks what Susan is seeking from the group and wonders what the payoff for her talking might be. Susan initially appears confused by the question but is soon able to communicate that she wants others to understand and appreciate how stuck she feels in her life. The counselor thanks Susan for her candor and asks the group members how they feel about Susan's identified goal for the group. The consensus of the group members is that this is the first time they have felt connected to Susan and understood what she needed from them.

We now turn to the process that resulted in this powerful group intervention occurring.

Planning a Group: Choosing a Format

When planning a group, the leader might consider whether a process group or psychoeducational group is indicated. In neuro-informed group counseling, however, process groups can be combined with psychoeducation, and should be. As noted in the preceding vignette, clients can often hide behind both silence and words that obfuscate their meaning. This is often done unintentionally, but these patterns of communication have likely contributed to the struggles they now face. Focusing on process-based education assists clients in identifying their blind spots by experiencing and elucidating what is happening in the here and now and offering them a chance to reconsider their interactive patterns and try something different.

As a holistic learner, the brain adapts best when multiple modalities are engaged. Siegel (2015) and Badenoch and Cox (2010) described the value of bilateral integration, also known as *interhemispheric integration* or *interhemispheric transfer,* wherein the right and left sides of the corpus callosum work in a complementary fashion. This results in the logical, literal left hemisphere of the brain working in tension with the creative, holistic, emotion-based right hemisphere. The balance in group is critical. This can also be seen in the concept of vertical integration, wherein the body, the emotions, and the mind are in synchrony. These integrations can also represent the cohesion and complementarity with members in group. We advocate for using experiential process-based group activities that facilitate learning of principles. Groups are uniquely able to implement experiential interventions and education because clients have the opportunity to practice new learning in the moment in group. In planning a neuro-informed, experiential group, it is important to recognize Susan's potential for success in this format and modality.

Reflective Questions

Would a process group or psychoeducational group be most helpful to Susan?

Is there something specific she needs to learn and, if so, is this best accomplished through cognitive assent or experiential learning?

Preparing Participants: Pregroup Meetings

Learned paralysis is a useful metaphor for clients' experiences as they enter the group counseling room. Clients who have experienced a variety of unresolved losses can acquire learned paralysis in social, emotional, and behavioral functioning; they may inhibit, restrict, and withdraw. When a person feels threatened, chemicals such as cortisol are released as the sympathetic branch of the autonomic nervous system is activated, which can restrict behavior. Gladding (2016) and Yalom and Leszcz (2005) advocated for helping clients know what to expect from a group experience to ease anxiety and defensiveness. Informing participants about the group ahead of time reduces a person's likelihood of feeling threatened and increases the likelihood that the person can be fully engaged from the outset. This preparation readies the autonomic nervous system for the experience. Informing participants about the group ahead of time reduces their likelihood of feeling threatened and thus the possibility of being overwhelmed. Group counseling offers these clients a way to rehabilitate psychological dimensions that have fallen prey to the survival reflex of paralysis. Sklare (2014) referred to this type of preparation as flagging the minefield. Susan's counselor will help Susan identify the ways in which a group counseling setting might activate defensive responses and what those responses would look like in session. These conversations will assist Susan to calibrate her expectations of both her own autonomic responses to group and the dynamics in the group milieu.

Setting the Stage: Establishing Group Norms

Talking to members about group norms is essential to setting up a group. In establishing group norms, two guidelines are essential, at least when considering neuroscience integration: (a) no storytelling and (b) no gossiping.

No Storytelling

The first rule of counseling is that it is the counselor's responsibility to teach clients how to be group members. This is critical to beginning—and finishing—well in counseling because group members do not know what is expected from them in this environment, nor do they know what they can or should expect from counseling. Group members often have a firm belief that for counseling to be effective, they have to tell the full story of their experiences, often in great detail. Members are right to believe this,

> **Reflective Question**
>
> What additional information could have been helpful for Susan to know before group?

in that they are attached to their stories. In the past, some counselors have been trained to inform group members that they have been misled in believing that telling their stories with all the details is crucial for success. Given the current state of neuroscience and

Reflective Question

What purpose might Susan's storytelling serve her in the world outside of group?

its integration with counseling, this may be erroneous reasoning. A group member's need to share his or her story may be linked to the memory's role in constructing a personal narrative when influenced by fluctuating perceptions and emotions.

In group, an individual's self-debasing storytelling, in an attempt to establish reasons for his or her helpless state, can have the effect of manipulating individual group members to agree with the client and enable the client's helplessness. In turn, this type of unhealthy collusion can negatively affect the group dynamics in general. As an alternative, we invite group members to describe how a particular story is affecting them in the present time and place. For example, as a member begins to tell a story, we might ask the member to pause in the telling of it and focus on his or her breathing and other autonomic responses (though we do not typically use words like *autonomic* in our groups) as the member recalls the situation. Not only is the impact of reconsidering the memory in the here and now of emotions and context much more informative than the member sharing the content of the story, but it also seems to have more positive clinical impact on the individual and the group as a whole.

Unbeknownst to Susan, her retelling of the reasons for her despair may actually be reinforcing it (Hayes, 2004) by creating the perception that the past is present in the present. Her counselor and the group describe the phenomenon of contagion, wherein the mirror neuron system in the brains of the group members simulates Susan's described experience. This can lead to the emotional experiences of one person encroaching on the emotions of the observer (Iacoboni, 2009), particularly in vulnerable individuals. Although there is nothing inherently wrong about Susan sharing her past, counselors in neuro-informed group process recognize the risks to Susan herself and to the other group members.

No Gossiping

Participants are encouraged to refrain from discussing in detail the behaviors of individuals who are not group members. Clients seem quite attentive to the actions of other people (non–group members) in their lives and will frequently use group time to discuss their antics. As an alternative, we have one therapeutic phrase that we often use in gossip situations: "Don't tell us; show us—show us how thinking about this experience is affecting you." As we have learned from gestalt therapy and other experiential approaches, words deceive, but the body rarely lies. Herein is the junction between group facilitation and neuroscience integration. In teaching and writing about the integration of neuroscience and counseling, we often ask clients and students to think about brain function in terms of the Internet rather than a telephone line. Despite descriptions of neurobiological structures, systems, and functions, the brain is best understood as a system of systems, constantly and inextricably connected. For the sake of simplicity, descriptions of neuronal communication are often reduced to neuron-to-neuron communication. In the same way, and in terms of gestalt therapy, accurate communication requires holism, the sense that words and behaviors are united (Perls, 1976). Counseling is more effective when clients can move out from behind their words (and words about others) to demonstrate their experience of relationships within the group environment.

Susan may have learned that indirect communication is the least risky way of getting her needs met. In group, the counselor will assist her in bringing her communication into direct contact with others, both by speaking directly to group members when talking to and about them and via role-plays in which she can practice direct communication. In the group, the counselor and members can supply Susan with cues that remind her to regulate her sympathetic response to this new type of communication.

Getting to the Working Stage: Focusing on Process

One of the challenges that can get counselors into trouble when facilitating groups is getting the "math" of group wrong. A group of five members is not like counseling five group members times one (individual) session. Group interactions are much more complicated than this simple math. Rather, it is more accurate to think of it as five group members times the number of individuals times the dyads and triads in the group, all multiplied by the group facilitator interactions! This exponentially increases the number of interactions and relationship dynamics occurring in the group counseling setting. Group work requires continual attention to each individual as well as to the interactions between any two or more group members, plus the potential responses of all group members to any comment or issue.

Managing this type of interactional dynamics requires a focused counselor. One way that we might leverage these dynamics in a group with Susan is to have each member of the group represent Susan's self-talk. For example, we have

Reflective Question

What purpose might Susan's gossiping serve her in the world outside of group?

asked clients like Susan to identify self-defeating statements and then assign each of these statements. Susan might stand in the center of the group and be asked to perform a Mini-Mental State Examination item. For instance, we ask Susan to count backward from 100 by sevens (reverse serial sevens). As she prepares for the task, we also ask

Reflective Question

What might have been the consequence if the facilitator had focused solely on Susan's story instead of asking other members to give input?

each group member to say aloud the self-statement they are portraying, increasing their volume each time. Rarely is a client able to complete this task without getting flustered, and for good reason. Susan was able to directly experience her negative self-talk during a basic task, highlighting her struggle to perform more complicated daily social tasks. She was just unaware of this noise before this intervention.

Impact of the Working Stage

Groups that reach the working stage experience numerous benefits, including the ability for participants to experience therapeutic factors of group work. Yalom (1995) identified 11 factors that make group therapy effective and lead to positive outcomes, and for decades these factors have driven the field of group counseling. Here, we briefly outline these factors, provide a brief definition, and make links to the literature on neuroscience and its integration with counseling.

Therapeutic Factors of Group Work

Altruism

Group counseling provides members the opportunity to share what they have learned and to offer selfless or mutually beneficial emotional support and encouragement to other group members. Displaying altruism in group results in gaining neural support. For example, neurochemicals associated with reward centers in the brain, such as the neuropeptides oxytocin and vasopressin, have been linked to altruistic behaviors (De Dreu et al., 2010; Insel, 2010). De Dreu and Kret (2016) described the role of oxytocin in what they called the "tend and defend" function of this neuropeptide. When given the opportunity to share their lived experience with another group member, participants can experience a reward, both anecdotally and neurologically (Andreoni & Rao, 2011).

Cohesion

In group counseling, a skilled facilitator can and must create an atmosphere and experience that draws individuals into a sense of "we-ness." In a body of literature reviewed by Inzlicht, Gutsell, and

Legault (2012), individuals who imitated the behaviors of those they perceived as significantly different (outgroup; us vs. them) demonstrated increased empathy—neurologically! Oxytocin is a neuropeptide that plays an instrumental role in social connectedness (Anacker & Beery, 2013). However, this role is mediated by the effects of early relationships and current contexts. For example, the researchers reviewed literature on primates and demonstrated in animal models that early attachment issues can be exacerbated by oxytocin during social interactions by increasing perceived threats.

Instillation of Hope
Group members benefit from being able to see a brighter future for themselves in the lives of fellow group members who have made progress in a particular area.

Universality
Group members benefit from sensing their individuality as well as their membership in a group. Membership helps members realize that they are not alone in their experiences. Michael and Luke (2016) described a phenomenon they called *projective sympathy*, in which an individual attempts to sense another's experience by comparing how she or he would feel in the described situation and then assumes that is how the other individual feels. Therapeutic universality, in contrast, is created in group by facilitators who enjoin members to take responsibility for their experiences as their own; the facilitator then assists members in making crucial connections to others (linking) while maintaining their experiences as their own.

Imparting Information
Psychoeducation is a function of most effective treatment approaches, whether expressed didactically (as in cognitive behavior therapy) or experientially (as in gestalt therapy). Clients need to experience cognitive growth as part of the group process to transfer group experiences to their lives outside of group. The development of insight is vital to transferring group learning to real-world emotional application. We feel that one of the most ethical, effective ways that counselors can begin integrating neuroscience into counseling is through the use of metaphors. Metaphors have been demonstrated time and again to be effective counseling tools (Tay, 2012; Wickman, Daniels, White, & Fesmire, 1999) and to have a neuroscientific impact (McGeoch, Brang, & Ramachandran, 2007). The metaphoric approach to integration and synthesis lends itself particularly well to group counseling. Clients can best learn information about their brain via concepts and ideas they already understand.

Corrective Recapitulation of the Primary Family Group
Group counseling creates a microcosm of social systems, especially family social systems, and as such it offers members the opportunity to revisit painful family issues in a safe environment. The first group

that humans typically experience is their family. Unfortunately, this first group experience is not always positive. As Schore and McIntosh (2011) have demonstrated empirically, early relationships shape later ones; brains develop around these relationships. Group counseling is a place for clients to unlearn old relational patterns and relearn (rewire the brain) new ones to increase their interpersonal efficacy. This can be accomplished through role-play, with group members taking on family members' roles and the client practicing different interactive patterns with mock family members. These interactive patterns can create healthier family dynamics and generalize to interactions outside the nuclear family, with friends, peers, partners, and so forth.

Imitative Behavior

One of the principal factors and main components of group efficacy is the opportunity to model adaptive behaviors between and among group members. From an evolutionary–developmental perspective, this imitation has been—and is—critical to survival, and therefore the brain has adapted in ways that facilitate imitation (Oberman, Pineda, & Ramachandran, 2007). Group leaders attend to the space between clients (discussed later) during group because of the implicit receptivity people's brains have to one another (Schermer, 2010). Mirror neurons are the neurons in the motor cortex that appear to fire when observing another's action, as though the observer had initiated the actions. This has been described as an adaptive mechanism for rapid learning (imitative behavior or social modeling) as well as for social functioning (Iacoboni, 2009). In the case of the latter, it is important that social organisms make inferences about the emotions and therefore the intentions of others rapidly.

Although mirror neurons have been heralded in the counseling field as evidence that humans are wired for empathy (Ivey, Ivey, & Zalaquett, 2013), they also seem to prove that humans are wired for imitation. Ramachandran (2000) described this in terms of the adaptive efficiency of seeing and then doing, compared with waiting for each individual in a group to discover skills individually. He noted that learning that would have taken generations to complete can now take place almost instantaneously through observation and imitation.

The role of the group leader is vital to blocking and protecting members from emotional contagion and excessive exposure. For example, group members can serve as mirrors to fellow members who have experienced losses in their lives. After mirroring other group members, these peers can then, while being observed, demonstrate or model healthy communications that can aid in relieving their own pain.

Socialization Techniques

A foundational component of any group is the opportunity it provides for members to interact with each other. Many clients enter group counseling either without ever having developed effective social skills or with diminished social skills as a result of life stressors. Groups create a laboratory of sorts for members to experiment with new ways of behaving in social environments.

Cozolino (2014) referred to the "social synapse" when writing about the social neuroscience of therapy. Nowhere is this more clearly illustrated than in group counseling. In the brain, a synapse is best thought of as a verb instead of a noun. An action potential stimulates a neuron to send its signal down the axon to the terminal, triggering the vesicles to release their neurotransmitters into the synaptic cleft (the microscopic space between axons and dendrites). This event (synapse) allows for the transmission of signals from one neuron to the next without them being in direct, physical, permanent contact. This happens in an instant through the 100 billion neurons in the human brain, resulting in trillions of these events in a relatively short period of time. The product of these events is cognition, emotion, behavior, and myriad involuntary processes vital to survival. In group counseling, the social synapse metaphor can be seen very clearly. In group, it is the space between members where therapy happens. Neurologically, the social synaptic connections are there, whether seen or unseen. Multiple bodies of literature (summarized by Cozolino, 2014) have demonstrated the implicit effects that humans have on one another. Group therapy illuminates these effects during interactive moments. It seems that, from a brain-based perspective, "we are made for group" (Carter, 2014, p. 49; Flores, 2010).

Interpersonal Learning

One of the most important skills a group facilitator can impart to group members is the power "to be" with others and with oneself (see literature reviewed by Oberman et al., 2007). Yalom and Leszcz (2005) explained that group leaders can facilitate interpersonal learning by getting out of the way of the group process. In this approach, the group facilitator is the process expert, and the group members are the content experts. Yalom and Leszcz suggested that the role of the group leader should be to activate the group and illuminate the here-and-now process of what is occurring between group members. Kottler (2000) and Kottler and Englar-Carlson (2015) reasserted the notion that the person of the group leader is the most useful tool ever present and available to the counselor.

Catharsis

Common emotional expressions experienced in counseling include anger outbursts, crying, and laughter. When expressing emotions (i.e., anger, sorrow, laughter), people feel relieved, and the brain's limbic system releases dopamine. Dopamine is a naturally occurring pleasure hormone released by the brain in anticipation of, or in response to, enjoyable stimuli.

190

Existential Factors

Group counseling provides an environment for members to wrestle with the likely sources of dysfunction, such as anxiety regarding the purpose and the ultimate end of life. Meaning-making and taking on responsibility are essential to living a life of purpose, not just to managing symptoms. Frankl (1959/2006) believed that finding a balance between freedom and responsibility was essential to optimal living. Finding such a balance often requires personal insight into one's choices and life course. The integration of the brain regions associated with survival (hindbrain), emotions (midbrain), and cognition (forebrain) enables the capacity for higher order thinking, such as the development of insight (Siegel, 2015).

> **Reflective Question**
>
> How might you draw on the power of the group to help Susan?

Our Brain-Based Approach to Group Counseling

Ramachandran (2000) suggested that human brains are best studied in relationship to one another rather than in isolation. When people observe another's perceived pain (e.g., being pricked with a needle), the mirror neurons in their brain exhibit the same firing pattern as though it happened to them. However, they do not experience the localized pain (the needle prick) because the brain sends a nullifying message that conflicts with (neutralizes) the mirrored experience. People have the capacity to understand the pain of others as separate from their own, at least under healthy circumstances. This chapter outlined an approach to group work that is experiential and process based, using neuroscientific findings to explain why such an approach can be beneficial.

In our brain-based approach to group counseling, we prepared Susan for the group during the planning and prescreening processes. We facilitated positive expectations for the group experience, assisting Susan to tolerate the ambiguity of the group experience. Once in group, we used experiential activities to engage Susan. For instance, when Susan experienced the intolerable state of not story-telling, we encouraged her to demonstrate what it felt like to hold back. In doing so, her behaviors signaled memories, cognitions, and emotions in

> **Reflective Question**
>
> How could a brain-based understanding of humans' interconnectedness help the group leader to intervene with Susan?

other group members as their brains connected to hers. Through this process, Susan came to develop a new skill set, that of bringing her behavior into harmony—congruence—with her verbalizations. In terms of vertical integration, Susan's body acted out the feelings in her limbic system, which up to this point had been circumvented by her cerebral cortex. This renewed sense of wholeness played out in her relationships with her group members. Eventually, Susan became more congruent in her relationships outside of group, in her personal life. By the close of her group experience, Susan's mixed messages, passive–aggressive comments, and relational dissatisfaction were all reduced.

Conclusion

This chapter outlined an approach to group work that is experiential and process based, using neuroscience findings to explain why and how such an approach can be beneficial. Group facilitators do not need extensive neuroscientific knowledge to use the principles of neuro-informed counseling. In fact, Yalom and Leszcz's (2005) admonition to stay in the here and now of group and for facilitators to illuminate the group process rings true in our brain-based approach to group counseling.

Quiz

1. What factors make group so complex?
   a. The numerous points of interactions (dyads and triads) between and among members to which a facilitator must attend.
   b. The sheer number of people in a group at a given time.
   c. Therapeutic factors that make it difficult for the group to come together to work on their goals.
   d. The need for group leaders to maintain control of the group at all times and members' unpredictability.

2. What is social synapse as it applies to neuroscience and group counseling?
   a. Social media for people interested in the brain and neuroscience.
   b. The connections among individuals that produce a network of functioning that is similar to neural networks.
   c. The primarily cognitive process in group counseling that requires the use of multiple neural synapses.
   d. Emotion-control neurons in the brain when in group.

3. According to the authors, what is the problem with storytelling from a neuroscience perspective?
   a. Nothing is wrong with storytelling because catharsis is one of the therapeutic factors.
   b. Group members are often disingenuous and should not be trusted to tell their story.

   c. Storytelling can activate group members' fight-or-flight response; a no-storytelling guideline is for their protection.

   d. Memory is not recall as much as it is reconstitution, so storytelling in the wrong context can bias the story and distort perception.

References

Anacker, A. M., & Beery, A. K. (2013). Life in groups: The roles of oxytocin in mammalian sociality. *Frontiers in Behavioral Neuroscience, 7,* 185.

Andreoni, J., & Rao, J. M. (2011). The power of asking: How communication affects selfishness, empathy, and altruism. *Journal of Public Economics, 95,* 513–520.

Badenoch, B., & Cox, P. (2010). Integrating interpersonal neurobiology with group psychotherapy. *International Journal of Group Psychotherapy, 60,* 462–481.

Carter, P. D. (2014). Phantoms in the brain. *Groupwork, 24*(2), 45–59.

Council for Accreditation of Counseling and Related Educational Programs. (2015). *2016 CACREP standards.* Retrieved from http://www.cacrep.org/wp-content/uploads/2012/10/2016-CACREP-Standards.pdf

Cozolino, L. (2014). *The neuroscience of human relationships: Attachment and the developing social brain* (2nd ed.). New York, NY: W. W. Norton.

De Dreu, C. K., Greer, L. L., Handgraaf, M. J., Shalvi, S., Van Kleef, G. A., Baas, M., . . . Feith, S. W. (2010). The neuropeptide oxytocin regulates parochial altruism in intergroup conflict among humans. *Science, 328,* 1408–1411. doi:10.1126/science.1189047

De Dreu, C. K., & Kret, M. E. (2016). Oxytocin conditions intergroup relations through upregulated in-group empathy, cooperation, conformity, and defense. *Biological Psychiatry, 79,* 165–173.

Flores, P. J. (2010). Group psychotherapy and neuro-plasticity: An attachment theory perspective. *International Journal of Group Psychotherapy, 60,* 546–570.

Frankl, V. E. (2006). *Man's search for meaning.* Boston, MA: Beacon Press. (Original work published 1959)

Gladding, S. T. (2016). *Groups: A counseling specialty* (7th ed.). New York, NY: Pearson.

Hayes, S. C. (2004). Acceptance and commitment therapy, relational frame theory, and the third wave of behavioral and cognitive therapies. *Behavior Therapy, 35,* 639–665.

Iacoboni, M. (2009). *Mirroring people: The new science of how we connect with others.* New York, NY: Macmillan.

Insel, T. R. (2010). The challenge of translation in social neuroscience: A review of oxytocin, vasopressin, and affiliative behavior. *Neuron, 65,* 768–779.

Inzlicht, M., Gutsell, J. N., & Legault, L. (2012). Mimicry reduces racial prejudice. *Journal of Experimental Social Psychology, 48,* 361–365.

Ivey, A. E., Ivey, M. B., & Zalaquett, C. P. (2013). *Intentional interviewing and counseling: Facilitating client development in a multicultural society* (8th ed.). Boston, MA: Cengage.

Kottler, J. A. (2000). *Learning group leadership: An experiential approach.* Boston, MA: Allyn & Bacon.

Kottler, J. A., & Englar-Carlson, M. (2015). *Learning group leadership: An experiential approach* (3rd ed.). New York, NY: Sage.

McGeoch, P. D., Brang, D., & Ramachandran, V. S. (2007). Apraxia, metaphor and mirror neurons. *Medical Hypotheses, 69,* 1165–1168.

Michael, T., & Luke, C. (2016). Utilizing a metaphoric approach to teach the neuroscience of play therapy: A pilot study. *International Journal of Play Therapy, 25,* 45–52.

Oberman, L. M., Pineda, J. A., & Ramachandran, V. S. (2007). The human mirror neuron system: A link between action observation and social skills. *Social Cognitive and Affective Neuroscience, 2,* 62–66.

Perls, F. (1976). *The gestalt approach and eye witness to therapy.* New York, NY: Bantam Books.

Ramachandran, V. S. (2000). Mirror neurons and imitation learning as the driving force behind "the great leap forward" in human evolution. Retrieved from https://www.edge.org/conversation/mirror-neurons-and-imitation-learning-as-the-driving-force-behind-the-great-leap-forward-in-human-evolution

Schermer, V. L. (2010). Mirror neurons: Their implications for group psychotherapy. *International Journal of Group Psychotherapy, 60,* 486–513.

Schore, A., & McIntosh, J. (2011). Family law and the neuroscience of attachment, Part I. *Family Court Review, 49,* 501–512.

Siegel, D. J. (2015). *The developing mind: How relationships and the brain interact to shape who we are.* New York, NY: Guilford Press.

Sklare, G. B. (2014). *Brief counseling that works: A solution-focused therapy approach for school counselors and other mental health professionals* (3rd ed.). Thousand Oaks, CA: Corwin.

Tay, D. (2012). Applying the notion of metaphor types to enhance counseling protocols. *Journal of Counseling & Development, 90,* 142–149.

Wickman, S. A., Daniels, M. H., White, L. J., & Fesmire, S. A. (1999). A "primer" in conceptual metaphor for counselors. *Journal of Counseling & Development, 77,* 389–394.

Yalom, I. D. (1995). *Theory and practice of group psychotherapy* (5th ed.). New York, NY: Basic Books.

Yalom, I. D., & Leszcz, M. (2005). *Theory and practice of group psychotherapy.* New York, NY: Basic Books.

Chapter 12

Neuro-Informed
Career-Focused Counseling

Chad Luke and Thomas A. Field

Neuroscience can inform effective practice in addressing career-related issues. To effectively integrate neuroscience into career counseling, counselors may need to adjust their perspective to see career issues as a clinical mental health counseling presenting problem, like and un-like other presenting problems, rather than as a stand-alone problem. Neuro-informed career-focused counseling[1] addresses career issues as a specific type of presenting problem in counseling, making them appropriate for integration with recent neuroscientific findings (Luke & Redekop, 2016). The field of neuroscience has yet to identify a "career region" of the brain; integration therefore requires taking a broader perspective by looking at indirect evidence. This is an issue of philosophical proportions, so to proceed carefully and as clearly as possible, it is helpful to use translational neuroscience to guide the process. Translational approaches, generally speaking, "examine how basic biological (i.e., brain-based mechanisms) and behavioral factors interact in initiating and sustaining positive behavior change as a result of psychotherapy" (Feldstein Ewing & Chung, 2013, p. 329). In other words, translational approaches assist with the process of applying basic scientific information to clinical practice (Woolf, 2008). One key approach to using translational neuroscience in career-focused counseling is through metaphors. The purpose of this chapter is to explore how neuroscientific literature and principles of-fer an innovative, metaphoric perspective on neuro-informed career-focused counseling.

---

[1] I (Chad Luke) owe a debt of gratitude to Seth Hayden for using this term in a panel presentation at the American Counseling Association Conference and Expo, ushering in new verbiage for describing the work counselors do with career-related issues.

2016 CACREP Standards

This chapter addresses sections of the 2016 Council for Accreditation of Counseling and Related Educational Programs (CACREP) Standards pertinent to the common core area of Career Development (Standard II.F.4.):

- Approaches for conceptualizing the interrelationships among and between work, mental well-being, relationships, and other life roles and factors (Standard II.F.4.b.)
- Strategies for facilitating client skill development for career, educational, and life-work planning and management (Standard II.F.4.h.)

This chapter also addresses the following Specialization Standard:

- Strategies to help clients develop skills needed to make life-work role transitions (Career Counseling, Standard V.B.3.b.)

■ ■ ■

Clinical Case Study: Larissa

Larissa is a woman in her 40s who meets with you for an intake to discuss phase-of-life issues. Your initial intake paperwork shows that she has been a stay-at-home mom rearing three children for the past 14 years. Larissa also recently separated from her husband of more than 15 years. She has a bachelor's degree in sociology but has never worked in a job that required this or any other degree. At this time, her children are in middle and high school and require a different type of active parenting, allowing her time to reflect on her role in the family, community, and world.

During the first session, she reports feeling some emptiness as she has entered her 40s and is no longer parenting small children. She thinks she wants to further explore occupational options (simple career advice, right?). As she has researched job options, she has been experiencing increased anxiety with disrupted sleep, including nightmares about getting fired from jobs. She has a history of generalized anxiety, although it has not been consistently treated or even diagnosed. She states that although her family is stable financially, she wants to make a tangible contribution to the household.

Larissa may or may not meet the criteria for a mental health disorder, but she definitely has psychosocial stressors impinging on her career decision making.

Is this a career or mental health issue?

Why?

Linking Career-Focused Counseling With Neuroscience of the Self

Neuroscience and career-focused counseling can be integrated using Busacca's (2002) career development problem taxonomy. Adapted from the work of Savickas (1998), this taxonomy can help counselors and clients make sense of career-focused counseling and neuroscience integration. Busacca's conceptualization includes two domains of functioning—interpersonal and intrapersonal—and, within these domains, three levels of functioning and related interventions. In essence, Busacca examined whether the career difficulty is located in the individual (intrapersonal domain) or in the individual's connections with others (interpersonal). Zunker (2016) echoed this in describing career-related issues in terms of work environment (inter) and worker traits (intra). This is useful in particular to counselors seeking integration because neuroscientific findings have application to personal (Siegel, 2012) and social (Cozolino, 2010) development. Busacca also identified three areas of career difficulties, broadening the perception of career issues beyond career decision making to career choice, career entry, and career transition. This chapter explores neuroscience applications for both intra- and interpersonal domains, as well as the different levels of career concerns.

The relationship between the intrapersonal and interpersonal domains can be understood through the theory of Frank Parsons and Donald Super. According to Parsons' (1909) seminal construction of the career guidance process, career development is influenced by a deep understanding of how one's environment, experiences, and relationships have shaped the self (intrapersonal) and how this self then seeks to project itself into the world of work (interpersonal). Following Parsons, Donald Super (1990) later established that career development was heavily influenced by a person's vocational identity:

The process of *vocational development is essentially that of developing and implementing a self concept* [italics added]: it is a compromise process in which the self concept is a product of the interaction of inherited aptitudes, neural and endocrine make-up, opportunity to play various roles, and evaluations of the extent to which the results of role playing meet with the approval of superiors and fellows. (Super, 1951, p. 190)

A person's vocational identity is essentially the self-at-work (Super, 1955, 1990), and it changes over time and across environments (i.e., life span, life space). Work performance and satisfaction are optimal when the self (intrapersonal) is able to be expressed in the work environment (interpersonal). The impor-

> **Reflective Question**
>
> How would you describe Larissa's vocational identity at the point at which she enters counseling?

tance of outwardly expressing a self-concept has been emphasized not only by Parsons and Super but also by other important career theorists such as Strong, Holland, and Savickas.

Vocational Identity in the Brain

So where might one find the self (or, alternatively, the identity) in the brain? One proposition is that the self is the totality of experiences and that these experiences are stored as memories—more specifically, as autobiographical memory. *Autobiographical memory* refers to the memories related to oneself in context: experiences, relationships, and environments. The self is a (re)construction of memories drawn from these key components; it is us. Memory is generally governed by the executive function of the hippocampus, in connection with the emotional memory governance of the amygdala. At the same time, autobiographical memory, a component of declarative memory, seems to recruit prefrontal lobe regions in constructing the self (Freton et al., 2014). Freton et al. (2014) noted that the precuneus and ventromedial prefrontal cortex involved in autobiographical memory have ramifications for "both emotional regulation and self-related processes" (p. 959).

The situation in which Larissa finds herself is an example of how career issues and mental health issues are interrelated. Larissa's vocational identity is most certainly tied to her personal identity. Neuro-informed career-focused counseling might assist her in exploring how early memories of self and work have contributed to the life and career decisions she has made along the way. In investigating further, you find that her anxiety has been a constant companion throughout her life. Larissa has frequently made life decisions that served the purpose of mitigating her anxiety rather than pursuing her career goals. Neuro-informed career-focused counseling will assist Larissa in exploring her memory function as well as her developmental perspective, as we show later in this chapter. The relationship between mental health and career issues results in and from work-related stress, which we consider next.

Neuro-Based Metaphors in Career-Focused Counseling

Research has demonstrated the clinical utility of metaphor use in counseling (Tay, 2012; Wickman et al., 1999), and counselors can take a metaphoric approach to the integration of neuroscience and counseling (Luke, 2015; Michael & Luke, 2016). Wickman, Daniels, White, and Fesmire (1999) offered a rationale for the use of metaphors in counseling:

> Traditionally, counselors have developed metaphors to demonstrate empathy and to suggest alternative interpretations of presenting problems. This use of metaphor, created by the counselor, does not change a client's problems; rather, it changes perception of the problem and allows for solutions as yet unconsidered. In this manner, metaphor has provided both a linguistic tool to facilitate empathy and an intervention technique with a history of therapeutic value. (p. 389)

From this perspective, metaphor is just a mnemonic; as such, in the metaphoric model, we use metaphor somewhat interchangeably with other linguistic–empathic devices such as similes, analogs, and examples. Brain and central nervous system structures, systems, and functions provide numerous analogs to human psychological and behavioral functioning. The metaphoric approach can be applied in two distinct ways: (a) using examples from everyday life as a metaphor for brain function to help clients understand that this is a "brain thing," not a character deficit, and (b) using brain function as a metaphor for client experiences.

Brain-Based Metaphors as Normalizing and Demystifying

As noted earlier, neuroscience offers ways for counselors to assist clients in accepting their career-related presenting problems as an often neurological phenomenon as opposed to a character-based one. The field of translational neuroscience (Feldstein Ewing & Chung, 2013; Fisher & Berkman, 2015) seeks to bridge the gap between neurobiological functions and psychosocial behavior and interventions. For example, Fisher and Berkman (2015) have identified multiple brain structures involved in the neural mechanisms of addiction. This translational approach has important implications for career-focused counseling. Clients can understand what happens in their brain and central nervous system when they are under acute or prolonged stress by examining the effects of the hippocampal–pituitary–adrenal axis as a function of the sympathetic branch of the autonomic nervous system. When stressed, the body goes into action by:

- Increasing heart rate, which fuels major muscle groups;
- Dilating pupils, to take in more light to see a threat;
- Stimulating adrenal glands, for sudden (brief) bursts of energy and clarity;
- Slowing or stopping digestion, to redirect the body's resources to life-saving functions; and
- Constricting blood vessels, to minimize blood loss from injury.

One of these components—stimulation of the adrenal glands—involves cortisol, and its impact on stress management can be applied to career-related issues. Cortisol functions as a glucocorticoid during stress responses, effectively speeding metabolism for energy. As you can imagine, the life-saving

Reflective Question

How can a counselor use this information about Larissa's mental ability in a session without treating Larissa as if she has a sort of brain damage?

utility of cortisol is balanced by its deleterious effects on the individual when the stress is unrelenting or traumatic stress occurs. In other words, stress, such as the kind Larissa has experienced in the transition from full-time stay-at-home mom to seeking employment outside the home, shows cortisol's darker side: decreased neuroplasticity (adaptability of the cells and synapses), dendrite degeneration (resulting in diminished message transfer), deficits in cell remyelination (cell insulation that promotes neural efficiency), cell death, and inhibition of neurogenesis and neural growth (Kindsvatter & Geroski, 2014). In addition, and perhaps most concerning with career-focused counseling clients who have lived with chronic anxiety, high levels of cortisol correlate with compromised hippocampal function. The hippocampus functions as the executive regulator of memory, so individuals with diminished hippocampal function demonstrate deficits in short- and long-term memory, as well as in capacity for new learning (LeDoux, 2003).

The implications of these neural phenomena are clear. Larissa may find her mental ability dulled in response to anxiety and acute stress, although it is a condition to which she may have grown accustomed. Any challenges in following through on counselor recommendations for moving forward in exploring potential careers may actually be less about her resistance and more about resilience. Neuroscience-informed career-focused counselors may begin interventions focused on self-care and wellness concerns before fully engaging in more traditional career counseling interventions.

Using a Metaphoric Approach to Understanding Brain Function

Amblyopia is an eye–brain condition wherein the eye and brain do not communicate effectively, if at all. In reaction, the brain assumes the eye is not functional or even present, so it limits connections between the eye and the occipital lobe of the brain. Amblyopia is an example of synaptic pruning. The brain trims back unused circuits and synapses. The result is the ironically termed "lazy eye" and even blindness. The treatment is to cover the working eye to compel the other eye to "see" and stimulate the brain to maintain connections. The eye is not actually lazy; it is understimulated and unsupported. Larissa will most certainly benefit from this reframing of motivation and effort in terms of her career.

This concept of synaptic pruning and synaptogenesis, both concepts related to neuroplasticity, can also be seen in maze completion. Many people have seen or completed a maze at some point in their lives, so the example has an element of universality. With Larissa, the counselor might produce a basic paper-based maze and ask her to complete it while I time her. This may produce some anxiety in her, so I would reassure her that this is a low-stakes activity. In the session, I would use three to five trials in succession, recording the time for each. In reflecting on the results, Larissa will likely notice a common occurrence: Overall, her time decreases with each attempt.

This simple activity demonstrates how the brain learns from both successes and failures. Maze trials offer clients such as Larissa hope for learning, which represents growth and change. In effect, her stronger, mothering "eye" has been covered, allowing the weaker, vocational "eye" to get stronger. As the expectation of this unused tool increases, so does its performance. Career-skills synaptogenesis takes place, wherein the necessary networks of career problem solving are formed and reformed, reminding Larissa of previous successes in these areas. This confirms that Larissa has been understimulated, as opposed to lazy or idle.

Your response to this reflection will drive the metaphor used. For example, one might conceptualize Larissa's dilemma as an overactive sympathetic response system in which anxiety is the dominant experience, leading to paralysis of action. In Larissa's situation, one would use the metaphor (technically, a simile) of memory as orange juice from concentrate (Luke, 2015). Orange juice from concentrate begins with oranges that are modified through a number of processes, the result of which is a tiny can of concentrated frozen substance that, when thawed and added to water, once again becomes orange juice. However, although it is technically still orange juice, it is not exactly the same as the juice it started from; that is, it has been reconstituted. Likewise, memory in the brain is a reconstruction of the original, which itself was created using perception. Clients retell stories that are reconstituted from earlier retellings of those stories. Here is the catch: Each time a memory is recalled (*recall* being a misnomer because it implies replication), the emotions of the individual and the context in which it is recalled influence its reconstitution. For instance, the same memory being retold in story form can serve to confirm a person's identity as the hero or the victim, depending on the emotions and psychological needs of the moment.

Larissa's memories constitute a view of herself that fits a familiar narrative and limits her belief in who she can be. The result is

Reflective Question

How would you as a counselor or helping professional frame Larissa's presenting problem?

stupefaction. Moving forward involves taking old memories, recalling them, and exploring how they might be modified to assist her in moving forward. For example, in the safety of the counseling room and relationship, Larissa may practice recalling memories of anxiety-filled experiences in which she was frozen or otherwise avoided action. Neuro-informed career-focused counseling invites her to rerememember (Savickas, 2012) experiences in a calming, safe context in which she can turn the memory over in her mind and examine it for inaccuracies. This process offers her the option to reconsolidate these memories, if nothing else, as neurological phenomena that are separate from her character or ability.

Stress and Wellness in the Workplace . . . and the Brain

Neuroscience can be readily applied to career-focused counseling practice when considering the self under stress. Stress has been described by neurodevelopmentalists as "circumstances appraised as threatening and as a burden to coping mechanisms" (Heim, Kletzko, Purselle, Musselman, & Nemeroff, 2008, as cited in Kindsvatter & Geroski, 2014, p. 473). Stress is both an objective, observable phenomenon and a subjective, internally experienced one. Not all stress and stressors are created equal. Depending on the individual's sense of self:

1. Clients with early trauma or non-nurturing environments can be more susceptible to stress in the work environment, in terms of perception and response;
2. Clients' stress-vulnerable brains can change and heal as a result of psychosocial interventions; and
3. Regardless of the objectivity of the stressor, nurture-deprived and therefore stress-vulnerable clients have a "blunted" cortisol response to stress, limiting the individual's ability to call on neurochemical resources to deal with stress (Bruce, Fisher, Pears, & Levine, 2009).

Take, for example, the experience of Larissa and the impact of her propensity toward anxiety in response to real or perceived stressors along with her current vocational struggle. This is seen most clearly in the case of two individuals: say, Larissa and a friend, who are exposed to the same stressor or trauma, wherein only Larissa experiences a breakdown in her coping behaviors. This seems to be a clear indicator of the necessity of the two components in the development of the stress response. This internal response is in part a reaction to the individual's perception of the event and is well informed by neuroscience and has important implications for career counseling with career-related stress.

In addition to world-of-work (external) factors, there are individual factors (or worker traits) that increase an individual's susceptibility and response to stressors (Zunker, 2016). In other words, work stresses can have an intrapersonal and an interpersonal component. The hope for Larissa and her career-anxiety dilemma is realized in Fisher and Berkman's (2015) findings that both acute and chronic stress show plastic responses to counseling interventions. Larissa's work-related stressed brain can change, grow, and improve.

The implications of the human stress response system and its limitations have ramifications for addressing work stress in career-focused counseling. The general stress mechanism in the brain and autonomic nervous system is found in the hypothalamic–pituitary–adrenal axis, identified early on in neuroscience research (Selye, 1955).[2] The system works by interpreting sensory material (input through the five senses from an external source) as threatening or nonthreatening. It is important to note that the hypothalamic–pituitary–adrenal axis does not discriminate in terms of stress response between perception and reality. In terms of its response, it is all real. Sensory input from the five senses is routed through the thalamus and limbic region, namely, the amygdala, to determine whether what is being perceived is similar in any meaningful way to stored material that has fear or anxiety salience. Once a threat (stress) is perceived, the hypothalamus activates the pituitary (the master gland), which triggers the release of adrenocorticotropic hormone, which stimulates the adrenal glands to release cortisol. During this time, epinephrine and norepinephrine are also released by way of the sympathetic–adrenal–medullary axis either to prepare the body for fight or flight or to prepare to freeze when the system is utterly overwhelmed (LeDoux, 2003).

The autonomic nervous system is an efficient system in terms of preparing the body to protect itself. It has, however, at least three specific characteristics that can serve as two double-edged swords:

1. It fires quickly but returns to homeostasis slowly.
2. It acts solely on the basis of perception, regardless of reality.
3. The long-term effects trigger the law of diminishing returns.

Regardless of the system's speed and accuracy, it has clear physical effects on the body, and work-related stress is no exception. McDonald and Hite (2016) reviewed the literature on stress and strain in the workplace, noting these effects: physiological, such as headaches, irritable bowel syndrome, high blood pressure, and so forth; psychological, including anxiety and depression; and behavioral, including substance use, being unpunctual, or missing work (McDonald & Hite, 2016).

---

[2]It is important to note that this description represents a fairly severe oversimplification of the process, but it is described in this way for the sake of clarity and clinical application.

It may be the case that Larissa's somatic symptoms are related to her career-related anxiety and stress. It may also be the case that her drive to find greater vocational meaning will conflict with these reactions— the preprogrammed messages of threat that activate her fight, flight, or freeze response system. Neuro-informed career-focused counseling will help to inform her of these biological processes in ways that help her to challenge these physi-ological stress responses.

Reflective Questions

How would you conceptual-ize Larissa's problem from a neuroscience integration per-spective: psychosocial stressors affecting career-related issues or career-related issues limit-ing her options and therefore creating stressors?

Does it matter?
Why?

Work–Life Balance and Strategies for Work–Life Role Transitions

Work–life balance has been touted as the goal for a healthy, successful life for as long as career-focused counseling has existed as a professional service. McDonald and Hite (2016) observed, "While this concept [work–life balance] is frequently used, there appears to be less agreement as to what work–life balance really means" (p. 162). Workers may feel confused about what work–life balance might look like in their lives.

Raskin (2006) listed several factors related to work–life or work–family balance, factors that extend beyond the generated conflicts often discussed:

1. Role conflict—tension between the role one plays in family and work contexts, contrasted with the roles one is expected to play;
2. Role overload—multiple, unsustainable long-term roles;
3. Spillover—positive or negative impact of one life role on another;
4. Work schedules and family-friendly policies—flexibility, or lack thereof, for employees with multiple life roles that potentially conflict with the work role;
5. Child care—increasingly a felt burden for the working poor, because child care quality correlates with household income;
6. Child outcomes—often investigated and discussed exclusively in terms of the effects on children of working mothers but could include the impact of paternal work schedule and presence or absence on child development;
7. Stress and illness—work–life balance issues can provide protective factors when balanced and illness and substance abuse when out of balance; and
8. Off- and on-ramping—a phenomenon in which life roles—moth-ering in particular but also elder care—limit the investment one makes in career building and may result in part-time and discon-tinuous employment.

As part of Larissa's experience in living in sympathetic arousal in response to environmental resistance, many of the factors identified here will need to be explored in counseling. For example, although her maternal role has shifted, she has not abdicated it. Therefore, her pursuit of her own vocational goals may trigger a type of guilt–conflict response to the avocational role in which she has invested much of her adult life. One tool from the field of adult education is prior learning, in which the individual uses the wisdom and skills gained in earlier life tasks in new ones (Luke, 2016).

Our Brain-Based Approach to the Case of Larissa

Let's take a closer look at what neuroscience integration might look like with Larissa. Two features of this integration stand out and bear reflection. As with all wellness-based counseling, career-related issues tend to be developmental in nature (Super, 1955, 1990). This developmental nature involves task completion at various stages. Completion of the task or tasks at one stage strengthens the individual in preparation for advancement to the next stage and with it the concomitant tasks therein. As with many counseling clients, Larissa entered the consulting room because the tasks she is facing have overwhelmed her capacity to complete them (i.e., stress). In counseling Larissa, I would use brain development as an analog to human development in general. For example, I might describe synaptic pruning, or apoptosis, the process by which synaptic connections are quite literally cut off because of lack of use. I might share with her a brief video of the eye condition known as amblyopia, discussed briefly earlier. In neuro-informed career-focused counseling, the metaphor highlights the need for Larissa to develop balanced strengths because of the tendency toward atrophy. The "eye patch" demonstrates the importance of recognizing her strengths without neglecting other areas of growth that are necessary for balance. In career-focused counseling, it is common for clients such as Larissa to thrive in their home environment while feeling less adept in dealing with challenges returning to school or work. The result can be overwork and ongoing neglect of family time and relationship development. Neuro-integrated career-focused counseling can support clients such as Larissa in exploring this dynamic and working toward increased harmony.

In the career domain, a strong and growing body of literature has supported the notion that career counseling involves career problem solving and goal setting (Sampson, Lenz, Reardon, & Peterson, 1999). Just as in amblyopia, however, problem-solving "muscles" or circuits in the brain can atrophy, leaving one feeling powerless to make decisions and solve problems. Larissa is a prime example of this. Four years ago, Larissa's life situation shifted radically. Before her separation, Larissa's job, income, and role in the family worked harmoniously together;

it made sense to her and for her. Up until her separation from her husband, she had cultivated skills related to her role in the home, without a focus or even awareness that she might need certain skills in the future. However, suddenly this arrangement, her job, and her role have changed. Larissa could explore the potential impact of this life-role change. In summary, neuroscience-informed career-focused counseling (a) aided Larissa in normalizing her experience of confusion, ambivalence, and generally feeling lost about what to do next; (b) demonstrated how her relational and vocational memories shaped her current perspective; and (c) assisted Larissa in reconstructing her life and career narratives.

As a result of this approach, Larissa was able to visualize the neural processes underlying her experience of anxiety as she began to explore occupational pathways. When those old, embedded memories triggered her fight-or-flight response, she sat down with a glass of orange juice and reflected on the "reality" of those memories. Her newfound power over anxiety-saturated career identity and narrative memories enabled her to choose the facets of early experiences she wanted to harness in moving forward toward her goals. She might post the maze activity on her refrigerator at home as a reminder of the brain's ability to learn and build new connections and that a career focus is within her reach at this time. Her threat-detection systems (sympathetic nervous system) have "cooled" in response to her re-remembering and new visualizations of her brain's processes. By the end of several sessions, Larissa had explored several viable career paths, applying for a dozen jobs in the realm of her sociology degree, and she had enrolled in a graduate course in nonprofit management.

Conclusion

The integration of neuroscience and career-focused counseling is in its infancy. As with the integration of neuroscience and counseling, neuroscience-informed career-focused counseling can offer valuable explanations of and therapeutic metaphors for assisting clients in navigating career-related issues, whether in the domain of career choice, career entry, or career adjustment. For counselors to be effective in this process, they need not be experts in neuroscience and neurobiology; rather, counselors need to embrace their curiosity so that they

Reflective Question

How might Larissa's understanding of the brain help her to be successful in her studies and next career?

become knowledgeable enough to assist clients in understanding their career-related issues from a brain-based perspective.

Quiz

1. According to Donald Super, vocational identity is:
   a. A projection of the self into the world of work.
   b. The status one attains as a result of one's job.
   c. A person's sense that he or she has selected the right career.
   d. An unnecessary component of career counseling.
2. Which system is activated during times of stress, including work stress?
   a. Parasympathetic nervous system.
   b. Autonomic nervous system.
   c. Mesolimbocortical dopamine system.
   d. Hypothalamic–pituitary–adrenal axis.
3. Busacca identified two domains and three types of career-related issues. What are they?
   a. Intrapersonal and interpersonal; career choice, career entry, and work adjustment.
   b. Dependence and interdependence; career choice, career entry, and work adjustment.
   c. Intrapersonal and interpersonal; self-knowledge, work knowledge, and true reasoning.
   d. Intradependence and interdependence; self-knowledge, work knowledge, and true reasoning.

References

Bruce, J., Fisher, P. A., Pears, K. C., & Levine, S. (2009). Morning cortisol levels in preschool-aged foster children: Differential effects of maltreatment type. *Developmental Psychobiology, 51,* 14–23. http://dx.doi.org/10.1002/dev.20333

Busacca, L. A. (2002). Career problem assessment: A conceptual schema for counselor training. *Journal of Career Development, 29,* 129–146.

Council for Accreditation of Counseling and Related Educational Programs. (2015). *2016 CACREP standards.* Retrieved from http://www.cacrep.org/wp-content/uploads/2012/10/2016-CACREP-Standards.pdf

Cozolino, L. (2010). *The neuroscience of psychotherapy: Healing the social brain* (2nd ed.). New York, NY: Norton.

Feldstein Ewing, S. W., & Chung, T. (2013). Neuroimaging mechanisms of change in psychotherapy for addictive behaviors: Emerging translational approaches that bridge biology and behavior. *Psychology of Addictive Behaviors, 27,* 329–335.

Fisher, P. A., & Berkman, E. T. (2015). Designing interventions informed by scientific knowledge about effects of early adversity: A translational neuroscience agenda for next-generation addictions research. *Current Addiction Reports, 2,* 347–353.

Freton, M., Lemogne, C., Bergouignan, L., Delaveau, P., Lehéricy, S., & Fossati, P. (2014). The eye of the self: Precuneus volume and visual perspective during autobiographical memory retrieval. *Brain Structure and Function, 219,* 959–968.

Kindsvatter, A., & Geroski, A. (2014). The impact of early life stress on the neurodevelopment of the stress response system. *Journal of Counseling & Development, 92,* 472–480.

LeDoux, J. (2003). *Synaptic self: How our brains become who we are.* New York, NY: Penguin Books.

Luke, C. (2015). *Neuroscience for counselors and therapists: Integrating the sciences of mind and brain.* Thousand Oaks, CA: Sage.

Luke, C., & Redekop, C. (2016). Supervision of co-occurring career and mental health concerns: Application of an integrated approach. *Career Planning and Adult Development Journal, 32,* 130–140.

McDonald, K., & Hite, L. (2016). *Career development: A human resource development perspective.* New York, NY: Routledge.

Michael, T., & Luke, C. (2016). Utilizing a metaphoric approach to teach the neuroscience of play therapy: A pilot study. *International Journal of Play Therapy, 25,* 45–52. http://dx.doi.org/10.1037/pla0000015

Parsons, F. (1909). *Choosing a vocation.* Boston, MA: Houghton Mifflin.

Raskin, P. M. (2006). Women, work, and family: Three studies of roles and identity among working mothers. *American Behavioral Scientist, 49,* 1354–1381.

Sampson, J. P., Lenz, J. G., Reardon, R. C., & Peterson, G. W. (1999). A cognitive information processing approach to employment problem solving and decision making. *The Career Development Quarterly, 48,* 3–18.

Savickas, M. L. (1998). Career style assessment and counseling. In T. Sweeney (Ed.), *Adlerian counseling: A practitioner's approach* (4th ed., pp. 329–359). Philadelphia, PA: Accelerated Development.

Savickas, M. L. (2012). Life design: A paradigm for career intervention in the 21st century. *Journal of Counseling & Development, 90,* 13–19.

Selye, H. (1955). Stress and disease. *Science, 122,* 625–631.

Siegel, D. J. (2012). *The developing mind: How relationships and the brain interact to shape who we are* (2nd ed.). New York, NY: Guilford Press.

Super, D. E. (1951). Vocational adjustment: Implementing a self-concept. *Journal of Counseling & Development, 30,* 88–92. http://dx.doi:10.1002/j.2164-5892.1951.tb02607.x

Super, D. E. (1955). Transition: From vocational guidance to counseling psychology. *Journal of Counseling Psychology, 2,* 3–9.

Super, D. E. (1990). A life-span, life-space approach to career development. *Journal of Vocational Behavior, 16,* 282–298.

Tay, D. (2012). Applying the notion of metaphor types to enhance counseling protocols. *Journal of Counseling & Development, 90,* 142–149.

Wickman, S. A., Daniels, M. H., White, L. J., & Fesmire, S. A. (1999). A "primer" in conceptual metaphor for counselors. *Journal of Counseling & Development, 77,* 389–394. http://dx.doi.org/10.1002/j.1556-6676.1999.tb02464.x

Woolf, S. H. (2008). The meaning of translational research and why it matters. *JAMA, 299,* 211–213.

Zunker, V. (2016). *Career counseling: A holistic approach* (6th ed.). Boston, MA: Cengage Learning.

Part V

SUMMARY

The text has described how neuroscience can be integrated into every aspect of neurocounseling practice. The fifth section of the text presents a brain-based approach to conducting research and evaluating neurocounseling programs before offering practical guidelines for the integration of neuroscience into the counseling profession, whatever the specialty within counseling may be.

■ ■ ■

Chapter 13

Conducting Brain-Based Research and Program Evaluation

Eric T. Beeson and Thomas A. Field

Counselors are well positioned to contribute to the growing body of brain-based research literature. This chapter provides an introduction to the principles needed to design brain-based research and program evaluation in counseling. The importance of evidence-based and ethical practice is emphasized. The chapter also explores the feasibility of conducting controlled experiments versus single-subject research.

 ## 2016 CACREP Standards

This chapter addresses sections of the 2016 Council for Accreditation of Counseling and Related Educational Programs (CACREP) Standards pertinent to the common core area of Counseling and Helping Relationships (Standard II.F.5.) and Research and Program Evaluation (Standard II.F.8.):

- Development of measurable outcomes for clients (Standard II.F.5.i.)
- Development of outcome measures for counseling programs (Standard II.F.8.d.)
- Evaluation of counseling interventions and programs (Standard II.F.8.e.)
- Analysis and use of data in counseling (Standard II.F.8.i.)
- Ethical and culturally relevant strategies for conducting, interpreting, and reporting the results of research and/or program evaluation (Standard II.F.8.j.)

This chapter also addresses the following Specialization Standards:

- Methods for evaluating counseling effectiveness (Counselor Education and Supervision, Standard VI.B.1.e.)
- Emergent research practices and processes (Counselor Education and Supervision, Standard VI.B.4.d.)

■ ■ ■

Case Study: Landry

Landry is a graduate student who recently attended a workshop on brain-based counseling techniques. Enraptured by the information, Landry finds himself generating ideas after the workshop for his capstone research project. He is particularly excited about researching the effects of counseling on brain activity. As he begins to formulate a research plan, he realizes that he knows little about how to conduct brain-based research and is unsure how to begin.

Much like Landry, counseling students and professionals may be interested in conducting brain-based research but think they are unprepared to do so. Although many counselors are curious about brain-based principles in counseling, they may struggle to make sense of a body of literature that can be very technical and difficult to comprehend. Others might think research is something completed only by those with doctoral degrees and question its relevance to their current practice. Nonetheless, the infusion of brain-based principles in research and practice is imperative if counseling is to remain a significant mental health profession (Myers & Young, 2012). Therefore, this chapter provides a step-by-step guide to interpreting existing brain-based literature, connecting this knowledge to practice, and creating a brain-based research agenda.

Conceptualizing Research

All research begins with a curiosity to determine what is known and what is not yet known. This curiosity leads to the discovery of topics of interest and potential research projects. Research ranges on a continuum of empiricism on the basis of the degree to which the methods are controlled and grounded in existing research. Using the brain-based research methods described in this chapter can increase the degree of empiricism in all forms of counseling research.

The research process follows several steps: (a) Identify a topic of interest, its context, and your motivation for this interest; (b) establish the relevance of the topic to the counseling profession; (c) review the current literature related to the topic; (d) identify gaps in the literature; (e) create a research question to fill in the gaps in the literature; (f) design research methods to answer the research question; (g) complete the research according to the design selected; (h) analyze and interpret the data; (i) compare findings with the previous body of literature; (j) discuss the implications of your findings; and (k) provide recommendations for future research. These steps can guide your exploration of brain-based research and are used to organize the remaining sections of the current chapter.

Exploring the Existing Body of Literature

After establishing the relevance of your brain-based topics to the counseling profession, it is necessary to explore existing literature related to these topics. Identifying brain-based literature can be difficult because most of it exists outside of the counseling profession. The following section provides a few strategies to assist your review of the brain-based literature.

The first step in conducting a review of the literature is identifying sources of information. During your search of the literature, you are likely to find an expansive body of knowledge related to your topics and brain-based terms. You will also find additional literature related to the brain and mental health, psychiatric diagnoses, and psychotherapy. However, you will likely find less brain-based literature related to the counseling field. In fact, it has been said that counseling researchers have "largely failed to use brain-based measures to substantiate their work" (Myers & Young, 2012, p. 26). This has led to a brain-based body of counseling literature that is largely conceptual in nature, attempting to theorize how neuroscientific findings might be applied within a counseling framework. These publications have argued for an increased infusion of neuroscience in the counseling process that ranges from a revision of existing theories to the implementation of brain-based interventions such as neurofeedback (e.g., Echterling, Presbury, & Cowan, 2012; Field, Beeson, & Jones, 2015; Fragedakis & Toriello, 2014; Kindsvetter & Geroski, 2014; Makinson & Young, 2012; Myers & Young, 2012). Despite these strong conceptual arguments and recommendations, they are only beginning to be empirically evaluated (e.g., Collura, Zalaquett, & Bonnstetter, 2014; Dreis et al., 2015; Field et al., 2016; Russell-Chapin et al., 2013). Although it is important to theorize about the application of brain-based research findings to counseling practice, it is imperative that these hypotheses be empirically evaluated using rigorous experimental designs.

Reflective Question

Where would you encourage Landry to look for information, and what resources would you recommend?

Creating a Research Question

While completing your review of the literature, you will notice gaps in the literature and recommendations for future research. The next step in the research process is to create a research question that aims to fill these gaps and extend existing lines of research.

Defining and Measuring Variables

Once research questions are created, it is important to operationally define each variable you want to include in the study. In the past, counseling research has used observations, psychometric instruments, and classification systems such as the *Diagnostic and Statistical Manual of Mental Disorders* (5th ed.; American Psychiatric Association, 2013) to define variables. These methods have been criticized for cultural bias and questionable validity, thus creating the need for a more objective, transdiagnostic system that focuses on the brain networks related to common symptomatology (Buckholtz & Meyer-Lindenberg, 2012; Insel et al., 2010). In response, the National Institute of Mental Health created the Research Domain Criteria (RDoC) as an organizing system for brain-based research that aims to detect subgroups of mental disorders, inform treatment selection, and facilitate more direct links from research to practice (Insel et al., 2010). The RDoC can guide counseling researchers in the identification and selection of variables for research. Although a complete review of the RDoC is outside the scope of this chapter, you can review the RDoC by visiting the institute's website (www.nimh.nih.gov/research-priorities/rdoc/index.shtml).

The RDoC include numerous functional constructs (e.g., response to acute fear) that are described through their related genes, molecules, cells, circuits and networks, physiology, behavior, self-report, and research paradigms. Constructs are organized into one of five functional domains: negative valence systems, positive valence systems, cognitive systems, systems for social processes, and arousal and regulatory systems. As shown in Figure 13.1, if you were interested in studying a functional construct (e.g., response to acute fear) of the negative valence system, you could choose to measure one or more of the characteristics of this construct (e.g., physiology) using one or more methods (e.g., heart rate). Examples of each characteristic are included in parentheses.

Once you have identified and operationalized variables, you will need to determine the method for measuring these variables. Brain-based methods give counselors the tools to collect more objective measurements that can be used in

Reflective Question

What is one research question that could guide Landry's exploration?

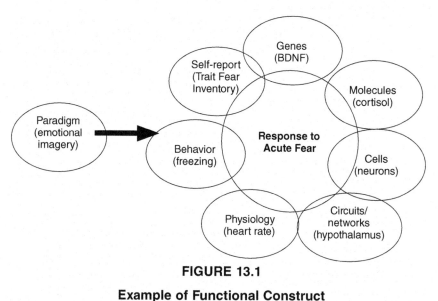

FIGURE 13.1

Example of Functional Construct

Note. Emotional imagery and acute fear response in phobias and related features for the Research Domain Criteria (RDoC) negative valence system domain are shown. Examples of each characteristic are included in parentheses. BDNF = brain-derived neurotrophic factor.

conjunction with existing measures (e.g., psychometric instruments) to produce a clearer picture of the human experience. The RDoC provide a useful structure to identify targets of measurement related to specific topics. For instance, if you are interested in the acute fear response of clients with specific phobias, then the RDoC can help the researcher identify behaviors, physiology, genes, brain circuits and networks, cells, and molecules to measure, as well as research paradigms to study them.

Measuring variables identified in the RDoC can be difficult and requires additional training, yet brain-based research methods are becoming more accessible to practicing counselors and researchers. For instance, small samples of clients' saliva and blood can be collected and analyzed for genetic and molecular information used to identify risk factors of mental illness, predict treatment response, and evaluate treatment outcomes (Bakker et al., 2014; Eley et al., 2012; Kennedy, Cullen, DeYoung, & Klimes-Dougan, 2015; Silverstein et al., 2015; Teche et al., 2013). Measurements of clients' skin conductance, cardiovascular responses, muscle activity, pupil diameter, eye blinks, and eye movements can measure physiological responses to specific interventions and the quality of the counseling relationship (Finset, Stensrud, Holt, Verheul, & Bensing, 2011). Neuroimaging techniques, such as computed tomography, functional magnetic resonance imaging (fMRI), structural MRI, positron emission tomography, single-photon emission computed tomography, and electroencephalography (EEG) are being used in psychotherapy outcome research to measure the effects of interventions on specific brain structure, function, and connectivity (Bunge & Kahn, 2009; Weingarten & Strauman, 2015). However, with the exception of EEG, neuroimaging techniques are seldom found in the counseling literature.

EEG is purported to be a direct measure of the real-time flow of electrical activity in the brain that is collected by placing electrodes on the scalp (Bunge & Kahn, 2009) and is much cheaper than other neuroimaging methods (e.g., fMRI). The quantitative analysis of EEG provides objective data that are accessible to counselors and can be used to measure brain activity, function, and connectivity across the counseling process (Myers & Young, 2012).

Despite the potential benefits of brain-based measurement strategies, the cost of training, equipment, and software is a barrier to including these methods in counseling practice and research. To conduct brain-based research, the counselor will need tools to collect the data from the participant (e.g., electrodes), supplies to ensure an adequate connection (e.g., conductive paste), and an amplifier that sends signals from the electrodes to a computer program designed to measure and evaluate the data. In addition to these professional tools, many home-use devices are becoming more accessible. A few examples of these tools include the HeartMath emWavePro (HeartMath Inc., Boulder Creek, CA), the PIP (Galvanic Ltd., Dublin, Ireland), and Muse (Interaxon, Toronto, Ontario, Canada). Clients who receive these in-office interventions may be able to purchase their own equipment for practicing at home. Although home-use devices have advantages (e.g., cost), researchers should be careful to evaluate the quality of the data compared with that from professional equipment before including them in research proposals. We recommend consulting with current neurocounseling practitioners and researchers before purchasing equipment for research use.

Selecting Research Methods

Your research question guides the selection of research methods and data analysis. There are three predominate approaches to research design: quantitative, qualitative, and mixed methods. Quantitative research involves the collection and analysis of numerical data that are statistically analyzed to test the research hypothesis. Qualitative research pertains to the collecting and analysis of non-numerical data, such as words, narratives, and

> **Reflective Question**
>
> Recall the research question you identified earlier.
>
> What functional domains, constructs, and methods (variables) from the RDoC could Landry use to explore his research question?

documents to identify common themes. Mixed-methods research involves the intentional mixing of quantitative and qualitative data. Although qualitative and mixed-methods designs can be beneficial to brain-based research, quantitative methods are most likely to be selected because the data collected

from brain-based measures (e.g., EEG) will be in numeric form.

Types of quantitative designs include true experiments, also known as randomized controlled trials (RCTs), which require control groups and randomization of subjects into groups to minimize error and bias; quasi-experiments, which are similar to true experiments except they lack the ability to randomize subjects into groups; single-subject designs, which compare a person's individual readings at different time intervals; ex post facto designs, which analyze data that have already been collected (thus limiting the ability to randomize subjects); and correlational studies, which evaluate the strength of the relationship between two variables in noncontrolled conditions. Counselors can design RCTs that measure the EEG of randomized samples of clients receiving randomized treatment conditions (e.g., cognitive behavior therapy, person-centered therapy, and no treatment) over the course of treatment. Single-subject designs can incorporate brain-based outcome measures that track the progress of individual clients over time. An example of a single-subject research design is collecting pretest skin temperature when teaching skin temperature control to clients and comparing these data with posttest skin temperature after the technique has been demonstrated and practiced. Ex post facto designs can be used to create normative databases of client brain activity. Correlational designs can be used to evaluate the relationship between brain activity and treatment outcomes.

Unfortunately, most practicing counselors are not usually in the position to conduct the most rigorous type of experimental research studies. It is typically difficult for counselors to randomly assign their clients or place clients in control groups because of the ethical conundrum of withholding a treatment from a client for research purposes (especially if the client is paying for those services). When counselors want to conduct more rigorous experimental studies, they should consider either obtaining grant funding so that research projects can offer free services to participants or partnering with other agencies, organizations, or universities that could provide free services to participants. If you are considering conducting a less controlled experimental study, we especially encourage you to consider single-subject research designs.

Analyzing and Interpreting Data

After designing the research methods, it is imperative to follow them exactly when conducting the study. Maintaining fidelity to the research design will increase the quality of data collected. Once brain-based data have been collected, they can be analyzed using descriptive (frequency, range, mean, standard deviation, etc.) and inferential (correlation, *t* test, analysis of variance) statistics. The research question chosen drives the selection of research methods and subsequent data analysis and interpretation. In brain-based research, the same statistical principles related to hypothesis testing apply, meaning that the goal is to determine whether any changes in the dependent variables were the result of the independent variables or of some unknown variable (e.g., chance). For example, if you were interested in the brain-based outcomes of counseling, you might ask the following research question: Is there a statistically significant difference in clients' EEG before and after counseling? You could use a single-subject design that takes EEG readings of all clients before counseling and at case closure. Software programs, such as Neurostat (Applied Neuroscience Inc., Largo, FL), can be used to conduct statistical analyses on these data to determine whether there is a significant difference between participants' EEG before and after treatment. A statistically significant result is typically indicated by a $p < .05$, depending on the nature of the study. Although statistically significant data are important, it is also necessary to calculate effect sizes (e.g., Cohen's *d*) to determine the degree of statistical impact of counseling (independent variable) on clients' EEG (dependent variable).

Discussing Implications

After data have been analyzed, it is important to discuss the implications of these findings in terms of clinical practice and future research. Although methods of collecting brain-based data are advancing, it is still difficult to make causal inferences. At best, researchers can make solid conclusions regarding what regions and networks of the brain are active during certain tasks, at rest, and in response to certain stimuli (Bunge & Kahn, 2009). Although researchers can see that the brain changes, it is difficult to attribute this change to treatment alone. Real-time methods of data collection in response to specific counseling interventions might yield a more direct cause–effect relationship to guide future practice.

Ethical Issues

Ethics are at the core of counseling practice and research. Counselors who conduct research should use

> ### Reflective Question
>
> Reflect back on the variables you identified earlier.
>
> What brain-based technologies could Landry use to measure his RDoC variables?

institutional review boards at local universities and hospitals to ensure that their research procedures meet the highest degree of ethical standards. All participants should be presented with an informed consent document that is approved by an institutional review board and have the opportunity to ask questions about the study before electing to participate. Counselors are encouraged to further consult with their institutional review board when researching new techniques to "protect the rights of research participants when research indicates that a deviation from standard or acceptable practices may be necessary" (American Counseling Association, 2014, p. 16). Counseling researchers engaging in brain-based research should ensure that counselors in the study have adequate training and supervision in the neurocounseling methods used.

Another important consideration is the participant's right to non-disclosed information. Although participants in research have the right to disclose or not, objective measures of the brain may indicate a specific reaction to certain content that the participant was not willing or prepared to disclose, thus raising the potential for harm. Participants should be fully informed of this potential in the informed consent document. Some brain-based studies require the participant to experience an aversive condition (e.g., fear-provoking stimuli) to measure the reaction. In vivo activation of aversive conditions raises additional ethical concerns that must be fully explained to the participant before the research (Linden, 2008). If invasive measurements or techniques are used, participants should also be informed of this, and the researcher must carefully weigh the relative risks versus benefits to the participant.

Development of Our Brain-Based Research Agendas

Reading the existing body of literature related to neuroscience and counseling has significantly influenced our research agendas. Drawing from the work of Albert Ellis and Aaron Beck (cognitive behavior theorists), alongside researchers such as Tom Collura, Daniel Kahneman, Jaak Panksepp, Dan Siegel, and Allen Schore, we collaborated with the second editor of this text, Laura Jones, to reconceptualize cognitive behavior therapy from a neuroscience perspective (n-CBT). The conceptual model was first published in the *Journal of Mental Health Counseling* in Spring 2015 (Field, Beeson, & Jones, 2016). Citing the work of Albert Ellis and Aaron Beck as a foundation, n-CBT integrates several findings from neuroscience, including top-down/bottom-up processing, implicit memory formation and reconsolidation, the hippocampal–pituitary–adrenal axis, and many others to create a true model of neurocounseling. Despite the anecdotal merits of this model, it was important to empirically evaluate n-CBT in naturalistic settings. Therefore, we developed a research project to evaluate the credibility and expectancy of treatment outcomes related to the model from the perspectives of clients and counselors (Field et al., 2016).

Our sample almost exclusively featured counselors (95.8%), which is rare in psychotherapy outcome research. The results of the study were encouraging, and we plan to conduct additional studies that include brain-based measurements of clients, alongside self-report, to determine whether n-CBT causes change in brain wave activity relative to other psychotherapies. We have intentionally planned to conduct smaller studies first before attempting a large-scale RCT because of feasibility and the enhanced ability to secure grant funding after successful smaller pilot studies. We are also currently developing an n-CBT treatment manual because RCTs typically need to train practitioners to conduct standardized interventions with clients to reduce the impact of variability among counselors. Variability would affect the validity of findings because of the study's potential internal inconsistency.

Conclusion

The counseling profession has come a long way to establish itself as a major mental health profession. Counselors' professional identity is stronger than ever, and practice privileges continue to increase. However, an independent body of knowledge is just beginning to be established. It is imperative for future generations of professional counselors to have the skills and competencies in research and program evaluation that will justify the practice of professional counseling and inform new theories and models of counseling. We hope that this chapter has provided you with some directions about how to conduct brain-based research that is relevant to your practice.

Quiz

1. You decide to conduct a study that compares the difference between brain wave activity taken from a sample of 100 clients at two intervals: immediately before and after a counseling session. All clients have depression and are receiving acceptance and commitment therapy, and activity in their prefrontal cortex is being measured by qEEG. Which of the following quantitative designs would you use for the study?
    a. True experiment.
    b. Quasi-experiment.
    c. Single subject.
    d. Ex post facto.
    e. Correlational.
2. You design a second study that now compares the relationship between time spent in the waiting room before the session and client brain activity taken from the first interval (immediately before the counseling session) of the same sample. Which of the following quantitative designs would you use for the study?

a. True experiment.
b. Quasi-experiment.
c. Single subject.
d. Ex post facto.
e. Correlational.

3. What are the limitations of both of the preceding studies?
   a. Lack of control groups.
   b. Lack of randomization.
   c. Too many confounding variables.
   d. a and b only.

References

American Counseling Association. (2014). *ACA code of ethics.* Alexandria, VA: Author.

American Psychiatric Association. (2013). *Diagnostic and statistical manual of mental disorders* (5th ed.). Arlington, VA: American Psychiatric Association Publishing.

Bakker, J. M., Lieverse, R., Menne-Lothmann, C., Viechtbauer, W., Pishva, E., Kenis, G., . . . Wichers, M. (2014). Therapygenetics in mindfulness-based cognitive therapy: Do genes have an impact on therapy-induced change in real-life positive affective experiences? *Translational Psychiatry, 4,* 1–10. http://dx.doi.org/10.1038/tp.2014.23

Buckholtz, J. W., & Meyer-Lindenberg, A. (2012). Psychopathology and the human connectome: Toward a transdiagnostic model of risk for mental illness. *Neuron, 74,* 990–1004. http://dx.doi.org/10.1016/j.neuron.2012.06.002

Bunge, S. A., & Kahn, I. (2009). Cognition: An overview of neuroimaging techniques. *Encyclopedia of Neuroscience, 2,* 1063–1067.

Collura, T. F., Zalaquett, C., & Bonnstetter, R. J. (2014). Toward an operational model of decision making, emotional regulation, and mental health impact. *Advances in Mind-Body Medicine, 28*(4), 4–19.

Council for Accreditation of Counseling and Related Educational Programs. (2015). *2016 CACREP standards.* Retrieved from http://www.cacrep.org/wp-content/uploads/2012/10/2016-CACREP-Standards.pdf

Dreis, S. M., Gouger, A. M., Perez, E. G., Russo, G. M., Fitzsimmons, M. A., & Jones, M. S. (2015). Using neurofeedback to lower anxiety symptoms using individuated qEEG protocols: A pilot study. *Neuroregulation, 2,* 137–148. http://dx.doi.org/10.15540/nr.2.3.137

Echterling, L. G., Presbury, J., & Cowan, E. (2012). Neuroscience, magic, and counseling. *Journal of Creativity in Mental Health, 7,* 330–342. http://dx.doi.org/10.1080/15401383.2012.739947

Eley, T. C., Hudson, J. L., Creswell, C., Tropeano, M., Lester, K. J., Cooper, P., . . . Collier, D. A. (2012). Therapygenetics: The 5HT-TLPR and response to psychological therapy. *Molecular Psychiatry, 17,* 236–237. http://dx.doi.org/10.1038/mp.2011.132

Field, T. A., Beeson, E. T., & Jones, L. K. (2015). The new ABCs: A practitioner's guide to neuroscience-informed cognitive behavioral therapy. *Journal of Mental Health Counseling, 37,* 206–220. http://dx.doi.org/10.17744/1040-2861-37.3.206

Field, T. A., Beeson, E. T., & Jones, L. K. (2016). Neuroscience-informed cognitive-behavior therapy in clinical practice: A preliminary study. *Journal of Mental Health Counseling, 38,* 139–154. http://dx.doi.org/10.17744/mehc.38.2.05

Finset, A., Stensrud, T. L., Holt, E., Verheul, W., & Bensing, J. (2011). Electrodermal activity in response to empathic statements in clinical interviewing with fibromyalgia patients. *Patient Education and Counseling, 82,* 355–360. http://dx.doi.org/10.1016/j.pec.2010.12.029

Fragedakis, T. M., & Toriello, P. (2014). The development and experience of combat-related PTSD: A demand for neurofeedback as an effective form of treatment. *Journal of Counseling & Development, 92,* 481–488. http://dx.doi.org/10.1002/j.1556-6676.2014.00174.x

Insel, T., Cuthbert, B., Garvey, M., Heinssen, R., Pine, D. S., Quinn, K., . . . Wang, P. (2010). Research domain criteria (RDoC): Toward a new classification framework for research on mental disorders. *American Journal of Psychiatry, 167,* 748–751. http://dx.doi.org/10.1176/appi.ajp.2010.09091379

Kennedy, K. P., Cullen, K. R., DeYoung, C. G., & Klimes-Dougan, B. (2015). The genetics of early-onset bipolar disorder: A systematic review. *Journal of Affective Disorders, 184,* 1–12. http://dx.doi.org/10.1016/j.jad.2015.05.017

Kindsvetter, A., & Geroski, A. (2014). The impact of early life stress on the neurodevelopment of the stress response system. *Journal of Counseling & Development, 92,* 472–480. doi:10.1002/j.1556-6676.2014.00173.x

Linden, D. E. J. (2008). Brain imaging and psychotherapy: Methodological considerations and practical implications. *European Archives of Psychiatry and Clinical Neuroscience, 258,* 71–75. http://dx.doi.org/10.1007/s00406-008-5023-1

Makinson, R. A., & Young, J. S. (2012). Cognitive behavioral therapy and the treatment of posttraumatic stress disorder: Where counseling and neuroscience meet. *Journal of Counseling & Development, 90,* 131–140. http://dx.doi.org/10.1111/j.1556-6676.2012.00017.x

Myers, J. E., & Young, S. J. (2012). Brain wave feedback: Benefits of integrating neurofeedback in counseling. *Journal of Counseling & Development, 90,* 20–28. http://dx.doi.org/10.1111/j.1556-6676.2012.00003.x

Russell-Chapin, L. A., Kemmerly, T., Liu, W. C., Zagardo, M. T., Chapin, T. D., Dailey, D., & Dinh, D. (2013). The effects of neurofeedback in the default mode network: Pilot study results of medicated children with ADHD. *Journal of Neurotherapy, 17,* 35–42.

Silverstein, W. K., Noda, Y., Barr, M. S., Vila-Rodriguez, F., Rajji, T. K., Fitzgerald, P. B., . . . Blumberger, D. M. (2015). Neurobiological predictors of response to dorsolateral prefrontal cortex repetitive transcranial magnetic stimulation in depression: A systematic review. *Depression and Anxiety, 32,* 871–891. http://dx.doi.org/10.1002/da.22424

Teche, S. P., Nuernberg, G. L., Sordi, A. O., de Souza, L. H., Remy, L., Mendes Cerese′r, K. M., Rocha, N. S. (2013). Measurement methods of BDNF levels in major depression: A qualitative systematic review of clinical trials. *Psychiatric Quarterly, 84,* 485-497. http://dx.doi.org/10.1007/s11126-013-9261-7

Weingarten, C. P., & Strauman, T. J. (2015). Neuroimaging for psychotherapy research: Current trends. *Psychotherapy Research, 25,* 185–213. http://dx.doi.org/10.1080/10503307.2014.883088

Chapter 14

Ten Practical Guidelines for Neurocounseling

Lori A. Russell-Chapin, Thomas A. Field, and Laura K. Jones

This concluding chapter applies information from the previous chapters to the clinical case study of Muna, first presented in the Preface. The case is considered again from a comprehensive neurocounseling perspective.

 Clinical Case Study: Muna

Muna is a 42-year-old Iraqi woman who is experiencing anxiety at her new job in an accounting firm. Muna lives and works in a metropolitan area of a large U.S. city. She is also struggling with feelings of inadequacy related to her long-standing dating relationship of nearly a decade. Her family lives in Iraq, and she emigrated to attend a U.S. college in her early 20s. She lives in constant dread of her family finding out that she is living with her boyfriend outside of marriage. She has been drinking alcohol to cope, mostly at night (four to five units). Muna also struggles with sleep at night, usually only getting 3 to 5 hours. She sometimes binge eats when she wakes up at night. Muna has a past diagnosis of attention-deficit/hyperactivity disorder and takes 20 mg of Adderall twice a day. In terms of her medical history, Muna was born prematurely at 28 weeks but otherwise has no history of medical issues. When asked about her family history, Muna mentions that she experienced psychological abuse from her father throughout her childhood. She is very warm and engaging during the initial interview, though her nonverbal fidgeting suggests she is somewhat anxious.

During the first day of Lori's Neurocounseling: Brain and Behavior course, students were given this case study and asked to conceptualize and create a treatment plan. The discussion was lively, and excellent plans were developed. The students knew that this same case study would be discussed at the end of the class as well. We put the case study away for a few months. The course unfolded, and we worked on neuroanatomy concepts and definitions, reasons for neurological dysregulation, self-regulation skills, head map of functions, and brain-based interventions. During the final class, we took out our old case study and treatment plans. The class was divided into small groups. Each group read through the case study again and created a new or edited treatment plan. Something remarkable occurred. All the groups discarded the old treatment plan and created new ones that were neurocounseling based. It was in that moment that Lori learned that once one truly understands the brain and its physiology and functions, one can never go back and see the world from the other vantage point. The traditional counseling viewpoint is not lost, but an additive and adjunctive neurocounseling viewpoint is gained. The major goal of this entire book is to share the additive value of neurocounseling with the essential and instrumental aspects of traditional counseling.

Ten Practical Guidelines for Neurocounseling

The following 10 practical guidelines for neurocounseling have been adapted from a previous article by Russell-Chapin (2016). We explore each guideline in this chapter by presenting our neurocounseling approach to the first clinical case study of Muna.

Guideline 1

Integrating neurocounseling offers clients a fuller opportunity for personal wellness and intrinsic locus of control through the practice of emotional, behavioral, and physiological self-regulation.

As with traditional counseling, neurocounseling values a wellness-based approach. After completing a wellness assessment and discussing how her current patterns were affecting her brain, Muna was receptive to addressing key aspects of wellness as counseling goals. Two major Therapeutic Lifestyle Changes (Ivey, Ivey, & Zalaquett, 2014) were initiated, pertaining to exercise and sleep. Muna began exercising on a daily basis, walking every day for 20 minutes. Muna received psychoeducation about adults needing 7 to 9 hours of sleep per night for memory consolidation, immune system functioning, and toxin removal in the brain. Muna's admission of sleeping 3 to 5 hours per night now seemed quite alarming to her. Muna was amazed that when people are sleep deprived for even one night, memory retention declines (Stickgold & Walker, 2015). Muna committed to a better sleep hygiene pattern every night by going to bed at the same time, cutting down on alcohol consumption in the evenings, and avoiding the use of screen time 1 hour before bed. For Muna, knowing about the brain and its functions empowered her to make more informed decisions about her treatment and her life choices from a complete wellness perspective.

Reflective Question

Think back to your initial thoughts about Muna in the Preface.

Because neurocounseling is now a part of your counseling foundation, how would your treatment of Muna be different?

- Review the Preface and Chapters 1 (Anatomy and Brain Development), 2 (Neurophysiological Development Across the Life span), and 8 (Wellness and Optimal Performance) for more information about neurocounseling, brain development, and wellness.

Guideline 2

Honoring the similarities and differences of each client is a core pillar of our professional identity and neurocounseling.

Listening to Muna's fears about her family was essential to Muna's feeling understood. Muna's main fear was that her family might discover she was living with her boyfriend. Although this concern is not unique to just the Iraqi culture, this fear had a large impact on Muna because her family considered cohabitation to be a grave sin. Helping Muna process her fears was essential to the counseling process.

- Review Chapter 3 (Biology of Marginality) and Chapter 5 (Neuroscience of Attention) to understand the importance of providing a safe space for clients who come from diverse cultural backgrounds, especially when they are marginalized and oppressed.

Guideline 3

Locating available licensed professionals and resources from other disciplines provides clients with more comprehensive and thorough care.

Neurocounseling suggests that physiological dysregulation influences the mental health of many clients. Professionals who could be part of a resource team include functional medicine physicians, integrative psychopharmacologists, dieticians, and holistic pharmacists. Counselors may want to request that clients have a complete physical with an integrated primary care practitioner or functional medicine specialist soon after beginning counseling. A complete physical with a comprehensive blood screen may be requested and recommended to ensure that both the psychological and the physical bidirectionality from the brain and body are being covered. If the presenting symptoms are chronic and severe, Gordon (2015), a functional medicine practitioner and brain trauma specialist, has recommended additional hormonal blood assays along with DNA swabs from neuroendocrinologists.

Muna called her insurance and found a functional medicine practitioner in her provider network. Muna's bloodwork assessment came back with astonishing results. Muna was anemic and vitamin D deficient, had progesterone levels below the normal range, and her thyroid was not working properly. Knowing those results seemed to reduce Muna's presenting symptoms of anxiety and sleeplessness; Muna acknowledged holding deep-seated fears that something was deeply wrong with her. Once her hormones were balanced and some symptoms were relieved, Muna was more receptive to counseling.

- Review Chapters 1 and 2 for additional information about human growth and development.

Guideline 4

Incorporating neuroscience into counseling provides additional insight into the physiological basis of interpersonal and therapeutic relationships.

When Muna began to discuss her family of origin, she quietly reported being physically abused by her father while seeking psychological safety from her mother. Often, this help did not come from her mother. She was not close to her siblings. As we discussed her past and present relationships, Muna realized her attachment pattern was to end relationships before the other person might call it quits. Muna stated that she is not very trusting of any person in her life. Treatment for Muna included discussing the effects of trauma from her abusive father. Muna learned how this influenced her overaroused physiology, her development, and her overall functioning. Using attachment theory and the polyvagal theory (Porges, 2011), the goal of neurocounseling with Muna was to create a safe environment in counseling and develop a therapeutic alliance.

- Review Chapter 2 for information on the influence of attachment relationships on brain development, Chapter 4 for information about the impact of trauma, and Chapters 5 and 6 (Neuroscience-Informed Counseling Theory) for information about helping relationships and counseling theory.

Guideline 5

Including neurocounseling information in group counseling adds another layer of depth to group work.

There were two very difficult issues that were addressed with Muna. Her two major counseling goals were to (a) curb her use of alcohol to control her anxiety and (b) explore her personal beliefs about her culture, spirituality, and organized religion. Sharing with Muna the biochemical aspects of alcohol and its impact on the brain and its chemistry was necessary and helpful to Muna's counseling treatment. Giving her the needed resources for open Alcoholic Anonymous groups assisted in exploration of possible addiction. Openly sharing her views on religion and spirituality empowered Muna to consider her own values and beliefs. Toward the end of the neurocounseling process, Muna was considering reconnecting with a mosque in the area.

- Review Chapter 9 (Clinical Neuroscience of Substance Use Disorders) and Chapter 11 (Neuro-Informed Group Work) for more discussions on addictions and the importance of group work in neurocounseling.

Guideline 6

The use of neurocounseling significantly widens the array of treatment strategies available for meaningful and more focused physical, emotional, and behavioral change.

In addition to traditional counseling conceptualization and treatment strategies, neurocounseling added basic biofeedback, neurotherapy, and neurofeedback skills to the counseling paradigm. One of the first neurocounseling techniques taught to Muna was skin temperature control. When I shook Muna's hand for the first time, her hands were cold and very limp. I gave her an inexpensive handheld thermometer and assessed a baseline temperature. Muna was similar to other anxious clients. Her baseline skin temperature was in the low 80 degrees. The desired goal was to achieve 90 degrees, the state of peak performance, relaxed but focused attention (Lowenstein, 2002). After a visualization exercise, Muna rechecked her temperature and stated, "Wow, it is 89 degrees. I can't believe I can do that." Much information was given to Muna with just this one biofeedback technique. Muna said she felt she had so much control.

- Review Chapters 5 on microskills and 8 on wellness and optimal performance.

Guideline 7

Integrating the world of work into neurocounseling is another essential aspect of neurocounseling.

Often, counselors may glide over career issues in neurocounseling. However, many counselors spend more time at work than at home or with our families. Considering work–life balance and stress from a neurocounseling point of view may be enlightening. Teaching clients that more than 80% of all symptoms reported to physicians are stress related is a powerful statistic (Ivey et al., 2014).

Understanding why Muna chose her accounting career was very insightful. Her father told her that a girl needed a steady income if she did not marry. Muna's father decided her major because she was good with numbers and mathematics. Muna had never enjoyed being an accountant, and this dissonance resulted in another layer of stress for her. Muna started considering other possibilities for an occupation, and she also brainstormed other outside resources that offered her pleasure and satisfaction.

- Review Chapter 12 (Neuro-Informed Career-Focused Counseling).

Guideline 8

The use of neurocounseling enables and almost mandates that counselors more fully evaluate and develop treatment plans and more effectively intervene in clients' physiological, psychological, and behavioral problems.

Muna's intake session was similar to the traditional psychosocial history, except that more in-depth information was gathered, including birthing history and screen time. Muna reported being a premature baby, delivered only after 28 weeks by cesarean section. Muna reported using her smartphone, laptop, and television for more than 10 hours per day. Both these pieces of information offered new information about her possible anxiety concerns and assisted in goal development.

Neurocounseling offers quantitative data that can improve counseling efficiency and efficacy. Another essential piece of helping Muna understand the process of self-regulation was to teach her the neurocounseling and biofeedback skill of diaphragmatic breathing (McCraty, Atkinson, & Tomasino, 2001). Muna was an extremely shallow breather, which exacerbated her anxiety. Muna was taught to breathe more deeply. With repeated practice, she gained control of another piece of her physiology, her breath. After using computerized heart rhythm software in our counseling office, Muna decided to purchase her own handheld unit for daily practice and reinforcement.

As Muna became more aware of self-regulation and intrinsic locus of control, she decided to engage in a full neurofeedback assessment with five-channel encephalography (EEG; Chapin & Russell-Chapin, 2014). Her assessment did show that frontal attention-deficit/hyperactivity disorder was present, so 20 sessions of neurofeedback were conducted. At that time, Muna had a second five-channel EEG administered as a posttest. Her nine listed presenting symptoms had all gotten better. Another 10 sessions of neurofeedback were conducted.

Using psychopharmacology when necessary was also an essential element in neurocounseling and in Muna's treatment. Muna learned about the physiology, chemistry, and physics of psychopharmacology. This gave her additional information about how her brain worked and offered more control over the use of prescribed medications. Another goal of integrating neurocounseling is the possible reduction and, at times, elimination of unneeded medications. As she entered counseling, Muna was already taking Adderall for her attention concerns. With more self-regulation skills and the assistance from neurofeedback, Muna consulted with her physician to wean off the stimulant medication. Once again, Muna was regaining more control over her life.

- Be sure to review Chapter 7 (Neurocounseling Assessment) and 10 (Psychopharmacology Basics).

Guideline 9

Being aware of the ethical issues in neurocounseling practices must continue to be at the forefront of our counseling practices.

Muna had many complicated and complex variables interacting with her presenting symptoms. Synthesizing and translating complex scientific information into something that was discernable and comprehensible to Muna required its own skill set. Counselors are encouraged to receive training to learn how to distill neuroscientific concepts without diluting critical information. Supervision could be very helpful in the development of competencies pertinent to translating neuroscientific knowledge to clients, and the field is in need of supervisors who understand how to translate neuroscience information.

Neurocounseling also requires attention to ethical issues. Counselors practice within their scope of competence, and appropriate training is vitally important for counselors who are using brain-based assessment instruments and interventions. Counselors require training before using assessment tools such as the quantitative EEG. Counselors also need training and supervision in the use of interventions such as neurofeedback and biofeedback before using these approaches independently with clients. These assessments and interventions require an understanding of neurobiology in addition to familiarity with the technological components (both hardware and software) of the interventions. Counselors who are interested in integrating neurofeedback and biofeedback into their work are encouraged to consider specialized credentialing to ensure the highest levels of training. The Biofeedback Certification International Alliance is recommended for credentialing in biofeedback and neurofeedback. All of Muna's professionals were licensed, and her counselor was board certified in neurofeedback.

- Review Chapter 7 for additional ethical information.

Guideline 10

Neurocounseling offers evidence-based research to support its teaching.

With every skill and technique taught to Muna, she was exposed to evidence-based research and its findings. Research studies and results give clients and students scientific theories and facts to validate and support their personal work. This offers strength to daily practice and credibility to neurocounseling and counseling. Some clients may not want to read articles, but most enjoy listening to the facts presented. Muna was very interested. The article that seemed to impress Muna and give her personal motivation was about sleep and understanding the role that melatonin plays in assisting neuronal health (Srinivisan, Spence, Brown, & Cardinalis, 2011).

- Review Chapter 7, Chapter 8 on wellness assessment and the importance of sleep hygiene, and Chapter 13 (Conducting Brain-Based Research and Program Evaluation).

Conclusion

As editors of this neurocounseling book, our goal was to assist your development into neuroscience-informed practitioners, educators, and supervisors. You do not necessarily have to become an expert in functional medicine, biochemistry, or neurofeedback. Having a foundation in neuroscience as presented in this text, understanding the benefits of this knowledge as discussed in every chapter, and even referring to another helping professional with a different knowledge base and skill set are all aspects of being neuro-wise. As you have seen throughout this text, once you understand how neuroscience informs and enriches case conceptualizations and clinical practice, it is difficult, if not impossible, to go back to the traditional way of counseling.

Quiz

1. Which is *not* a key feature of neurocounseling?
   a. Bridging brain and behavior.
   b. Using other disciplines to add to wellness.
   c. Focusing on the medical model.
   d. Realizing that many mental health concerns have a physiological basis.
2. Neurocounseling allows the client to:
   a. Focus on building an intrinsic locus of control.
   b. Rely heavily on prescribed medications.
   c. Only use cognitive counseling.
   d. Minimally integrate therapeutic life changes.

3. Integration of neurocounseling into counseling:
   a. Adds value to the counseling profession.
   b. Teaches personal accountability to clients.
   c. Builds client self-regulation skills.
   d. All of the above.

References

Chapin, T., & Russell-Chapin, L. (2014). *Neurotherapy and neurofeedback: Brain-based treatment for psychological and behavioral problems.* New York, NY: Routledge.

Gordon, M. (2015). *Traumatic brain injury: A clinical approach to diagnosis and treatment.* Retrieved from http://www.tbimedlegal. com

Ivey, A. E., Ivey, M., & Zalaquett, C. (2014). *Intentional interviewing & counseling: Facilitating client development in a multicultural society* (8th ed.). Belmont, CA: Brooks/ Cole.

Lowenstein, T. (2002). *Stress and temperature.* Port Angeles, WA: Stress Market.

McCraty, R., Atkinson, M., & Tomasino, D. (2001). *Science of the heart: Exploring the role of the heart in human performance.* Boulder Creek, CO: Institute of HeartMath.

Porges, S. (2011). *The polyvagal theory.* New York, NY: Norton.

Russell-Chapin, L.A. (2016). Integrating neurocounseling into the counseling profession: An introduction. *Journal of Mental Health Counseling, 38,* 93–102. http://dx.doi.org/10.17744/ mehc.38.2.01

Srinivisan, V., Spence, D.W., Brown, G. M., & Cardinalis, D. P. (2011). Melatonin in mitochrondrial dysfunction and related disorders. *International Journal of Alzheimer's Disease, 2011,* 1–16.

Stickgold, R., & Walker, M. (2015). Sleep on it. *Scientific American, 313,* 52–57.

Explanation of Quiz Answers

Chapter 1
Anatomy and Brain Development

1. Which of the following lobes of the brain is in charge of executive functioning?
   a. Frontal.

   The frontal lobe of the brain is responsible for executive functioning.

2. Which functional system of the brain is primarily known for helping people to respond to emotionally salient cues and threats in their environment but also plays a role in memory, social processing, motivation, addiction, and sexual behavior?
   c. Limbic system.

   The limbic system is made up of brain structures such as the hippocampus, the amygdala, and the basal ganglia, which play a role in memory, social processing, motivation, addiction, and social behavior.

3. The theory detailing the social engagement system suggests that which of the following nerves evolved in such a way as to optimize interpersonal functioning?
   b. Vagus nerve.

   Porges's polyvagal theory details the importance of the vagus nerve to the ventral vagal system (also known as the social engagement system).

Chapter 2
Neurophysiological Development Across the Life Span

1. During which stage of development do synapses begin developing at a rate of approximately 40,000 per minute?
   c. Third trimester.

   During the third trimester, synapses begin developing at the amazing rate of approximately 40,000 per minute.

237

2. During adolescent brain development, which of the following is true?

   a. Subcortical limbic regions of the brain develop before the prefrontal cortical areas.

   Because subcortical limbic regions of the brain develop before the prefrontal cortex, adolescents can struggle with cognitive control and tend to make emotionally driven decisions.

3. In older adults, which of the following *do not* seem to be impaired by healthy aging?

   b. Emotion regulation.

   Healthy aging leads to declines in memory and processing speed, but not in emotional regulation. Changes in emotional regulation can be characteristic of a neurocognitive disorder.

Chapter 3

Biology of Marginality: A Neurophysiological Exploration of the Social and Cultural Foundations of Psychological Health

1. Which of the following statements does not accurately characterize what is known about psychoneuroimmunology?

   b. Chronic stress causes inflammatory shutdown.

   Research in psychoneuroimmunology has shown that in response to chronic stress, acquired immunity is suppressed, and inflammation increases in intensity. Excessive inflammation can lead to psychological symptoms such as depressed mood, anxiety, and social withdrawal, and it can also lead to numerous debilitating chronic illnesses including cancers, arthritis, and heart disease.

2. Which of the following statements is not a characteristic of chronic stress?

   d. It initiates negative-feedback systems to control cortisol.

   The damage caused by chronic stress is related in part to the failure of negative-feedback systems to function properly, which results in a failure to control blood cortisol levels. Over time, the abnormal cortisol levels result in physical and psychological challenges.

3. Epigenetic changes can explain which of the following?

   a. A decrease in neuroplasticity.

   Under conditions of chronic stress, epigenetic mechanisms result in a decrease in brain-derived neurotrophic factor, which causes decreases in neuroplasticity that result in cognitive and emotional challenges.

4. Which of the following best describes the notion of predispositional vulnerability?

   c. It can change over time as a result of the impact of environmental forces.

   Although genetic predisposition is a component of predispositional vulnerability, environmental forces can raise or lower vulnerability, creating either more resilience in the face of stressors in the case of the former or increased vulnerability to stress in the case of the latter.

Chapter 4
Neurophysiology of Traumatic Stress

1. In the face of extreme or chronic stress, which of the following statements regarding cortisol is true?
   d. The negative-feedback loop for the HPA axis is disrupted, which impairs the body's ability to regulate levels of cortisol.
   Cortisol disrupts the HPA axis, impairing communication to the hypothalamus for corticotropin-releasing factor to be reduced. This results in chronically high levels of cortisol.

2. Which of the following structures is not implicated in impaired traumatic memories?
   b. Pineal gland.
   The amygdala, thalamus, and hippocampus are all implicated in traumatic memories. The hippocampus is responsible for storing memories, which can result in implicit recall of past traumatic events and heightened sensitivity to threats in one's environment. The thalamus relays messages to different parts of the brain, and, after exposure to trauma, may interpret incoming sensory information as threatening. Messages of potential threats are then routed to the amygdala, which activates the stress-response alarm system. This results in neurophysiological survival responses is known as fight-or-flight. The pineal gland is not implicated in traumatic memories.

Chapter 5
Neuroscience of Attention:
Empathy and Counseling Skills

1. Which of the following is *not* one of the considerations that Porges (2011) suggested is helpful to consider in establishing safety?
   d. Open-ended questions.
   Unlike the other three choices, Porges (2011) did not identify open-ended questions as helpful in establishing safety.

2. Which of the following is *not* a form of empathy?
   b. Situational.
   The three components of empathy are cognitive empathy, affective empathy, and mentalization.

3. In helping a client deal with microaggressions, the central goal is to:
   b. Provide a safe environment so that the client can talk easily.
   Although listening carefully and fully is important to all relationships, clients who experience microaggressions need to feel safe so that they can process what has happened to them. In such cases, close listening is not enough—the counselor's body language and nonverbal behavior must also help the client to feel safe in the room. Although providing psychoeducation is also useful, the client must first feel safe (the central goal). The last choice does not assist the client to process his or her experience nor does it address the injustice of the client's situation.

Chapter 6
Neuroscience-Informed Counseling Theory

1. Researchers began studying the neurobiological outcomes of the use of therapeutic interventions by investigating:
   c. Phobias.
   > Phobias were first studied when researchers began examining the neurobiological outcomes of counseling interventions.

2. The primary brain structure affected during the application of therapeutic interventions such as CBT and IPT is:
   d. b and c.
   > The brain structures primarily affected by counseling interventions such as CBT and IPT are the PFC and the limbic system.

Chapter 7
Neurocounseling Assessment

1. Which statement about validity and reliability is most true?
   a. The test needs to be valid and reliable.
   > Both reliability and validity are equally as important to test selection. Tests that are reliable and not valid will produce the same results over and over again, but the results will not be relevant or applicable to the client's problem.

2. The main goal of a neurocounseling assessment is:
   b. Physiological, emotional, and behavioral self-regulation.
   > Neurocounseling assessment aims to help clients achieve improved self-regulation. Although neurocounseling often includes comprehensive evaluation, this is not the main goal of neurocounseling practice.

3. Which of the following are possible sources of brain dysregulation?
   d. All of the above.
   > Genetic predisposition, substance abuse, and high fever are all possible sources of brain dysregulation.

Chapter 8
Wellness and Optimal Performance

1. Which of the following is not one of the six dimensions of Hettler's model of wellness?
   d. Health.
   > The six dimensions are occupational, physical, social, intellectual, spiritual, and emotional.

2. Which of the following is not a healthy lifestyle strategy?
   a. Moderate use of alcohol.
   > Healthy lifestyle strategies are diet, dietary supplements, exercise, sleep, and screen time.

3. Which of the following mental activities does not help clients to regulate their emotions?
   b. Focus time.

   Focus time is not necessarily linked to emotional regulation. In contrast, time-in and mindfulness, playtime, and adequate sleep time all help clients to regulate their emotions.

Chapter 9
Clinical Neuroscience of Substance Use Disorders

1. DAergic neurons in the mesolimbic pathway are largely associated with:
   a. Reward prediction.

   DA neurons in the mesolimbic pathway have been linked to reward prediction. In contrast, DA neurons in the mesocortical and nigrostriatal pathways are associated with executive function and movement disorders. Last, the insular cortex has been linked to attention and decision making.

2. Which of the following is *not* an evidence-based counseling intervention for addiction?
   d. Interpersonal and social rhythm therapy.

   Interpersonal and social rhythm therapy is a variant of interpersonal psychotherapy designed to target the pathogenic factors underlying bipolar disorder. However, this intervention has not been applied to addiction.

3. Which of the following elements make up the addiction cycle?
   c. Binge–intoxication, withdrawal and negative affect, and preoccupation–anticipation.

   Koob and Volkow (2010) proposed that the transition from voluntary to compulsive drug use may be understood through the lens of positive and negative reinforcement. Their framework consists of three stages of the addiction cycle: binge and intoxication (positive reinforcement), withdrawal and negative affect (negative reinforcement), and preoccupation and anticipation (craving).

Chapter 10
Psychopharmacology Basics

1. When the amount of the drug available to the body is the same as the amount being eliminated, then _____ has been achieved.
   c. Steady state.

   When a person takes medication on a regular basis, there is an ongoing process of drug absorption from each dose and, at the same time, an ongoing process of drug removal by the metabolism and elimination. Steady state is achieved when the amount of the drug going in is the same as the amount of the drug being eliminated . Drug side effects can be less severe or even eliminated after a steady state is reached. For example, selective serotonin reuptake inhibitors have reduced gastrointestinal side effects after reaching steady state (Kramer, 2003).

2. Which of the following is not a pharmacokinetic process?
   d. **Accumulation.**

   Absorption, metabolism, distribution, and excretion are the four pharmacokinetic processes.

3. What type of receptor would a serotonin neurotransmitter bind to?
   a. **Serotonin receptor.**

   Neurotransmitters have receptors with matching names so serotonin neurotransmitters bind to serotonin receptors.

Chapter 11
Neuro-Informed Group Work

1. What factors make group so complex?
   a. **The numerous points of interactions (dyads and triads) between and among members to which a facilitator must attend.**

   The number of members is not what makes group challenging; rather, it is all the exchanges and interchanges to which a facilitator must attend that takes so much energy.

2. What is social synapse as it applies to neuroscience and group counseling?
   b. **The connections among individuals that produce a network of functioning that is similar to neural networks.**

   Social networks mimic neural networks.

3. According to the authors, what is the problem with storytelling from a neuroscience perspective?
   d. **Memory is not recall as much as it is reconstitution, so storytelling in the wrong context can bias the story and distort perception.**

   Memory retrieval is context dependent and infused with present emotion that distorts perception of the memory.

Chapter 12
Neuro-Informed Career-Focused Counseling

1. According to Donald Super, vocational identity is
   a. **A projection of the self into the world of work.**

   Super believed that vocational identity is a projection of the self into the world of work. It is important because it implies that successful career development is predicated on self-identity.

2. Which system is activated during times of stress, including work stress?
   d. **Hypothalamic–pituitary–adrenal axis.**

   Stress and work stress are similarly experienced in the brain because they are governed by the hypothalamic–pituitary–adrenal axis. Physiological response to stress does not vary by type of stress.

3. Busacca identified two domains and three types of career-related issues. What are they?
   a. **Intrapersonal and interpersonal; career choice, career entry, and work adjustment.**

   Busacca (2002) adapted the work of Savickas (1998) to develop a taxonomy that helps counselors to determine whether career problems or issues are located within the individual (intrapersonal domain) or located within the individual's connections with others (interpersonal domain). Busacca further identified three areas of career difficulties: choosing a vocation or career (career choice), entering the desired vocation (career entry), and changing one's established career path (career transition).

Chapter 13
Conducting Brain-Based Research and Program Evaluation

1. You decide to conduct a study that compares the difference between brain wave activity taken from a sample of 100 clients at two intervals: immediately before and after a counseling session. All clients have depression and are receiving acceptance and commitment therapy, and activity in their prefrontal cortex is being measured by qEEG. Which of the following quantitative designs would you use for the study?
   b. **Quasi-experiment.**

   Measuring the same participants at two intervals (e.g., pre and post) is characteristic of a quasi-experimental study because there is no comparison or control group and thus no ability to randomize participants (a key criterion of a true experiment or RCT).

2. You design a second study that now compares the relationship between time spent in the waiting room before the session and client brain activity taken from the first interval (immediately before the counseling session) of the same sample. Which of the following quantitative designs would you use for the study?
   e. **Correlational.**

   Evaluating relationships between two variables (time spent in waiting room, brain activity) is characteristic of a correlational study. We are not seeking to understand differences between groups, common to true and quasi-experiments.

3. What are the limitations of both of the preceding studies?
   e. **a and b only.**

   Both of these studies lack control groups and the ability to randomize participants. The first study has defined the variables that will be evaluated: All clients have depression (and clients without depression will presumptively be excluded), are receiving only acceptance and commitment therapy, and qEEG readings are solely measuring prefrontal brain activity. In contrast, the second study has not properly defined the variables to be measured, only mentioning "time in waiting room" and that prefrontal brain activity is being measured. The absence of a comparison condition is problematic because it provides a natural control for confounding variables. When a comparison condition is not included, other variables should be defined and thus controlled for (e.g., diagnosis, treatment, number of sessions, demographic variables, time of day) to limit the number of confounding variables. Without this step, the study's findings may be uninterpretable.

Chapter 14
Ten Practical Guidelines for Neurocounseling

1. Which is *not* a key feature of neurocounseling?
   c. **Focusing on the medical model.**
   Neurocounseling incorporates wellness, bridges brain and behavior, and underscores the physiological basis of mental health. However, neurocounseling does not emphasize the medical model and actually promotes the wellness and strengths-based orientation of the counseling profession.

2. Neurocounseling allows the client to:
   a. **Focus on building an intrinsic locus of control.**
   Neurocounseling empowers clients, building an intrinsic locus of control by building on success experiences. Neurocounseling favors a wellness-based approach that assists clients to integrate life changes. It does not rely heavily on prescribed medications and may actually assist clients to eliminate unnecessary medications. Neurocounseling is not restricted to cognitive counseling.

3. Integration of neurocounseling into counseling:
   d. **All of the above.**
   This one was easy! Integrating neurocounseling into counseling practice adds value to the profession, teaches personal accountability to clients, and builds client self-regulation skills.

GLOSSARY

Action Potential. The basic electrical signal of a neuron and the likelihood that a neuron will transmit a signal. Important in the neurotransmission of messages from one neuron to another.

Agonists and Antagonists. An agonist is a chemical agent that binds to and activates a receptor. An antagonist is a chemical agent that impedes or blocks the physiological functioning of a receptor or another substance.

Allostasis. A person's ability to physiologically adapt in the face of changing psychological, physical, or environmental pressures and in anticipation of future stressors.

Allostatic Load. The wear and tear on the body and brain from a persistent allostatic response in the face of chronic or extreme stress or environmental pressures.

Amblyopia. This vision development condition better known as "lazy eye" is an example of synaptic pruning, whereby the brain limits connections between the eye and the occipital lobe of the brain.

Amygdala. A central subcortical brain structure that is responsible for detecting and responding to both innate and learned threats in the environment.

Autonomic Nervous System. A part of the peripheral nervous system that consists of two different branches, the sympathetic and parasympathetic nervous systems. The enteric nervous system, which innervates the gastrointestinal tract, is also considered a branch of the autonomic nervous system.

Axon. A long, hairlike projection that carries chemical messages away from the soma or cell body to the neighboring neurons, glands, or muscles on the other side of neuron.

Axon Terminal. The axon terminal is the area at the end of the axon where the axon branches and extends to come in close proximity to the neighboring structure (e.g., other neurons, muscles, glands).

Basal Ganglia. A coordinated set of subcortical nuclei consisting of the caudate nucleus and putamen (together known as the striatum), nucleus accumbens, globus pallidus, substantia nigra, and subthalamic nucleus. These structures play a considerable role in learning and memory, particularly implicit learning of automatized responses. The basal ganglia also inhibit and motivate movement.

Bilateral Integration. The integration of information, by way of the corpus callosum, coming from the left and right hemispheres of the brain.

Binding Potential Values. A crucial measure in positron emission tomography studies to establish the density of available receptors.

Biofeedback. An assessment and intervention approach that provides direct feedback to clients about certain markers of their physiological functioning, such as breathing patterns, heart rate variability, skin temperature, galvanic skin responses, and muscle tension. The goal of biofeedback is to help clients modify and enhance their neurophysiological functioning and performance, a process known as self-regulation.

Brain-Derived Neurotrophic Factor (BDNF). A class of proteins in the central nervous system integral to neuronal and synaptic development and survival and that plays a central role in neuroplasticity.

Brain Stem. The brain stem connects the brain to the spinal cord and the rest of the body and is vital for survival, regulating such integral processes as breathing, heart rate, blood pressure, and circadian rhythms.

Brain Wave Alpha. Alpha waves are categorized as 8 to 12 Hz and are needed for idling and transitioning from one brain wave state to another.

Brain Wave Beta. Beta waves go from 13 to 30 Hz. They are considered busy waves. Low beta waves from 12 to 15 Hz assist in focused attention and problem solving. Anxiety may be present when beta waves are too high.

Brain Wave Delta. Delta waves are often 0 to 3 Hz or 0 to 3 cycles per second. These waves are slow, low waves and are associated with sleep and sometime trauma-related problems.

Brain Wave Gamma. Gamma waves are 30 Hz or more and are often found in bursts of insight.

Brain Wave Theta. Theta waves are typically 4 to 7 Hz and are associated with drowsiness and meditation. They are also slower waves.

Brain Waves. Electrical impulses of the brain produced by neurons firing at certain characteristic frequencies. The five basic brain wave categories are delta, theta, alpha, beta, and gamma.

Broca's Area. An area of cortex in the frontal lobe, located at the base of the primary motor cortex that is associated with language production.

Cell Body. The soma or cell body is the core part of the neuron, containing the nucleus and other cellular structures such as mitochondria used in energy production.

Cerebellum. Meaning "little brain," the cerebellum is the cauliflower-shaped structure at the back base of the brain. The cerebellum is thought to be responsible for a range of functions related to cognition, emotion, sensory perception, attention, threat, and pleasure.

Cingulate Cortex. Lies underneath the outer surface of the cortex following the line of the corpus callosum. The job of the cingulate cortex is varied, given its role in learning, memory, reward, and social and emotional processing, with the anterior (frontal) and posterior (back) sections controlling diverse functions.

Corpus Callosum. A thick band of nerve fibers that connects the two hemispheres of the brain.

Cortisol. A hormone that helps to restore homeostasis after stress and is essential to life.

Cranial Nerves. Twelve pairs of nerves that function in sensory, motor, and parasympathetic control, with most of the nerves controlling muscles of the face and neck or regulating visual, olfactory, and auditory sensations.

Default Mode Network. A system of functionally connected brain regions that become engaged when the brain is in a resting state and is not involved in a specific attention-demanding, goal-oriented task.

ΔFosB. A protein thought to influence behavior change via alterations in gene expression and to play a role in drug addiction.

Dendrites. Branches extending out from the cell body that bring chemical messages or information into the cell body from neighboring neurons.

Diaphragmatic Breathing. Both an assessment and intervention tool. A client's number of breaths per minute can be compared with norms to offer clues about anxiety, body tension, and muscle rigidity. It can also regulate autonomic functioning and enhance absorption of glucose and oxygen.

Differentiation. The process by which stem cells develop into mature specialized cells. During brain development, it is the process of stem cells becoming either neurons or glial cells.

DNA. Molecules that carry the instructions or codes that direct the synthesis of proteins needed for growth, development, and other life-sustaining functions.

Dopamine. A neurotransmitter thought to play a role in movement, goal-directed behavior, cognition, attention, and reward.

Electroencephalography (EEG). A method for recording the brain's electrical activity, brain waves, through electrodes placed on the client's scalp.

Epigenetics. An array of mechanisms in which aspects of the environment are able to manipulate how genes are expressed. Several epigenetic mechanisms are linked to the harmful psychological outcomes of chronic stress.

Epinephrine. A hormone, also called adrenaline, that is primarily produced by the adrenal glands and prepares a person for action during times of threat as a form of self-protection. This fight-or-flight response involves changes in heart rate and breathing, among other physiological effects.

Functional Medicine. A holistic approach to medical treatment that focuses on addressing underlying causes of disease, using a systems-based approach that examines interactions among genetic, environmental, and lifestyle factors in the development of diseases.

Functional MRI (fMRI). A brain-imaging technique that measures changes in levels of oxygenated blood across various brain regions. The amount of blood flow into a particular area is said to denote the activity level of that brain region.

Gamma-Aminobutyric Acid (GABA). The body's primary inhibitory neurotransmitter. GABA plays a role in stress responses and the regulation of anxiety.

Gene Expression. The process by which the genetic information from a gene becomes a functional gene product, most often a protein; the activation of genes in a person's DNA sequence via epigenetic influences.

Glial Cells. The nervous system has two major forms of cells, neurons and glial cells. Glial cells provide insulation, nourishment, repair, and structural support to neurons. They also remove waste from the nervous system.

Glutamate. An amino acid that neurons use to send signals to other cells.

Gyri, Sulci, and Fissures. The cerebral cortex structurally contains ridges of tissues known as gyri, shallower grooves between the gyri known as sulci, and fissures, which are similar to sulci but are deeper grooves within the tissue that more clearly divide brain regions.

Half-Life. The half-life of a drug refers to the rate at which the drug is metabolized; it is the amount of time it takes for the plasma concentration of the blood to be reduced by one half.

Healthy Mind Platter. A wellness model developed to explain how optimal brain functioning can be maintained through daily healthy mental habits. Those mental habits include connecting time, downtime, focus time, physical time, playtime, sleep time, and time-in.

Heart Rate Variability. A measure of the variation in time between heart beats that can be used to determine the amount of stress the body is under. A lower heart rate variability signifies a predominant activation of the sympathetic nervous system. This measure can also be used as a biofeedback technique to aid in self-regulation.

Hippocampus. A subcortical brain region that is located in the medial (i.e., interior) region of the temporal lobes and is responsible for the formation (i.e., consolidation) of long-term declarative memories.

Hypothalamic–Pituitary–Adrenal (HPA) Axis. The functional connection between three endocrine glands that allows a person to adapt to both emotional and physical stress. When the HPA axis is activated, a chain of events occurs that eventually results in cortisol being released.

Hypothalamus. An almond-sized structure of the diencephalon that links the endocrine and nervous systems in the body. It assists the body in maintaining a state of internal balance or equilibrium known as homeostasis, such as controlling body temperature, food intake, and water intake. The hypothalamus is also responsible for the release of various key hormones in the body, sexual development, and the ability to respond to stress.

Immediate Early Genes (IEGs). Activated very quickly in response to cellular stimuli as part of the process of gene expression and have an important role in such functions as learning, brain development, and drug use and addiction.

Immunity. Immune function is generally divided into two types, acquired and innate. Acquired immunity refers to the ability to target and destroy specific disease-producing microorganisms such as specific viruses. Innate immunity is naturally occurring, does not require previous exposure to a pathogen, and mounts a defense that is typically generalized and nonspecific.

Inflammation. Inflammation, part of humans' innate immune functioning, involves a generalized rallying of cells (i.e., leukocytes or white blood cells) that travel to a site of tissue damage. Regardless of how the tissue became injured, the damage signals a generalized response that attempts to destroy and clear any invading microorganisms and foreign debris and initiates tissue repair.

Insula. This area of cortex, located in the frontal lobe near the confluence of the frontal, parietal, and temporal lobes, has a range of functions, such as homeostatic regulation, self-awareness, motor control, interoception, empathy, and emotional processing. It also helps with translating the emotions that people feel in their bodies into their cognitive understanding of those emotions, or what are known as feelings.

Interoception. The cognitive awareness of internal bodily states.

Lobe, Frontal. The frontal lobe is the largest brain region, located at the front of the skull. It is involved in problem solving, decision making, planning, moral reasoning, attention, emotion regulation, and even priming in memory. The primary motor cortex is located in the frontal lobe, along with Broca's area, which is responsible for language production.

Lobe, Occipital. The occipital lobe sits at the very back of the brain, is the smallest of the four lobes, and is the primary visual center of the brain.

Lobe, Parietal. The parietal lobe is located approximately halfway between the frontal lobe and the occipital lobe. This part of the brain contains the primary somatosensory cortex, regulating the sensations that are perceived by the physical body, such as touch and the awareness of bodily movement and the orientation of the body in space, known as proprioception.

Lobe, Temporal. The temporal lobe is located just behind the ears, below the parietal lobe and between the frontal lobe and occipital lobe. The temporal cortex has multiple functions, including hearing and language comprehension. Wernicke's area is located in the temporal lobe.

Memory. Memory is composed of several different theoretical components. Short-term and working memory are defined as the capacity for a person to remember a certain amount of information that was received in recent history. *Long-term memory* refers to the consolidation of events into long-term storage that are retrieved later. These memories are either consciously retrieved (known as declarative or explicit memory) or preconsciously experienced (known as nondeclarative or implicit memory). Different memory systems are regulated by different areas of the brain.

Microbiota–Gut–Brain Axis. The bidirectional connection network between the central nervous system and the gut microbiota in the gastrointestinal tract. The functioning of the microbiota–gut–brain axis has implications for depression, posttraumatic stress disorder, memory, pain, concentrations of brain-derived neurotrophic factor helpful in the development of brain cells and intercellular connections, and immune functioning.

Myelin Sheath. The fatty sheath, made out of fatty glial cells, that covers the axon of neurons and helps speed the transmission of electrochemical messages.

Necrosis. The death of a nerve cell (neuron).

Neural Plate, Groove, and Tube. During the development of a human embryo in the womb, the embryo develops a neural plate, or the structure that will eventually become the nervous system, including the brain and spinal cord. A neural groove later begins to form on the neural plate, which later becomes the brain. The two sides of the groove begin to curl, folding in on themselves and becoming a tubelike structure known as the neural tube.

Neurofeedback. A treatment method designed to alter brain functioning by providing feedback to the client about changes in their real-time electroencephalogram. Neurofeedback is grounded in the behavioral learning theory of operant conditioning.

Neurons. Cells of the nervous system that carry electrochemical messages. A neuron has four primary parts, namely the dendrites, cell body (soma), axon, and the presynaptic or axon terminal.

Neuroplasticity. The ability of the brain to alter its structure and function in response to external or internal changes in the environment, including development, learning, memory, brain injury, and disease.

Neurotransmission. Otherwise known as synaptic transmission, neurotransmission is the communication of neurotransmitters from one neuron to another.

Neurovegetative Symptoms. Symptoms of depression that appear to have a neurophysiological basis, such as changes in sleep, appetite, concentration, anhedonia, hypoactivity, and loss of energy.

Norepinephrine. As with epinephrine (i.e., adrenaline), norepinephrine is a chemical released by the adrenal medulla that prepares a person for action. Unlike epinephrine, noradrenaline is also a neurotransmitter in the sympathetic nervous system.

Olfactory Bulbs. The sensory organs that are responsible for the sense of smell.

Oxytocin. A neuropeptide that plays an instrumental role in social connectedness and bonding.

Pharmacokinetics. The study of how a drug moves through the body, which consists of four processes, namely absorption, distribution, metabolism, and excretion. Every drug has a unique kinetic profile composed of these four factors.

Pituitary Gland. A pea-sized structure that is the master gland of the body, both producing and regulating the functioning of numerous hormones. The pituitary gland is highly active in the production of sex hormones and is vital to the body's ability to respond and adapt to stress.

Polyvagal Theory. A theory proposed by Stephen Porges (2011) that suggests that evolution has led to a functional neural organization of the brain that regulates autonomic states to best support social behavior. Porges proposed that the vagus nerve consists of two branches, namely the ventral and dorsal vagal complex, that represent diverse states of autonomic regulation and functioning.

Psychoneuroimmunology. The field of scientific inquiry that studies the complex associations among the psychological state of a given individual, the neurological and hormonal processes that respond to that state, and the immunological mechanisms that communicate with those neurological and hormonal processes.

Quantitative EEG (qEEG). The comparison of a client's electrical activity in the brain with a norm group to determine whether electrical activity is within the normal range or may represent difficulties in certain areas of functioning.

Research Domain Criteria (RDoC). An organizing system created for brain-based research by the National Institute of Mental Health that aims to detect subgroups of mental disorders, inform treatment selection, and facilitate more direct links from research to practice. Includes numerous functional constructs (e.g., response to acute fear) that are described through their related genes, molecules, cells, circuits or networks, physiology, behavior, self-report, and research paradigms.

Reuptake. The process by which neurotransmitters that are released into the synaptic cleft and do not bind to the postsynaptic neuron are recycled back into the presynaptic neuron.

RNA. RNA is essentially a photocopy of certain portions of DNA genetic codes. RNA is involved in protein synthesis and regulating cellular processes. It can also serve as an enzyme to speed chemical reactions. Molecules are involved in the transmission of genetic information and expression of genes.

Self-Regulation. The ability for a person to intentionally regulate his or her emotions, cognitions, behavior, and related physiology.

Serotonin. A neurotransmitter that has an important role in regulating mood, appetite, and sleep.

Siegel Hand Model. A psychoeducational tool for explaining how the brain developed evolutionarily and developmentally.

Signal Transduction. The transmission of molecular signals from the exterior of cells to the interior that leads to a functional change within the cell.

Skin Temperature Control. A biofeedback technique that assists clients in self-regulating skin temperature to gain a state of peak performance (relaxed and attentive). A temperature of 90° is considered peak performance.

Steady State. When a person takes medication on a regular basis, there is an ongoing process of drug absorption from each dose and, at the same time, an ongoing process of drug removal by metabolism and elimination. Steady state occurs when the amount of drug taken is equivalent to the amount of drug eliminated.

Subcortical. Literally, "underneath the cortex"; subcortical brain structures are those that lie beneath the outer surface of the cortex.

Synapse. The region between two neurons that consists of the axon terminal, the synaptic cleft, and the dendrites.

Synaptic Cleft. The small space between two neurons.

Synaptic Pruning. The process by which the brain trims back unused synapses between neurons (and, as such, is an example of neuroplasticity).

Thalamus. The primary relay station of the brain.

Theory of Mind or Mentalization. The ability to attribute mental states to others and to grasp the perspective of another, considered one dimension of empathy.

Therapeutic Lifestyle Changes. Seventeen stress management strategies identified by Ivey, Ivey, and Zalaquett (2014) that enhance wellness.

Tonic and Phasic Firing. During neurotransmission, neurons fire in either a tonic or a phasic manner. Low frequency (1–8 Hz), tonic firing represents background activity of neurons that release neurotransmitters into the extracellular space. In contrast, phasic or bursting firing refers to a series of high-frequency bursts (15 Hz; induced by glutamatergic stimulation), which flood the synaptic cleft.

Wernicke's Area. A subcortical structure in the temporal lobe associated with language comprehension.

White Matter and Gray Matter. These terms are used to describe visually distinct areas of the brain as viewed on brain imaging scans. The gray areas are the neuronal cell bodies, and the white areas represent the axonal tracts, in particular myelinated axons. The myelin is what gives the white matter its characteristic white color.

INDEX

Figures and tables are indicated by "f" and "t" following page numbers.

A

ABC model of CBT, 108
Abilify (aripiprazole), 173
Absorption (drugs), 168
Abuse
    child abuse, xii, 64, 70–71, 227, 230
    of drugs. *See* Substance use and
        addiction
    partner violence, 64
ACA (American Counseling Association),
    vii
    Conference and Expo, 195*n*1
ACC. *See* Anterior cingulate cortex
Acceptance and commitment therapy,
    158
Acquired immunity, 50
ACTH (adrenocorticotropic hormone),
    13–14
Action potential, 16, 190, 245
Acute stress, 34, 199. *See also* Fight-or-
    flight response
ADD/ADHD. *See* Attention deficit/
    hyperactivity disorder
Adderall, 227, 232
Addiction. *See* Substance use and addiction
Adolescence
    brain development during, 33–35
    case study on preadolescent, 4, 21,
        38–39
    developmentally informed
        interventions for, 37–38
Adrenal glands, 14, 66, 199, 200, 203
Adrenocorticotropic hormone (ACTH),
    13–14, 155, 203

Affective empathy, 88–89, 92
Affective prosody, 69
Affect regulation/dysregulation, 64, 67,
    71, 72–73
African Americans. *See also* Marginality,
    biology of
    social determinants of health, 47–48
Aging adults
    brain changes in, 35–37, 83
    developmentally informed interventions
        for, 38
    exercise and, 136
    meditation and, 138
    neurofeedback and cognitive decline
        in, 141
    psychotropic medication and, 166,
        170
Agonists, 167, 173, 245
Alcohol use, 158, 159. *See also* Substance
    use and addiction
    in case study, 227, 229, 231
Alerting network, 85–86
Alexithymia, 155
Allostasis, 63, 66, 151, 245
Allostatic load, 63, 245
Alpha brain waves, 124–125, 127, 141,
    246
Alprazolam (Xanax), 172
Altruism in group work, 187
Alzheimer's disease
    aging brain and, 37
    benzodiazepines and risk of, 172
    dietary supplements and, 139
    focused attention and, 136
    neuroplasticity and, 18

255